MORAL EMPOWERMENT

MORAL EMPOWERMENT
IN QUEST OF A PEDAGOGY

SONA FARID-ARBAB

Bahá'í
PUBLISHING
Wilmette, Illinois

Bahá'í Publishing
401 Greenleaf Avenue, Wilmette, Illinois 60091

19 18 17 16   4 3 2 1

Library of Congress Cataloging-in-Publication Data

Names: Farid-Arbab, Sona, author.
Title: Moral empowerment : in quest of a pedagogy / by Sona Farid-Arbab.
Description: Wilmette, IL : Bahá'í Publishing, [2016] | Includes
   bibliographical references and index.
Identifiers: LCCN 2016024963 | ISBN 9781618511119 (hardcover :
alk. paper)
Subjects: LCSH: Bahai Faith—Education. | Bahai education of chil-
dren. |
   Bahai ethics. | Moral education. | Fundacion para la Aplicacion y
   Ensenanza de las Ciencias.
Classification: LCC BP388.E42 F37 2016 | DDC 297.9/35—dc23
LC record available at https://lccn.loc.gov/2016024963

Cover design by Bita Farid-Mohebati
Book design by Patrick Falso

CONTENTS

CONTENTS

FOREWORD

Those of us who in the early 1970s created the *Fundación para la Aplicación y Enseñanza de las Ciencias (FUNDAEC)*, were all engaged in an intensive effort to transform a university in a province of Colombia into a highly sophisticated modern institution in accordance with North American standards of excellence. The endeavor was well on its way; the school of medicine had already achieved recognition throughout the continent and other departments were following in its footsteps. Yet, several of us were overtaken by the fear that, no matter how successful, our university could never address the real challenges of the vast majority of the Colombian people. At the root of the problem was oppression, and oppression is perpetuated when knowledge is the possession of the few and not accessible to most segments of society. Could not arrangements be made, we asked ourselves, that would allow people in the rural areas and the marginalized neighborhoods of cities to participate meaningfully in the generation, application, and diffusion of knowledge—arrangements that would take us beyond the contributions of programs of non-formal education and the valuable yet inadequate achievements of government agencies, each working through their own agents of change? To answer this question, we gradually undertook lines of research and action concerned with a process of capacity building that later we referred to as moral empowerment.

As academics, we were familiar with prevalent theories and ideologies concerned with social change. In our new work, however, we were not interested in the kind of studies of social phenomena that a "relevant" modern university with which we were still associated was supposed to undertake. As activists, we decided, we were to avoid becoming the instruments for the defense and application of one or another ideology. We wished to learn systematically in collaboration with specific populations how to enhance capacity to contribute to the transformation of society. We engaged in a process of action and reflection within a conceptual framework that we knew would evolve as we gained experience. This framework would be informed by current theories in various fields, but it would not be attached to any; it would use theory as a source of insight and not as the final word on truth. This view we applied consistently, particularly in the field of education, which for us was a victim of fads and fashions, sometimes driven by the forces of the market.

As our work advanced and we began to achieve results that were surprising even to us, we discussed often the philosophical underpinnings of the framework that was progressively emerging. But we were faced with the demands of action, and had to be content with incorporating ideas we encountered in academic discourse into our educational materials and methods. This we did as we gained deeper understanding of the implications of each set of ideas for the social space we had called *University for Integral Development*, in which people learned to take charge of their own paths of development. The systematic philosophical treatment of the elements of the desired framework, we always hoped, would be pursued by others in some unspecified future. To see that Dr. Sona Farid-Arbab has now initiated such a project is a source of immense pleasure.

This book, of course, is not about FUNDAEC. It is concerned with the wider field of Bahá'í-inspired education, of which Sona has intimate knowledge after more than a decade's work at the Office of Social and Economic Development at the Bahá'í World Center, and to which FUNDAEC has made modest contributions. She has used our experience to identify the elements of the conceptual framework that will have to be elaborated as Bahá'ís learn to contribute more and more to the progress of material as well as spiritual civilization. She has, then, used insights gained from philosophical literature to give shape to certain crucial concepts, advancing on many fronts and pointing to challenges that lie ahead. Admitting partiality, I am convinced that the groundwork is now done. I can only hope that others will join her in furthering the development of the conceptual framework of educational processes that aim at the moral empowerment of their participants.

Farzam Arbab

CHAPTER 1

ORIGINS

The Source of Inspiration

The Bahá'í Faith, the youngest of the world's independent religions, does not see itself as one more religious system to be superimposed on the conflicting creeds that divide humankind, but rather as a restatement of the eternal verities underlying all the religions of the past. It upholds the unity of God, recognizes the unity of His Prophets, and inculcates the principle of the oneness and wholeness of the entire human race.[1]

A fundamental principle enunciated by Bahá'u'lláh is that religious truth is not absolute but relative, and that Divine Revelation is progressive.[2] Bahá'ís—constituting a worldwide community of several million and representing most of the nations, races, and cultures on earth—believe that the unification of humankind is inevitable, although the path to its realization is tortuous.

Bahá'í experience in the field of development stretches back to the beginnings of the Faith in Iran. In that country, the community of adherents was able, in just a few generations, to move to the forefront of major philanthropic and intellectual undertakings in diverse spheres of human endeavor. Much of this rapid advance was the result of achievements in processes of social and economic development, particularly in the area of education, set in motion in that community. By 1973, for example, Iranian Bahá'ís had achieved a literacy rate of 100 per cent among women followers under the age of forty; this in contrast to a national literacy rate among women of less than 20 per cent.[3] Worldwide involvement in social and economic development entered a new stage in the early 1980s, chiefly because of a substantial increase in the Bahá'í population of many nations.

Bahá'í development efforts in villages and towns throughout the world often begin as simple grassroots initiatives to address some of the challenges faced by local communities through a process of action and reflection that relies on insights drawn from the spiritual and social teachings of the Bahá'í Faith. Several hundred substantial projects have already emerged from thousands of grassroots initiatives, frequently in collaboration with governmental and nongovernmental organizations. Most of these initiatives are in the field of education, typically taking the form of academic schools; a smaller number have learned over time to address development issues from the perspective of multiple disciplines.

The Bahá'í teachings themselves do not include what might be called educational theory or, for that matter, a structured educational philosophy. Yet a discourse on education has always existed in the Bahá'í community and, in recent years, it has acquired a new dimension in the conversation among a growing number of groups and organizations around the world engaged in educational processes that have come to be designated as "Bahá'í-inspired."

An Evolving Conceptual Framework

The contribution of one organization, the *Fundación para la Aplicación y Enseñanza de las Ciencias (FUNDAEC)*—an organization that has been able to dedicate its resources over several decades to a search for content and methods inspired by the Bahá'í teachings in the context of education for development—to an advancing discourse on education in the Bahá'í community is particularly noteworthy. FUNDAEC was founded in 1974 by a group of scientists and professionals trying to understand the role of science, technology, and education in the social and economic development of a micro-region; its efforts initially focused near the city of Cali in Colombia. It expressed its primary aim as the creation of a social space in which specific populations could actively engage in learning about their own path of development. The name given to this social space is *University for Integral Development.* In pursuance of this aim, FUNDAEC focused in the first decade of its existence on action and research, assisting various groups in the aforementioned micro-region to participate in the generation, application, and diffusion of knowledge about the different processes of community life and how to improve them. Many of the processes of individual, family, and community life are not directly related to education, but analyzing chains of daily activity involved in each, and the factors determining their unfoldment, generated a body of knowledge that was progressively incorporated into educational materials. For example, examining chains of activity related to the production of crops and animal husbandry gave rise to participative research on alternative systems of production on small farms. Similar research and action was carried out in areas of health, formal education, socialization, community organization, local economies, environment, and appropriate technology. A set of some eighty textbooks based on this experience were prepared constituting the core of a curriculum for secondary education that, in the ensuing two decades, reached tens of thousands of students in several Latin American countries. The secondary school program became known as *Sistema de Aprendizaje Tutorial (SAT);* to make its largescale implementation possible, two other programs were also developed, one for the training of secondary school teachers and the other for raising human resources with competence at the Masters level. In recent years, FUNDAEC has focused on a revised portion of the SAT curriculum to create a program for the training of "Promoters of Community Well-Being," which is now being adopted by a growing number of organizations in Africa, Asia, and the Pacific.

The intention of this inquiry is to help advance what is being referred to here as a "Bahá'í-inspired" discourse on education. To do so, we first identify a number of key concepts that can be considered crucial elements of an evolving framework for the educational programs contributing to this discourse. At this early stage, many of the elements will have to be sought in the ideas elaborated by FUNDAEC, while drawing to the extent possible on a number of other experiences. The founders of FUNDAEC were, of course, aware from the beginning that they would not be defining the framework for Bahá'í-inspired education. All they hoped to do was to take a few steps in the desired direction and initiate a process of action, reflection, and research that would lead to the creation of a framework and the corresponding educational programs in a series of approximations. The field of education, they believed, has been subject to too many theoretical fads. While the succession of theories that have achieved temporary prominence during the past decades have contributed to progress, much more can be achieved through systematic action—drawing insight from a diversity of pedagogical perspectives—accompanied by profound reflection within an evolving conceptual framework.

Repeated reference to FUNDAEC does not mean that the purpose of this inquiry is to analyze its experience; the aim is to present a set of ideas that may assist those involved in Bahá'í-inspired endeavors to achieve greater coherence as they strive to translate their ideals into effective educational programs. Emphasis is on the gradual development of a conceptual framework to which an increasing number of groups can contribute, based on experience and reflection—two ingredients of any attempt to tackle philosophical problems. Naturally, there is also the hope that this book may make some contribution, no matter how small, to the discussion of certain themes in the general discourse on education.

The several key concepts that are identified and discussed throughout the book as possible elements of an evolving framework for educational processes inspired by the Bahá'í teachings are all in need of philosophical scrutiny. The approach employed here is to search the relevant literature, to examine the concepts in question in that light, and to find ways to express them in a language that lends itself to philosophical exploration. By its very nature, such an approach involves reference to several authors rather than an exhaustive treatment of the works of one or two. While a sufficiently deep understanding of the work of each author is required, the aim is not to treat his or her arguments comprehensively, but to use insights gained from them to elaborate, to a reasonable extent, the key elements of the conceptual framework under consideration.

Generating Premises

The term "Bahá'í-inspired" is in need of some clarification: The educational endeavors thus designated do not include religious instruction. Like followers of other religions, Bahá'ís, too, engage in the study of the history of their Faith, its laws, principles, and tenets. These are not, however, the topics addressed in the kind of programs with which we are concerned. Nor is the object of study individual and social codes of conduct "inspired" by the teachings of the Faith—a Bahá'í version of moral education. "Inspiration" in this case refers to the framework of thought and action within which educational experience unfolds, a framework that, as already mentioned, is to be continually elaborated and refined. Programs are expected to develop through a dynamic process of action and reflection on action, a process well informed of various theories and practices in the field of education. Those involved in such programs are not exclusively Bahá'ís; they include a range of like-minded individuals who agree on the fundamental elements of the evolving conceptual framework.

At the heart of the framework under consideration is the concept of moral empowerment. A brief examination of the genesis of the concept as used by FUNDAEC—sometimes denoting the principal aim of the educational process it proposes and sometimes referring to the process itself—seems necessary in these introductory remarks. Discussions with individuals who have played significant roles in the creation of FUNDAEC underscore the importance of two interrelated sets of Bahá'í teachings that gradually led them to their conception of moral empowerment. The first has to do with the principle of the oneness of humankind and the second with the evolution of human society.

The oneness of humankind is the central principle of the Bahá'í Faith and the pivot around which all its teachings revolve. The widespread acceptance of this principle, Bahá'ís believe, is indispensable if humanity is to overcome its present formidable challenges. Oneness, they are quick to point out, does not imply uniformity; on the contrary, it should bring to mind the image of a garden in which the diversity of colors and shapes increases its beauty. Yet, with all the diversity, the flowers are "refreshed by the waters of one spring, revived by the breath of one wind," and "invigorated by the rays of one sun."[4] At the same time, "the consciousness of the oneness of humankind" should not be construed as a "mere outburst of ignorant emotionalism" or "an expression of vague and pious hope." The principle while requiring the recognition of the gains humanity has made in building harmonious relationships, both interpersonal and collective, cannot be "merely identified with a reawakening of the spirit of brotherhood and good-will among men." It is "applicable not only to the individual, but concerns itself primarily with the nature of those essential relationships that must bind all the states and nations as members of one human family." It envisions a world "organically unified in all the essential aspects of its life, its political machinery, its spiritual aspiration, its trade and finance," without stifling "the flame of a sane and intelligent patriotism in men's hearts," abolishing "the system of national autonomy so essential if the evils of excessive centralization are to be avoided," or suppressing "the diversity of ethnical origins, of climate, of history, of language and tradition, of thought and habit, that differentiate the peoples and nations of the world." It calls for a "wider loyalty" and implies "an organic change in the structure of present-day society, a change such as the world has not yet experienced."[5]

As to the evolution of society, Bahá'í teachings suggest that humanity's collective life can be seen in terms of stages analogous to the different phases in the life of a human being: infancy, childhood, adolescence, and maturity. This analogy, Bahá'ís believe, captures "the millennia-long process that has carried humanity to this culminating point in its collective history,"[6] the beginning of its passage to maturity. Accordingly, the agitations of today's society are understood as the necessary manifestations of an age of transition. Each period in the biological, cognitive, and emotional life of the individual is marked by certain conditions characteristic of a particular degree of intelligence and ability, and entering a new phase requires advances in capacity well beyond former conditions and needs. It is envisioned that the transformation called for in social relations and social structures in this stage of transition are as profound as the transformation that marks the passage from adolescence to maturity. In this light, the destructive and constructive forces operating in the world today are associated with parallel processes of disintegration and integration of a society in rapid transformation, and are interpreted as forces that are simultaneously compelling humanity to abandon the habits of childhood and to adopt ways that are commensurate with its approaching maturity. It is important to note that, for Bahá'ís, such a view of history does not imply an ideology and a political program that would force the appearance of a mature humanity. They are well aware that ideologies based on deterministic visions of history have wrought havoc in the world, particularly during the twentieth century. That humanity undergoes a process of maturation is a conviction that influences thought and behavior as would the knowledge that a growing tree has the potential to bring forth luscious fruits if it receives the necessary light, nutrients, and water. It is in the makeup of a child to become an adult, and the consciousness of such a potential is indispensable particularly during the turbulent age of adolescence.

Everything seems to indicate that the interplay of the two sets of teachings stated above—on the oneness of humankind and on the evolution of society—created in the minds of the founders of FUN-DAEC the conception of a *telos*: a twofold moral purpose of personal transformation—the becoming "imbued with new virtues and powers, new moralities, new capacities"[7]—and of the transformation of society. The aim of the educational process set in motion was thus expressed as the empowerment of the individual to assume responsibility for developing those virtues and powers required of her as a member of a human race now entering its age of maturity, on the one hand, and of consciously contributing to organic change in the structures of society, on the other.

History, both past and contemporary, offers examples of how religious teachings are reinterpreted by certain groups in order to focus them on the problems of society at a given time. Liberation theology, already in full bloom in Latin America in the years FUNDAEC was being formed, is a good example of this phenomenon in the Christian Faith. The nature of the Bahá'í Faith and its organization is such that its followers have not felt the need for such alternative readings. However, those who join the worldwide community do evince the various mindsets through which religion in general is experienced. The pathways to a central religious experience represented by these mindsets have been explored by students of religion and include ritualism, legalism, evangelism, social reform, and mysticism. Aware of these tendencies that have, in fact, caused many a division in most religions, the Bahá'í community strives to achieve and maintain harmony in its application of the various aspects of the teachings it espouses. Indeed, the proper integration of the mystical, moral, administrative, and social teachings of their Faith is an ongoing theme of discussion. For the founders of FUNDAEC who were active participants in such discussions, conscious effort by members of the community not to function in an inward-looking congregational mode was a moral obligation. Bahá'ís are required by the very teachings of their Faith to abandon narrow conceptions of religion that merely associate it with a set of beliefs and customs. As 'Abdu'l-Bahá states, religion "is not a series of beliefs, a set of customs; religion is the teachings of the Lord God, teachings which constitute the very life of humankind, which urge high thoughts upon the mind, refine the character, and lay the groundwork for man's everlasting honor."[8] Moreover, the practice of religion is not to be reduced to the construction of a virtuous life focused on one's own affairs. "Do not busy yourselves in your own concerns; let your thoughts be fixed upon that which will rehabilitate the fortunes of mankind and sanctify the hearts and souls of men,"[9] is Bahá'u'lláh's admonition. Thus Bahá'ís are to concern themselves with the broad sphere within which religion exerts influence on the life of the individual and society and to transcend borders that have been created among peoples of different faiths, and between them and those who adhere to no particular religion.

The Bahá'í teachings that inspire the category of educational programs being considered here, then, are to a great extent on the theme of "civilization building" and the indispensable role that individuals, communities, and the institutions of society play in propelling the advancement of civilization. The intimate relationship between the two dimensions of the moral purpose mentioned above—seen in the context of the gradual emergence of a world civilization that embraces both the spiritual and material dimensions of human existence—is to be considered a fundamental element of the conceptual framework of these programs. As FUNDAEC puts it, a profound awareness of the reciprocal relationship between personal growth and organic change in the structure of society is essential to the civilization-building process:

One cannot develop virtues and talents in isolation, but only through effort and activity for the benefit of others. Idle worship and prolonged withdrawal from society, advocated by some philosophies of the past, can neither promote individual development nor aid humanity's progress. To focus one's sense of purpose only on the development of one's own potential is to lose objectivity and perspective. With no outside interactions and social goals, one has no standard by which to judge personal progress and no concrete results by which to measure one's development. A person forgetful of the social dimension of moral purpose is prone to subtle forms of ego—combinations of guilt, self-righteousness, and self-satisfaction.

Conversely, a sense of purpose driven only by the desire to transform society, with no attention to the need for personal growth and transformation, is easily distorted. The person who blames society for every wrong and ignores the importance of individual responsibility loses respect and compassion for others and is prone to acts of cruelty and oppression. Social transformation, if divorced from the desire to transform one's own character, is an extremely fragile enterprise.

Social Action, then, must transcend the limitations of unfettered individualism and of suffocating collectivism and direct energies towards a balanced approach to personal and collective transformation—complementary dimensions of a single process.[10]

This formulation of the complementarity between the individual and collective dimensions of a moral purpose resonates with a passage written on behalf of Shoghi Effendi, the implications of which are discussed in a number of places in this inquiry:

We cannot segregate the human heart from the environment outside us and say that once one of these is reformed everything will be improved. Man is organic with the world. His inner life moulds the environment and is itself deeply affected by it. The one acts upon the other and every abiding change in the life of man is the result of these mutual reactions.[11]

The foregoing remarks on the Bahá'í community's involvement in social and economic development of peoples, on the approach adopted in the present exploration of a conceptual framework that would inform educational programs seeking moral empowerment and on the nature of religious beliefs that would inspire certain organizations to work within such a framework, pave the way for an analysis in chapter 2 of the notion of moral empowerment and the identification of a series of concepts to be examined in subsequent chapters.

CHAPTER 2

On Moral Empowerment

This chapter is dedicated to a preliminary analysis of the concept of moral empowerment—a term indicating both the process and the goal of educational programs that seek to enable students to take charge of their own intellectual and moral growth and to contribute to the transformation of society. Since the transformation in question is perceived in the context of humanity's transition from childhood to maturity, this analysis begins with a brief description in the first section of the nature of certain relationships fundamental to human existence, suggesting that transition to collective maturity is marked by the profound change these relationships will necessarily undergo. This change, it is argued, entails a willingness to leave behind narrow conceptions of power. In the section that follows, a brief examination of certain views of power and of the corresponding educational approaches seeking political empowerment is undertaken. The limitations of the political dimensions of power, identified in that section, demand a search for an expanded notion of power on which educational processes concerned with moral empowerment could draw. With insights emerging from a discussion of such an expanded notion in the background, a series of concepts are introduced, to be elaborated in subsequent chapters, as key elements of the conceptual framework being explored in this book.

Essential Relationships

Being impelled by a twofold purpose to pursue one's own intellectual and spiritual growth and to contribute at the same time to the trans-

13

formation of society implies that there is no tension between the two; they are interwoven aspects of one necessary movement. What is being argued here is that advancing in both entails change in those essential relationships that define societal existence—among individuals and groups, and between the individual, community, and institutions of society. Underlying these is humanity's relationship with nature and, more fundamentally, the bonds that connect the human being with God. Any search for the content and methods of Bahá'í-inspired educational programs must address, not infrequently, three interrelated questions: What will these relationships be like once humanity has entered its age of maturity? What is the nature of the changes that will occur in these relationships as the transition from childhood to maturity advances through successive stages? And what kind of educational activities will enable the individual to participate in transformative processes at any given stage? None of the three questions have immediate answers; a long process of research, action, and reflection—all carried out within a philosophical framework which itself must evolve—can shed light on the issues at hand as an effective pedagogy is gradually developed.

What can be argued with relative ease at this point is that the principle of the oneness of humankind gives direction to the process of transition and offers insights into the nature of the changes that must occur in each of the above-mentioned relationships. An example from the Bahá'í teachings illustrates this point. In the physical world, the human body has evolved to a degree of complexity that makes the emergence of consciousness possible. The modes of operation that guarantee the biological functioning of the body and its well-being are characterized by the perfect integration of diverse cells: "No cell lives apart from the body, whether in contributing to its functioning or in deriving its share from the well-being of the whole." It is the wholeness of the system that allows for the complete development of the capacities inherent in each of its component elements. The physical

14

well-being thus achieved finds its purpose in channeling the expression of individual consciousness; "that is to say, the purpose of biological development transcends the mere existence of the body and its parts."[1]

It is worthwhile to consider whether the same conception does not apply to the organization of humanity's collective existence, even though, unlike the cells of the body, the individuals constituting society are endowed with intelligence and volition. Will not the essential relationships that define human existence evolve during the passage from childhood to maturity, one can at least ask, in such a way that the capacities of each human being are given room to fully develop as the bonds among individuals, communities, and the institutions of society are strengthened? And if so, can one not assume that such development will lead to an increasingly more complete expression of human consciousness with the aid of complex social structures, themselves undergoing evolutionary change?

The metaphor of the human body,[2] if earnestly taken into consideration, points to the inadequacy of the conception of human society either as an aggregate of competing elements or as a conglomerate of differentiated sectors, each trying to exploit the achievements of others. As transition to maturity advances, humanity will need to move away from the vision of society as the arena of negotiations among individuals defending personal or group interest. The steady increase in the number of people living in conditions of "absolute poverty," the growing gap between the rich and the poor, and the economic crisis affecting even the richest countries of the world, in an era of globalization so focused on competitiveness, seem to indicate that numerous challenges have to be overcome if the aspirations of the individual are to be harmonized with the interests of society. The condition in which the state as the embodiment of collective will would crush individuality to defend some conception of a higher purpose is not compatible with the type of relationships the principle of the oneness of humankind seems to demand either. Much of the argument in this book will assume that "the advancement of the race has not occurred at the expense of human individuality. As social organization has increased, the scope for the expression of the capacities latent in each human being has correspondingly expanded. Because the relationship between the individual and society is a reciprocal one, the transformation now required must occur simultaneously within human consciousness and the structure of social institutions."[3]

Conceptions of Power in Political Empowerment

Given the centrality of power to the way relationships among individuals, groups, and the institutions of society have taken shape during the evolutionary process that has brought humanity to its present state, and in light of the long established association of the very concept of power with domination, competition, and conflict, it seems reasonable to suggest that the transformation being envisioned requires a fundamental revision of the conception of power. A first step in such an endeavor would be to look at the prevalent views of political power and ask if they exhaust the meaning of power in all the relationships in which a human being enters. Our analysis of political power, although brief, will lead to the conclusion that there are other dimensions to power—notably those expressing the nobility of the human spirit—that a process of moral empowerment would have to recognize and draw upon. But appealing to these dimensions of power alone does not prove to be sufficient. The conception of political power itself needs to undergo a transformation if the essential relationships defining human society are to evolve in keeping with the maturation of the human race. These relationships cannot be neatly divided, for example, into those that involve political power as generally accepted today and those that depend on other forms of power. Power structures that fill the political landscape, whether incorporated in governmental institutions or organizations of civil society, exert a great influence on other spheres of human life; the struggles they engender penetrate every facet of individual and social existence.[4] Humanity is impelled, as it advances toward maturity, to aspire to higher and higher degrees of consistency in thought and action across the private and the public sphere. The notion of power that a politically active individual adopts has to become coherent with one embraced by a comprehensive conception of human well-being; the powers that reside in the individual and the collective—through the release of which social and material progress is achieved—will have to be allowed to play their part in shaping political life in general.

Although power is a highly contested concept, there is an underlying tendency of many political theorists to associate it with domination. Whether it is "the production of intended effects"[5] and the capacity to produce them, or the "probability that one actor within a social relationship will be in a position to carry out his own will despite resistance,"[6] power aspires to be a quantitative concept, empirically measured in terms of the resistance—actual or potential—that it can overcome. For the concept thus conceived to be viable, conflict, whether observable or not, needs to be ever present. In other words, conflict seems to emerge in one way or another as an indispensable condition that makes the exercise of power possible; it is intrinsic to power in its actual state. Our purpose here, of course, is not to analyze power in this form. What we need are insights from an examination of power in prevalent notions of political empowerment, particularly when they are associated with educational processes, to see if we can move toward an expanded concept of power that would enter our conception of moral empowerment. One source that can help us carry out this analysis is Steven Lukes' treatment of the three dimensions of power.[7]

As a prototype of the one-dimensional view of power, Lukes cites Robert A. Dahl's "intuitive idea of power," according to which "A has power over B to the extent that he can get B to do something that B would not otherwise do."[8] Dahl's analysis of power is carried out within the context of western liberal democracy and involves the careful examination of a series of decisions. The emphasis is on behavior, on the exercise of power, rather than on its possession. His method entails determining "for each decision which participants had initiated alternatives that were finally adopted, had vetoed alternatives initiated by others, or had proposed alternatives that were turned down." These actions are then "tabulated as individual 'successes' or 'defeats.' The participants with the greatest proportion of successes out of the total number of successes" are deemed to be "the most influential."[9]

To introduce the two-dimensional view of power, Lukes draws on the observation that power has two faces.[10] While power is obviously exercised by individuals participating in the making of decisions that affect others, it is also exercised when persons or groups limit the scope of issues to be considered, allowing room only for those matters that are not detrimental to their set of preferences. The one-dimensional view of power, then, is concerned with "decision-making," where a decision is "a choice among alternative modes of action."[11] The two-dimensional view also examines "nondecision-making," where nondecision is "a decision that results in suppression or thwarting of a latent or manifest challenge to the values or interests of the decision-maker." Nondecision-making is "a means by which demands for change in the existing allocation of benefits and privileges in the community can be suffocated before they are even voiced; or kept covert; or even killed before they gain access to the relevant decision-making arena; or, failing all these things, maimed or destroyed in the decision-implementing stage of the policy process."[12]

Lukes points out that both views place undue emphasis on "observable" conflict, be it overt or covert, and both are individualistic in essence. The two-dimensional view of power does acknowledge the operation of "a set of predominant values, beliefs, rituals, and institutional procedures"[13] which systematically and consistently benefit some at the expense of others. Yet it falls short by ignoring the fact that such bias "is not sustained simply by a series of individually chosen acts, but also, most importantly, by the socially structured and culturally patterned behaviour of groups, and practices of institutions, which may indeed be manifested by individuals' inaction."[14]

To overcome the shortcomings of the one- and the two-dimensional views of power, Lukes argues that it is the hidden face of power in its three-dimensional representation that needs to be exposed. Conflict, which acts as fuel for the exercise of power in its one- or two-dimensional sense, is transformed into "willing compliance" to domination in the three-dimensional view of power. Power operates unseen by securing willing compliance. Certain Marxist thinkers seek to provide an explanation of this phenomenon by elaborating on the theme of "false consciousness." Antonio Gramsci's elaboration underscores the consciousness developed by the subordinated social groups who borrow and internalize their conception of the world from the ideology of dominant groups. Internalization is manifested either in the form of belief in the values such a conception holds or in the inability to conceive of alternatives to the prevalent social norms.

A more in-depth study of Lukes' view of power than the above would have to address certain fundamental questions, for example, how he can reconcile two potentially contradictory conceptions of human beings: as autonomous calculating rational agents exercising power in its first two dimensions, and as malleable creatures of social conditions dominated by power in its third dimension.[15] It would also have to consider modifications he has made to his original view by stating, for example, that power is "a capacity" and "not the exercise of that capacity (it may never be, and never need to be, exercised)," that "you can be powerful by satisfying and advancing others' interests," and that "everyone's interests are multiple, conflicting and of different kinds."[16] However, we will not undertake such a study in this inquiry; what we have already mentioned allows us to identify the views of power implicit in educational approaches concerned with political empowerment. Let us consider two examples: citizenship education in liberal democracies and Paulo Freire's account of education as conscientization.

There are clear connections between power in its one- and two-dimensional manifestations and some of the objectives of citizenship education. In a liberal democracy, one may assign to citizenship education the task of enabling students to participate actively in the cultural, social, and political domains. The focus can vary depending on the views of the dominant social or political group at the time, which may attach supremacy to the market and the operation of individual choice or emphasize social welfare and social obligation. But no matter what the dominant view, there are common values inherent to liberal democracies that the citizen must learn to cherish. All parties would agree, to cite an example, that in order to resolve conflicts and achieve some degree of consensus in a pluralistic society, "appreciation of the paramount importance of democratic decision making" has to be cultivated. Citizenship education, of course, does not confine itself to the teaching of democracy; it incorporates "knowledge, attitudes, moral codes, and values, thereby placing spiritual and moral education explicitly within its scope."[17] Yet, irrespective of other moral attributes, the citizen of a liberal democracy is to uphold democratic values; she should be politically empowered to participate in the processes of decision making, to identify those policies and practices that are biased toward certain groups, and to bring these biases to the attention of the public. The parameters of this type of empowerment, one can argue, are defined to a great measure by the value placed on "free and fair competition," and the kind of power with which the citizen is to be invested belongs mostly to Lukes' one- and, occasionally, two-dimensional views.

The most notable educational approach which deals with the representation of power in its third dimension is Paulo Freire's. Given that in this dimension both the observable and unobservable conflicts are to be considered, any attempt at empowerment would necessarily involve the cultivation of critical consciousness. Freire examines in a most insightful manner how the oppressed can defeat the false consciousness they have adopted. Human beings begin in a state of "semi-intransitive" consciousness, solely concerned with "survival" on a biological level, lacking "a sense of life on a more historical plane." They enter a "transitive" state, as they "amplify their power to perceive and respond to suggestions and questions arising in their context," and as they "increase their capacity to enter into dialogue not only with other men but with their world."[18] However, this is only a "naïve transitive" state in which consciousness of people is "part of a mass," within which "developing capacity for dialogue is still fragile and capable of distortion." This state of consciousness is characterized:

> . . . by an over-simplification of problems; by a nostalgia for the past; by underestimation of the common man; by a strong tendency to gregariousness; by a lack of interest in investigation, accompanied by an accentuated taste for fanciful explanations; by fragility of argument; by a strongly emotional style; by the practice of polemics rather than dialogue; by magical explanations.[19]

Consciousness must progress from a naïve to a "critical transitive" state if it is not to be distorted. The critically transitive consciousness is characterized:

> . . . by depth in the interpretation of problems; by the substitutions of causal principles for magical explanations; by the testing of one's "findings" and by openness to revision; by the attempt to avoid distortion when perceiving problems and to avoid preconceived notions when analyzing them; by refusing to transfer responsibility; by rejecting passive positions; by soundness of argumentation; by the practice of dialogue rather than polemics; by the receptivity to the new for reasons beyond mere novelty and

21

by the good sense not to reject the old just because it is old—by accepting what is valid in both old and new.[20]

Only when the oppressed have reached a state of critical transitive consciousness will they have the power to act on society.

Freire criticizes the type of education he calls "banking education" as one in which the act of teaching and the relationship between the teacher and the students perpetuate an intransitive or naïve transitive state of consciousness and reinforce the domination exercised by the oppressor. Banking education assumes a dichotomy between human beings and the world: "A person is merely in the world, not *with* the world or with others; the individual is spectator, not re-creator"; he possesses an empty "mind" passively open to "the reception of deposits of reality from the world outside."[21] For education to liberate, it should become problem posing, allowing students to become "critical co-investigators in dialogue *with* the teacher."[22] The problem-posing method recognizes a movement in which the "point of departure" constitutes "the situation within which they (men and women) are submerged, from which they emerge, and in which they intervene." For this movement to occur people must not perceive their state as fated and unalterable; instead they need to view their situation as "an historical reality susceptible of transformation." The movement is necessarily one of inquiry. "Any situation in which some individuals prevent others from engaging in the process of inquiry is one of violence." Freire therefore describes this movement of inquiry as one "directed towards humanization—the people's historical vocation."[23] In chapter 9, we will examine Freire's arguments more critically, but this brief description helps demonstrate how his approach to education takes into account the exercise of power in its third dimension.

Search for an Expanded Concept of Power

With the above two examples in mind, we may now ask if it is possible to elaborate a conception of moral empowerment that can enter domains not covered by, say, citizenship education and education as conscientization. Clearly, the intention is not to ignore the elements of these and other approaches to empowerment. A program wishing to foster the twofold purpose at the heart of moral empowerment would also try, for example, to cultivate an appreciation of the paramount importance of consultative decision making and to assist in the movement from a state of semi-transitive consciousness into a critically transitive one. The question is the extent to which the kind of educational process being sought in this inquiry would need to explore other forms of power which could in turn modify the view of power in the three dimensions proposed by Lukes.

It is important to mention that the notion of domination seems to have taken center stage in most analyses of power in accordance with the assumption that other representations have less theoretical value. Lukes has expressed the view that "revisionary persuasive redefinitions" of power are not aligned with the "central meanings of "power" as traditionally understood and with the concerns that have always centrally preoccupied students of power." As a result, they end up "concealing from view the (central) aspects of power which they define out of existence."[24] What are these central meanings of power, we may ask, as traditionally understood? To what extent does Thomas Hobbes' legacy continue to exert influence on today's discourse on power? Hobbes wrote in the Leviathan:

> In the broadest and most general sense, a man's power is his present means to obtain some future apparent good. Power is either original (natural) or instrumental. . . . Natural (original) power is outstandingness in the faculties of body or mind, such as extraordinary strength, good looks, prudence, practical skill, eloquence, generosity, nobility. Instrumental powers are acquired through natural powers or through luck; they are means and instruments to acquire more, for example riches, reputation, friends, and the secret working of God which men call good luck.[25]

There is no question that "riches joined with liberality," "friends," "success," "noble rank," "eloquence," "good looks," and "what quality soever maketh a man beloved or feared of many, or the reputation of such quality"[26] can, and have, been used as means of yielding a certain kind of power. But how can one justify incessant pursuit of this power as the defining factor of the human condition based on such observations, no matter how many times and under how many differing circumstances they have been made?

One might wish to set aside Hobbes' analysis as an extreme. Yet the same pattern of thinking can be seen in others who, in one way or another, attempt to understand human relations in purely materialistic terms. Foucault's declaration that by power he does not mean "mechanisms that ensure the subservience of the citizens of a given state," "the mode of subjugation which [. . .] has the form of the rule" or a "general system of domination exerted by one group over another"[27] promises a possible break from the notion of power so closely associated with domination. But as one examines carefully what he claims to be methodological precautions—rules that would help us "eschew the model of the Leviathan" and shift our study of power from the "limited field of judicial sovereignty and State institutions" to the "techniques and tactics of domination"[28]—one begins to see a familiar vision of human existence. Power is omnipresent because it is "produced from one moment to the next, at every point, or rather in every relation from one point to another." Relations of power are not to be seen in "a position of exteriority with respect to other types of relationships,"[29] but are inherent to them. Foucault's disagreement with Hobbes does not seem to be on the nature of power and its omnipresence, but the points at which it should be studied—not in its "central location," but at "its extremities, in its ultimate destinations": points "where it becomes capillary."[30] A different interpretation of Foucault's ideas may be possible, but while even a limited reading of his work indicates the brilliance with which he analyzes power relations, it is doubtful if his articulation can offer us the kind of insight we seek in order to explore an expanded notion of power, one that frees it from its close ties to domination.

The claim being made in this brief discussion is that to assign domination such a central role in the discourse on power—with its corollary that conflict is vital to its exercise—is to limit the philosophical investigation of the concept to perceptions and habits that belong to the stage of humanity's childhood. According to Barry Hindess, Western political thought has mostly dealt with two conceptions of power. In the first, power is a simple quantitative phenomenon, nothing more than "a generalized capacity to act." In the second, more complex conception, the right to act also receives attention, "both capacity and right being seen to rest on the consent of those over whom power is exercised."[31] It is true that a government, for example, may "exercise" power "over" its people with their consent. But it seems legitimate to ask, in the context of a search for an expanded concept of power, why "being exercised over," although a historical fact, should continue to define in its totality the nature of power. This is the kind of question, we may assume, that led FUNDAEC to look for something more than political empowerment in the first place. The following statement is indicative of the organization's anxiety over the issue of power:

That change and transformation entail the operation of power is an undeniable fact. That numerous issues in the field of development have a significant political dimension is also irrefutable. But the premise that political and economic power—interpreted as advantage enjoyed by persons or groups or as an attribute of individuals, factions, peoples, classes, and nations used to acquire, to surpass, to dominate, to resist, and to win—is the agent that will bring prosperity to the entire human race is untenable. Despite all claims to the contrary, there is no convincing historical evidence for this supposition. . . .

The rapid expansion of Western civilization takes to every corner of the world both the blessings and the curses of the Enlightenment. The blessings include the systematic removal of the veils of superstition. But, unfortunately, this is accompanied by a coarseness of mind that tends to dismiss the ideal and to call real that which is ugly and base. The result, after a few centuries of insistence, is widespread forgetfulness of those many powers of the human spirit that are in fact responsible for some of the greatest accomplishments of humanity's past. Among these are the power of unity, of humble service, of noble deeds, of love, and of truth. But even to mention the word *truth* in respectable discourse has become unacceptable; truth has been dethroned and reduced to something that is negotiable or a mere expression of dominance. The loudest message broadcast all over the world for an entire generation to hear is "he who is successful is right."[32]

While the assertions made in these paragraphs clearly require philosophical scrutiny, the passage does suggest a dimension of power absent in Lukes' analysis, which needs to be examined in relation to moral empowerment. To begin, it questions a widespread assumption in the field of development that acting according to a conception of power that solely values political and economic advantages for which individuals and groups have to compete will ultimately lead to an acceptable degree of prosperity for the majority of the human race. To what extent, we too would ask, did the herculean efforts to give the disempowered masses of humanity access to such power help them free themselves from the yokes of oppression? But the more interesting implications of the quoted passage for this inquiry lie in the introduction of what it calls the powers of the human spirit. The question before us is whether an educational endeavor that seeks to help students become effective channels, for example, for the "power of unity, of humble service, of noble deeds, of love," can engender a process that indeed goes beyond political empowerment. Are these, we need to ask, not powers at work in the harmonious interaction of individuals, communities, and institutions when they do not wish to focus on the conflict of interest that may or may not exist, but are willing to find new channels for the expression of collective aspiration to advance civilization? Will not these powers over time transform the very decision-making process from unending cycles of dominance of one group over another into genuine consultation: collective investigation of reality? And will not a movement in this direction require the capacity to transcend one's own interests, one's particular perspective and one's preferences, if groups of people are to reach maturity of understanding through consultation?

Bahá'í-inspired educational efforts can gain valuable insights in their quest for a conception of power congruent with the coming of age of the human race in the rich metaphors of the Bahá'í Faith's spiritual teachings and, in fact, of many religious traditions: A pure, kindly and radiant heart is likened to a sovereignty ancient, imperishable and everlasting; humility is said to exalt the human being to the heaven of glory and power; a thought of peace is regarded as more powerful than a thought of war; idle disputation to advance oneself over one's brother is seen as unworthy of a human being. Apart from reflections on such spiritual teachings, insights need to be gained from philosophical approaches in which the subject of power is studied in new ways. One such approach involves the analysis of the positive and non-exhaustive nature of power. Admittedly in Hobbes characterization, too, "power is like fame in that it increases as it proceeds; or like the motion of falling heavy bodies, which go faster as they go further." Nevertheless, as it grows, power in this form continues to belong to the few "to whom most men have agreed to hand over their individual powers."[33] When viewed, in line with predominant discourses, as a substance that one or more people can possess, power is a measurable and circumscribed quantity to be distributed. If A gets filled with so much power, B will be emptied of a corresponding amount of it. Even in the case of Lukes' three-dimensional conception, political emancipation is meant to take power away from the "oppressors" and redistribute it among the "oppressed."

There are, however, forms of power tied to resources that are limitless; drawing on such resources enhances reciprocity and interconnectedness. When these forms of power are recognized, empowerment can become a process that calls for the development of one's capacity to accompany others and to release their powers and capacities. The process advances as power is generated and increased "through cooperation, sharing responsibility and working together."[34] To describe empowerment in this way is to acknowledge the possibility of power as a concept that is difficult to pin down, one which covers the release or actualization of a wide range of potentialities in the individual and in peoples. That it is fuzzy and therefore not susceptible to quantification in the way power as domination is, is to its advantage. Hannah Arendt reminds us that power is always "a power potential and not an unchangeable, measurable, and reliable entity like force and strength." It is actualized when people are together "in the manner of speech and action" and when in their being with one another they have reached a state in which "word and deed have not parted company," "words are not empty and deeds not brutal," and "words are not used to veil intentions but to disclose realities, and deeds are not used to violate and destroy but to establish relations and create new realities."[35] Power in the sense that Arendt describes is "boundless" and intimately connected to action. It is the condition of unity that ties power to action: "power corresponds to the human ability not just to act but to act in concert. Power is never the property of an individual; it belongs to a group and remains in existence only so long as the group keeps together."[36] It is this power which is the antithesis of violence. As Arendt writes: "the will to power, as the modern age from Hobbes to Nietzsche understood it in glorification or denunciation, far from being a characteristic of the strong, is, like envy and greed, among the vices of the weak."[37]

Key Elements

The way we perceive empowerment, associating it intimately with a vision of the evolution of those essential relationships that shape individual and collective existence, although not fully developed in the above, allows us to begin the next task of this inquiry: the identification of the main concepts that would constitute some of the elements of the framework for educational processes that pursue moral empowerment. The premise that humanity is approaching its stage of maturity holds within it claims about the evolution of the collective powers of the species; the conviction that such powers are increasingly manifesting themselves is at the heart of the optimism with which the possibility of something beyond political empowerment has been discussed in the previous section. It is common to refer to the explosion of knowledge as a characteristic of our times, but the sheer quantity of knowledge available to humanity is only a sign of the more profound transformation anticipated. Particularly, the capacity to manifest such powers as thought, comprehension, insight, reflection, and vision—as well as other powers of the human spirit like the power of unity, of humble service, of noble deeds, and of love mentioned earlier—must increase enormously. If the metaphor of the human body is to express the desired relationship between the individual and the collective in a society that embodies the principle of the oneness of humankind, these powers have to manifest themselves in greater and greater measures in both the individual and in the species as a whole. Educational processes must emerge, then, that enable a vast number of people to develop intellectual and spiritual powers, already present in potential, to a degree far surpassing the achievements of past generations.

Our conception of power is clearly an element of the philosophical framework explored here; a related element has to do with the role knowledge plays in the process of moral empowerment. One of the most valuable contributions FUNDAEC has made to Bahá'í-inspired discourse on education is its analysis of widespread oppression in terms of

29

worldwide structures and processes that in the end deny the majority of humanity access to knowledge. Based on this perception, it has examined how moral empowerment needs to occur in the context of participation in the generation, application, and diffusion of knowledge—driven by the twofold purpose of pursuing personal growth and contributing to the transformation of society—and not in the struggle for power *per se*. For such participation to lead to moral empowerment, the intellectual excellence associated with the acquisition of knowledge should be freed from the chains of "self-centeredness." Knowledge has to be acquired in light of a profound understanding of social reality by one not aloof from society but intimately involved in its ongoing transformation. The way reality is understood, described, and acted upon is integral to the dual processes of individual and social transformation. We stand in need of a conception of "understanding" that takes into account the intellectual and moral powers of the individual, the varying complexities of the "objects of understanding" that need to be grasped and acted upon, as well as the process by which greater measures of insights into reality and its transformation are gained. Such a conception of understanding is an essential element of the framework being sought here, and will be explored in the next three chapters. In chapter 3 we begin to search for the desired characteristics of the "subject of understanding," the protagonist of moral empowerment. In this search, we will necessarily have to take a critical look at certain predominant theories of learning and cognition and make explicit the assumptions they hold regarding the powers of the human mind and the nature of understanding. We will also seek insights into the dynamic relationship between the subject of understanding and the cultural environment. This can only be done if we recognize that "generation of meaning" is a complex process. Meaning is neither entirely produced within the subject, nor does it completely reside in the culture. The relationship between the individual mind and the outer environment is not simply one of precedence, in which arguments are made either in favor of an "inside out" or an "outside in" process through which meaning is generated. Not until we transcend such reduction, will we be in a position to explore the intricate interconnectedness of the powers of the human spirit and the elements of the environment as well as the transformation which their mutual interactions engender. We will develop further our conception of understanding in chapter 4 by considering its unboundedness, both as a process in which one may systematically advance and as a faculty of the human soul with its endless potentialities. We will propose that "nurturing understanding," so central to a process of moral empowerment, is inseparable from "fostering spiritual qualities." The connection is not just consequential, to ensure that knowledge is not used to perpetuate oppression; there are underlying bonds that unite understanding with various "spiritual qualities" at the level of "being." By spiritual qualities we do not mean the wide range of qualities, attitudes, and skills that the term "virtues" brings to mind. Spiritual qualities are inherent to the human soul as heat is to the sun and warmth to fire. The concept becomes muddled when specific spiritual qualities are placed under the broad and relatively vague category of virtue; it becomes difficult to distinguish a spiritual quality from a host of culture specific dispositions, social dexterities, and mental skills. A brief analysis of Alasdair MacIntyre's account of virtues embedded in practice will help us clarify the distinction being made and elaborate a conception of spiritual qualities, which together with understanding can be seen as permanent constituents of being. In chapter 5, we will undertake an exploration of the "object of understanding" in its most general sense—physical, social, and spiritual reality. Drawing on insights from the works of John R. Searle, Thomas Nagel, and John McDowell, as well as advances made by FUNDAEC in dealing with the problem of fragmentation in education, we will identify significant connections between the subject, the object, and the process of understanding.

In examining the question of knowledge in the context of moral empowerment, it soon becomes necessary to look at the way the framework for the desired educational process would establish the necessary connections between reason and morality. To see what we mean by links between the power of reason and the moral act, let us look briefly at two well-known rationalist approaches, namely, utilitarianism and the formalism originated from Immanuel Kant's views. The two approaches have been subjects of intense and sophisticated analysis in the field of ethics, and it is not necessary at this point to delve into this ongoing philosophical investigation. We need only draw on the most obvious features of the two in order to highlight the role that reason plays in the moral domain in each perspective.

In utilitarianism, human reason and morals are linked through utility: "The creed which accepts as the foundation of morals *utility* or the *greatest happiness principle,* holds that actions are right in proportions as they tend to promote happiness, wrong as they tend to produce the reverse of happiness."[38] By "happiness," is meant pleasure, and the absence of pain, and by "unhappiness," pain, and the privation of pleasure. According to Jeremy Bentham, our standard of right and wrong is completely governed by pain and pleasure:

Nature has placed mankind under the governance of two sovereign masters, *pain* and *pleasure.* It is for them alone to point out what we ought to do, as well as to determine what we shall do. On the one hand the standard of right and wrong, on the other the chain of causes and effects, are fastened to their throne. They govern us in all we do, in all we say, in all we think: every effort we make to throw off our subjection, will serve but to demonstrate and confirm it. In words a man may pretend to abjure their empire: but in reality he will remain subject to it all the while. The *principle of utility* recognizes this subjection, and assumes it for the foundation of that system, the object of which is to rear the fabric of felicity by the hands of reason and law. Systems which attempt to question it deal in sounds instead of sense, in caprice instead of reason, in darkness instead of light.[39]

John Stuart Mill admits that greater clarity needs to be achieved about what is to be included in the concepts of pain and pleasure if the utilitarian theory is to yield moral standards. However, according to him, such "supplementary explanations" do not affect the broader theory of life on which utilitarian morality is based. In this broader theory, the only desirable ends are pleasure and freedom from pain and the worth of anything depends either on the pleasure inherent in it, or as "means to the promotion of pleasure and the prevention of pain."[40] Mill acknowledges that there are higher and lower pleasures, while Bentham sees no such distinction; for him "the quantity of pleasure being equal," all human preferences should be regarded as equivalent in value. With pain and pleasure governing our standard of right and wrong, reason becomes the means by the aid of which happiness is maximized.

In the Kantian approach, the "categorical imperative"—as opposed to "hypothetical imperative" which treats reason instrumentally—brings into light the rational dimension of moral action: "if the action is represented as *in itself* good, hence as necessary [for] a will in itself conforming to reason, as its principle, *then it is categorical.*"[41]

Here, reason is not the means for gaining happiness and fleeing from pain; it is the end that makes human beings autonomous, free from the captivity of desire and passion. Although it often seems we are the authors of our own decisions when pursuing personal preferences, we are in fact slaves to already determined values. Reason renders us free according to a law we give ourselves—not divine law—which, in turn, determines our will to act. "But what kind of law can that be, the representation of which must determine the will, even without regard for the effect expected from it, in order for the will to be called good absolutely and without limitation?"[42] The Kantian answer is universal law conformity with which "serves the will as its principle."[43] This "single categorical imperative" is summarized as *act only in accordance with that maxim through which you can at the same time will that it become a universal law."*[44] Not all maxims can attain the status of universal law. For example, making a false promise to pay back the money one has borrowed is not a categorical imperative; it is not a maxim that could become a universal law. To test such a maxim one has to imagine the condition that would be created by its universal application: a world in which everyone made false promises in order to get some money. The universalization of this maxim, it can thus be concluded, nullifies the very conception of a "promise," which acquires meaning only if it is intended to be fulfilled by the one who makes it. This logical contradiction in the maxim, were everyone to follow it, would obliterate altogether the practice of making and accepting promises. Further, its universalization derails the purpose of the act of promising which is to create trust and cooperation among people.

Charles Taylor points out how these two perspectives, notwithstanding the substantive moral insights they offer, have regrettably attained the status of meta-theory. A meta-theory is formulated with an "already formed model of valid reasoning, all the more dogmatically held because we are oblivious to the alternatives."[45] The model, thus framed, prevents the operation of reason in its fullest. In the utilitarian perspective, what validates an ethical position is "hard evidence." Reality is cut and chopped down to fit "the Procrustean bed" of this mode of validation. The consequences for human happiness of one or another course of action are counted and the one with the highest total is chosen. Human happiness is considered as "something conceptually unproblematic, a scientifically establishable domain of facts like others. One could abandon all the metaphysical or theological factors—commands of God, natural rights, virtues—which made ethical questions scientifically undecidable. Bluntly, we could calculate."[46] In the Kantian perspective, according to Taylor, one is to "ignore the problematic distinctions between different qualities of action and modes of life, which play such a large part in our actual moral decisions, feelings of admiration, remorse, etc., but which are so hard to justify when others controvert them." There is the assumption that all possible sets of desirable and undesirable actions can be tested for their universalizability in isolation from their qualitative aspects, and "principles that would be adopted by free rational agents in certain paradigm circumstances" be delineated.[47]

The framework we are exploring needs to be informed of rationalist approaches to ethics. However, being inspired by the teachings of the Bahá'í Faith, it cannot shy away from religious conviction. When religious conviction is present, to act in a certain way in a given situation would not be simply desirable because it would increase total happiness, or because it follows the Kantian maxim, although it may fulfill some formulation of such conditions. A crucial consideration will be consistency with the pattern of conduct understood to be prescribed in the scriptures. What is more, religious teachings offer their own definitions of, and insights into, such concepts as happiness, will, freedom, duty, and law. Yet, understanding what is prescribed in the scriptures is not a straightforward matter. We must acknowledge that a rationality that places undue emphasis on a given interpretation of a set of religious teachings is as narrow as the one that marginalizes religious conviction, and the educational process based on it would suffer from a suffocating rigidity which can only lead to rebellion. Exclusive dependence on the reading of the "text," which admittedly must have a place in a system of thought inspired by religion, would distort experience; the role of science, both its methods and its content, in the educational process would at best become blurred. Given the centrality of the principle of harmony between science and religion in the Bahá'í teachings, such an approach—always in danger of a fundamentalism arising from literal interpretations at war with each other—would be untenable. On the other hand, an approach that considers the insights of religion irrelevant is equally unacceptable. We cannot resolve this apparent dilemma unless we come up with a reasonably satisfactory explanation of the complementary relationship between science and religion. Thus the conception of the "complementarity between science and religion" is an important element of the framework under consideration. This theme is addressed in chapter 6 at some length, but a few words should be said here about the contrast between the notion of complementarity as advanced by FUNDAEC and certain prevalent views of the relationship between science and religion.

According to one perspective, whatever truth is expounded by religion about spiritual phenomena will someday be explained by science. Religion in this case is an institution of the childhood of humanity that will finally be made irrelevant by scientific explanation. An opposing view may hold that religion is the outcome of God's Revelation, and that—as God knows everything—scientific truth is ultimately attainable by penetrating the mysteries of religious text. Neither of these two views is considered valid in this inquiry. There is another perspective according to which science and religion are so distinct that there is no possibility of significant conflict between them. Science studies the material universe. Its accomplishments serve to push forward the frontiers of technological possibility, opening the way for innovations that can be employed either for the good of humanity or to its detriment. Science in itself does not have the ability to point the way. Religion, on the other hand, is concerned with the spiritual dimension of human existence. Its task is to throw light on the inner life and to engender a code of ethics that can appropriately guide human behavior. So long as each remains within the sphere of its own genus, they can coexist in harmony. This "view of the harmony between science and religion is valid, but only at the level of application. Ultimately, in this approach, science and religion are separated and allowed to pursue their own ways, and what assumes importance is the interaction between technology and morality."[48] Arguing for complementarity between science and religion as two systems of knowledge and practice with a somewhat fluid overlap addresses at a more profound level the harmony between the two. Complementarity, moreover, implies that an educational process concerned with moral empowerment has the freedom to look to both sources in order to engender understanding of various aspects of reality and to cultivate the appropriate attributes in the students.

A question that arises naturally once issues related to sources of knowledge are to some degree analyzed is how, in nurturing understanding and fostering spiritual qualities, one brings the "objects of understanding" from various fields and disciplines together to create the proper teaching-learning experience that would empower students to pursue their own development and, at the same time, contribute to the advancement of society. An important element of our evolving framework is a conception of "integration" which takes into account the interconnections between structures of the human mind, objects of understanding, and active participation in transformative processes that lead to progress. In other words, an educational process focused on the moral empowerment of its participants is required to seek those deeper ties that fuse together "being," "knowing," and "doing." In this context, a major challenge of integration is to move away from a vision of knowledge that largely considers it as a sum of contents and methods of fields and disciplines separated by rigid boundaries without losing the rigor of education. One tantalizing prospect is to use social practices as the axis around which educational activities can be organized. However, as Michael Young points out, the trend in curriculum studies focused solely on social practices has led to the marginalization of knowledge because it does not provide a basis upon which a distinction between curriculum knowledge and everyday knowledge could be made. Young identifies two other co-culprits: first, the work begun in the 1970s in the sociology of education, to which he himself contributed, sidelining the role of knowledge by conceptualizing subject-based curriculum in terms of social interests that define its content, and second, postmodernism with its critique of school curriculum, claiming that it leaves no space for any voice except those of the professional and the academic elite. All three developments, he mentions, "collude, albeit unintentionally, with the marketization that now drives educational policy." He adds that "in denying a distinctive role for knowledge that transcends specific social practices, interests, and contexts, these approaches remove the grounds for a critical relationship between theory and curriculum policy and practice."[49]

Integration as discussed in this inquiry is not only concerned with issues related to the disciplines of knowledge and social practices. It also addresses more fundamental questions. We will deal with this theme in chapter 7, first at the level of knowledge—drawing on Paul Hirst's theory of forms of knowledge and his later views on the priority of practical knowledge—then at the level of values inherent in knowledge, and finally through a brief presentation of the inseparability of thought and action.

Chapter 8 is dedicated to the examination of yet another element of the conceptual framework being explored: the conception of "capability." In its attempt to deal with the various dimensions of the challenge of integrating the content and methods of a morally empowering educational experience, FUNDAEC introduced the notion of capability. It used the word in a very specific way, as "developed capacity to think and act in a particular sphere of activity and according to an explicit purpose." Capability refers to "complex spheres of thought and action each requiring a number of related skills and abilities," but its acquisition, in addition to the mastering of skills, is dependent on the assimilation of "relevant information," advancement in the "understanding of relevant concepts," and the development of "certain attitudes, habits and spiritual qualities."[50] Others, of course, have used the notion of capability, notably Amartya Sen and Martha Nussbaum. At a first glance, this seems to be a coincidence, two unrelated uses of a word in different contexts. But as we will see in chapter 8, there are common ideas as well as differences in philosophical outlooks, the examination of which sheds further light on the question of moral empowerment.

FUNDAEC's own account of the concept of capability limits it to the area of curricular design. In fact, it speaks of it mostly in relation to the analysis of the content of the programs it has developed over a few decades corresponding to secondary education. FUNDAEC's particular focus on the ages between 12 and 18 reveals by itself an interesting view of empowerment. In a world where adult literacy/conscientization on the one hand and universalization of primary education on the other occupied center stage, the founders of FUNDAEC, after an initial attempt to create an accelerated program to train generalists in integrated rural development, came to identify youth in their teens as the most promising group whose education could spearhead the social and economic development of the communities in which they were working. This, of course, was not meant to diminish the importance of primary education, but their experience convinced them that all was not lost, as was often said, when children did not go to a "good primary school"; they encountered numerous youth who, while lacking certain skills typically developed in childhood, possessed the intellectual ability and the spiritual resilience to make up for lost time and advance rapidly in the process that was later to be called moral empowerment. Further, they rejected the prevalent notion that vocational education was the most reasonable answer to the needs of the youth from the so called "disadvantaged" populations; they reacted with indignation to what they perceived as "learning to think" for the children of the rich and "learning to carry out orders" for the children of the poor. They were concerned with the capacity of a given population to apply and generate knowledge as it walked its own path of development and were searching for an educational program that would equip the youth of the community to participate effectively in such a process and, ultimately, to lead it. "Capability" has proven to be a sufficiently robust concept to give shape to such a program. Although capabilities are to be developed in individuals, a major criterion for their selection is their relevance to capacity building in the community. Not necessarily apparent in the case of every capability, sets of interrelated capabilities are concerned with the essential relationships briefly discussed in the beginning of this chapter, and as such with the transformation of the social environment and its structure.

The last two chapters of the book will focus on the implications of the notion of capability in pedagogical and philosophical spheres. In chapter 9 we will examine the role it can play in making pedagogical choices, specifically its usefulness as an integrating strategy to overcome certain deeply rooted dichotomies in the field of education. These dichotomies arise when an idea with some degree of validity is taken too far and placed at the center of an approach which opposes another with its own exclusive and rigid central dogma. Thus endless debates on such dualities as traditional versus progressive education, banking education versus problem posing, child-centered versus teacher-centered, and logical order versus psychological method. Finally in chapter 10, by focusing on capabilities that bear directly on moral issues, we will examine a conception of "continuity of thought, language, and action," itself a significant element of our philosophical framework. Two defining ideas in this respect will be the oneness of heart and mind and the interplay between the individual and the collective.

CHAPTER 3

THE SUBJECT OF UNDERSTANDING

In the previous chapter "understanding of reality" emerged as a central concept to be examined in the context of educational programs seeking moral empowerment of their students. In this and the next two chapters, we will treat various facets of this complex theme, making explicit significant philosophical underpinnings that give shape to the structure of the entire book. We will begin our argument by locating a major cause of superficiality in education in the failure to nurture understanding. This failure can be attributed to incomplete and, at times, faulty views of what understanding entails. More often than not, the interconnectedness of the "subject," the "object," and the "process of understanding" is ignored, and one is overemphasized at the expense of the other two. A quick analysis of the longstanding tension between learner-centered and content-centered approaches will be presented to illustrate the problems to which such inadequate views give rise in educational theory. A premise of this inquiry is that, in order to meet the challenge of nurturing understanding, educational programs need to contribute to the development of the intellectual and spiritual powers of the student, be rich in content both conceptual and informational, and pay attention to the process of understanding in all its complexity.

To admit in abstract that intricate threads bind the subject, the object, and the process of understanding is not significant by itself; to make certain that they are taken fully into account in an educational process that seeks to nurture understanding is a formidable challenge.

A brief discussion of Joseph Dunne's incisive critique of the "behavioral objective model of learning" in this chapter will demonstrate the undesirable consequences of an approach that tries to marry the three elements, and yet treats them superficially. It will become clear that the way the process of understanding and its objects are analyzed in any educational approach invariably projects a vision of the "subject of understanding." One of the tasks to be accomplished here, then, is to identify the attributes of the subject of understanding in the context of moral empowerment. We embark on our search for such attributes with an examination of the way understanding has come to be viewed in a particular development that started with the so-called cognitive revolution, and of the subject of understanding implied by computationalism and culturalism as analyzed by Jerome Bruner. We will then move on to make explicit some of the characteristics of the subject of understanding promoted by the emotivist culture as described by Alasdair MacIntyre and by subjectivism as suggested, for example, by Søren Kierkegaard. None of the contenders measures up fully to the protagonist of moral empowerment envisioned in this book. But each offers a partial view, from which emerges a sketchy but suggestive picture of who she or he may be, a picture that will be rendered more complete in later chapters.

Avoiding Shallow Treatments of Understanding

If we are to combat the superficiality to which the practice of education has proven itself vulnerable over the decades, we must learn to nurture understanding. The desire to remedy superficiality, of course, has driven the work of a number of educators who have begun their inquiry with the criticism of educational processes that fill the students' minds with facts and pay little attention to the development of their powers. But the remedy does not prove potent enough when the alternatives proposed focus mostly on the transformation and manipulation of information. The blurring of the distinction between assimilation of information and understanding of concepts is, in part, responsible for lack of depth in education.

Bits of information are finite things that are necessary to impart in an educational process. Being finite, they should be assimilated fully in a finite number of steps. Concepts, on the other hand, although not necessarily infinite in meaning and implication, often have to be understood progressively. According to FUNDAEC, "one must ask the question whether, for a given object of understanding, the dimensions [to be grasped] are finite or infinite. Are there certain concepts, for example, that we can understand and be done with? Do all objects of understanding call for the same depth of understanding? Does it make sense, for example, to design an activity the objective of which is for the student to understand precisely and completely a given object of understanding? These are not trivial questions and some kind of answer to them is necessary if we are to design educational activities the purpose of which is to enhance understanding."[1]

One of the obstacles to nurturing understanding in students is the more or less equal treatment given to profound concepts and trivial ones. The problem is further exacerbated when understanding is confused with mastering learning techniques. These techniques are often taught with the help of trivial examples, assuming that their application is the key to the understanding of complex concepts as well.[2] And even deeper problems appear when understanding itself is reduced to mere achievement, and its unboundedness as a process in which one continuously advances is ignored. These interrelated challenges can be met only if issues related to the powers of the human spirit and the interconnection between understanding and the development of these powers are adequately addressed.

Understanding seems to be a notion that defies all manner of definition. It is not synonymous with how the human mind sorts out and processes information; it is not merely a culminating point, at which one arrives once certain facts are assimilated; it is not simply the conclusion reached after following one or another procedure; nor is it reducible to judgments by way of sound reasoning based on the beliefs one holds. Understanding differs from physical action, say, planting a tree, and mental occupation, say, thinking about what to do. It is also distinct from mental activity involved in gathering and sorting information. All these contribute to understanding, especially when carried out purposefully, but they do not make up the process in its entirety.

FUNDAEC begins its exploration of the theme with the innocent statement that "the verb *to understand* assumes a subject and an object."[3] The verb also implies a process through which one advances, at least in relation to substantive concepts, as well as significant moments of insight and the grasp of specific facts and meanings. The process can be likened to moving forward along a path, which, though marked by certain milestones corresponding to levels of comprehension of vital aspects of reality, has by no means a predetermined end. What is required in order to advance in understanding is not independent of the object of understanding. It makes little sense to say, "I understand" without any reference to what it is that I am understanding. Attempts to reduce the process of understanding of every object to the application of a single approach—cognitive, cultural, empirical, constructivist, and so on—is the cause of great difficulty in educational theory and the ensuing pedagogies. Moreover, it does not seem reasonable to conceptualize the process of understanding without any reference to the qualities of the subject of the verb "to understand." Nor can the subject, at any given instance, be sharply separated from the object of understanding. For, does not the understanding of a specific set of scientific concepts contribute to the development of certain qualities and attitudes, intellectual and even spiritual, and is not the presence of specific qualities essential to the understanding of a set of scientific concepts?

Despite the positive response that many would probably give to the above suggestions, the field of education continues to follow theoretical constructs that place one element of the complex process of understanding in opposition to another. The longstanding tension between two major positions—one predominantly concerned with knowledge and information, and another primarily focused on the individual learner—is an instructive example. A number of pejorative terms such as "rote learning" and "banking education" have been used against pedagogies following the former. The accusations are unfair when we consider, for example, that much of the discourse on liberal education, which by no means can be identified as banking education, is centered on the subject matter. Implicit in any form of liberal education is the premise that exposure to a rich body of knowledge is vital to the development and training of the mind.

Richard S. Peters sheds light on what led to the sharp division between the learner and the content of education. The so-called "child-centered" movement emerged as a reaction to traditional teaching approaches that fill up the brain with items, using coercive techniques, if necessary. The alternative models offered by progressive trends have focused on the *manner* rather than the *matter* of education. Peters argues that although, on moral grounds, it is only correct that students be accorded respect and their liberty be preserved, the manner in which these principles are upheld cannot serve as a substitute for content, namely, the forms of knowledge which nurture a full range of understanding in pupils. In other words, there is no foundation holding up the assumption that an emphasis on worthwhile content would have to be accompanied by a "rigid" and "unreflective" method of education. On the contrary, Peters claims that "the talk about growth, self-realization, and the development of the individual potentiality,"[4] has glossed over what is worthwhile and in the interest of the child to learn.

Hannah Arendt provides another perspective on the origins of this extreme talk about child-centered education. She considers the recurring crisis in education as the most characteristic and suggestive aspect of the general crisis that has overtaken every sphere of life in the modern world. According to her, the measures that have given rise to the current condition of education can be traced back to three basic assumptions. "The *first* is that there exist a child's world and a society formed among children that are autonomous and must insofar as possible be left to them to govern." The adult can only tell the child "to do what he likes and then prevent the worst from happening." The *second* assumption relates to teaching: "Under the influence of modern psychology and the tenets of pragmatism, pedagogy has developed into a science of teaching in general in such a way as to be wholly emancipated from the actual material to be taught. A teacher . . . is a man who can simply teach anything; his training is in teaching, not in the mastery of any particular subject." The *third* assumption closely related to the second is that "you can know and understand only what you have done yourself," the application of which to education is "to substitute doing for learning," inculcating skills in place of teaching knowledge. Another consequence of this assumption is the obliteration of the distinction between play and work in favor of the former. Play is "looked upon as the liveliest and most appropriate way for the child to behave in the world, as the only form of activity that evolves spontaneously from his existence as a child. Only what can be learned through play does justice to this liveliness."[5] Our intention here, of course, is not to question the fact that children do learn through play, but to point out the danger inherent in the trend that systematically marginalizes every other way of learning.

Arendt's analysis focuses on the crises encircling elementary schools in which these assumptions shape the way children are educated, but the more disquieting consequence for our purposes is how they fashion ideas about education beyond childhood. The effect on children of education based on this kind of thinking may be that, in the name of autonomy and independence, they would not develop those powers appropriate to their stage of growth by being "debarred from the world of the grown-up." But what will happen when by "making absolute the world of childhood,"[6] we extend its values to the entire life cycle? Will not learning by hard work then be disdained by youth? Will not education be plagued by superficiality when disciplined study gives way to playfulness at every level, when a few techniques constitute the method for dealing with every object of understanding, irrespective of its degree of complexity, and when teachers are not continually advancing in their own understanding of the content of the subject matter they teach?

The unending debate about the merits of child-centered versus subject-centered approaches to teaching as well as a number of other similar debates seem unresolvable unless we learn to pay appropriate attention to the subject, the object, and the process of understanding in an integrated way. This proves extremely difficult in an environment that constantly polarizes them. One challenge is to ensure that understanding itself is not reduced to mastering some cognitive skills or achieving some predetermined narrow objectives. Any perspective on learning represents, in the final analysis, only a glimpse into the astonishing and often unpredictable power of understanding. But when a model is built on small fragments and supported by elaborate explanations of how it reflects reality, reality is reduced to fit the model. Then the subject, the object, and the process of understanding exist but only in shadows. The "behavioral objectives model" is a good example.

The behavioral objectives model focuses on objects of understanding in the form of carefully defined learning objectives; it pays attention to how these are achieved, often in a predetermined manner; and it is concerned with "demonstrable changes" in the pupil, changes that are possible to measure and assess. In an attempt, as Joseph Dunne has put it, to rescue "teaching from woolly-mindedness and muddle and of constituting it as a truly rational practice,"[7, 8] the content of education ends up being organized according to measurable objectives in taxonomies of cognitive and affective domains.[9] Objectives are expressed "in terms which identify both the kind of behaviour to be developed in the student and the content . . . in which the behaviour is to operate."[10] What constitutes an objective has been subsequently revised and made more specific: "A statement of an objective contains a verb and a noun. The verb generally describes the intended cognitive process. The noun generally describes the knowledge students are expected to acquire or construct." For example, the "students will learn to distinguish (cognitive process) among the confederal, federal, and unitary systems of government (the knowledge)." The verb *distinguish* "provides clues to the desired cognitive process," as it "is associated with the cognitive process category *Analyze*." The noun phrase *confederal, federal, and unitary systems of government* "gives clues to the desired type of knowledge." In this case, *systems* are associated with theories, models, and structures, the knowledge of which constitutes a sub-type of *conceptual knowledge*. The cognitive process contains several categories: *Remember, Understand, Apply, Analyze, Evaluate*, and *Create*. These categories represent growing complexity along a continuum. *Understand* is supposedly more cognitively complex than *Remember*, and *Apply* is considered more complex than *Understand*. Likewise the "knowledge dimension" has four categories along a continuum from concrete to abstract: *Factual, Conceptual, Procedural*, and *Metacognitive*. Students remember factual knowledge, understand conceptual knowledge, and apply procedural knowledge. In the case of the example presented above the objective involves *Analyze* and *Conceptual Knowledge*.[11]

Although the term *behavior* was originally used in defining an objective, a qualification was made later to distinguish the behavioral objectives model from behaviorism. In this model, it was claimed, a change in behavior was the result of instruction. "Specifying student behavior was intended to make general and abstract learning goals more specific and concrete, thus enabling teachers to guide instruction and provide evidence of learning. If the teacher could describe the behavior to be attained, it could be recognized easily when learning occurred." "Behaviorism, in contrast, was a means by which desired ends could be achieved." For that reason, principles of instruction included "instrumental conditioning and the formation of stimulus-response associations."[12]

Notwithstanding the explanations provided by its proponents to free the behavioral objectives model from the defects of behaviorism, the model continues to be criticized for its assumptions, its instrumental rationality, and its hidden values. Dunne, for example, points out that its most acknowledged characteristic is "operationalism" which demands that all teaching objectives be translated into "operational terms." There is an underlying claim that "cognitive processes can be adequately and exhaustively resolved into behavioural performances." Further, operationalism assumes that "knowledge can be analysed into a definite number of component elements." When applied to teaching, "a sequence of atomistic objectives will aggregate over time into intellectual virtues such as the habit of inquiry, rigour, judgment, and style. . . ." Most significantly, the feature that is supposed to make this model of teaching a respectable science is its verificationism, "the stipulation that a well-formed statement of objectives must contain an indication of the evidence that would be required to verify whether or not it has been fulfilled."[13] Dunne's criticism is not directed toward setting educational objectives in general, but to the way an objective is defined:

The pressure for such verification seems to stem from the concept of an objective; it seems to be a necessary feature of an objective that one should always have a means of knowing exactly whether, or to what extent, it has been achieved. Thus, the really significant point about operationally-stated objectives is not just that they indicate the operations that the student is to perform, if the objective is to be judged as fulfilled; their real point is that they indicate the operations that must be carried out by anyone who would verify whether an objective has been achieved. As Gagne and Briggs put it: "When defined in this precise way, definitions of objectives communicate to another person 'operations' he must carry out in order to observe the achievement of the objective. Precisely described objectives are those which make observations of another person possible."[14] Or, in the words of Bloom: "The overt behaviour or the procedure for observing it must be described so that all who read the description can agree whether or not a given student's performance or product testifies to the presence of the objective in question."[15, 16]

In the behavioral objectives model emphasis is laid on the *form* of verification that can be carried out, "unencumbered, by the detached observer."[17] A teacher would have to envisage being in virtual communication with a "detached observer" not situated in the particular context in which the teaching-learning experience is taking place. The main purpose of Benjamin Bloom in constructing a Taxonomy of Educational Objectives is precisely to facilitate communication between a teacher and potential observers who are not bounded by his or her situation. To achieve this end, educational objectives have to be classified with the aid of a technical language. Such a language is to eliminate ambiguity and is not in need of interpretation: "Carefully defined objectives . . . should have only a single meaning and the same meaning for all literate persons . . . they must in a sense have a technical meaning, conveying precise information about human performances."[18] A statement of an objective is, for example, "be able to write a musical composition with a single tonal base, within four bars. The composition must be at least sixteen bars long and must contain at least twenty-four notes," and "at least three rules of good composition" must be applied in the development of the score.[19] As Dunne points out "the fact that the system only permits ends that are student-behavioural outcomes and that these must, moreover, be stated precisely enough to allow accurate evaluation, entails that all objectives are essentially closed. Thus, they circumscribe the degree of initiative that can be exercised by the student."[20]

The purpose of these few paragraphs has not been to examine in detail the behavioral objectives model. Given that behaviorism is generally known and its limitations are by and large recognized, we are not including here any discussion of it either. Its conception of science that led it to look only at observable behavior and ignore the inner state of the learner and the working of his or her mind is already discredited. What the above analysis shows is that the mere claim of dissociation from a dominant theory without addressing its underlying assumptions does not guarantee freedom from it. In the behavioral objectives model, the superficial treatment of the subject, the object, and the process of understanding persists despite the apparent sophistication introduced in the elaborate scheme of educational objectives and the corresponding cognitive skills for achieving them. The powers of the mind are compartmentalized into memory, comprehension, application, analysis, evaluation, and creativity according to operations they presumably entail from simple to complex. Admittedly, a distinction is made between factual knowledge and conceptual knowledge, ostensibly to differentiate between discrete, isolated "bits of information" and the more complex and interconnected body of information organized around "models," "schemas," and "theories." Yet, from the outset, rigid restrictions are placed on the range of understanding to be attained by the student, and the process of understanding of every object, regardless of its complexity, is reduced to a series of steps according to one or another technical prescription. Moreover, the precise definitions of "objectives," as well as the predetermined operations the students are expected to perform in each instance, limit significantly categories of objects of understanding to those that fit the configuration dictated by the model. And finally, notwithstanding the proclaimed lack of commitment to the "metaphysical denial of the reality of inner events"[21] that distinguished behaviorism, the subject of understanding is still defined in terms of a number of observable operations, behaviors, or performances. Thus we see behaviorism living through a model of learning that claims to be distinct. Taylor points out how this can happen: "The best, most insightful, practice of history, sociology, psychology is either devalued or misunderstood, and as a consequence we find masses of researchers engaging in what very often turns out to be futile exercises, of no scientific value whatever, sustained only by the institutional inertia of a professionalized discipline. The history of behaviorism stands as a warning of the virtual immortality that can be attained by such institutionalized futility."[22]

Computational and Cultural Dimensions of Cognition

The cognitive movement[23] is a clear attempt to set aside the cold mechanical stance toward the learner springing from the stimulus-response of behavioral models of learning. It ousts the outer stimulus as the central factor in learning and assumes that, by examining the processes of sorting and encoding information within the brain, the person can be brought back into the picture in the most worthy manner. However, learning theory, despite the progress achieved by shifting the focus to the individual learner, continues to suffer from mechanistic presuppositions.

Bruner's prolific work in educational psychology, beginning with contributions that gave rise to the cognitive revolution, is a source of insight into certain facets of the process of understanding and its subject in the progressive development of this strand of educational thought. In *Culture of Education,* Bruner describes two fundamental views that have altered "conceptions about the nature of the human mind in the decades since the cognitive revolution":[24] the "computational" view, the hypothesis that "mind could be conceived as a computational devise," and what he calls "culturalism," the proposal that "mind is both constituted by and realized in the use of human culture." The computational view is concerned with "information processing: how finite, coded, unambiguous information about the world is inscribed, sorted, stored, collated, retrieved, and generally managed by a computational device. It takes information as its given, as something already settled in relation to some pre-existing, rule-bound code that maps onto states of the world." The aim of computationalism is to "devise a formal re-description of any and all functioning systems that manage the flow of well-formed information."[25] The human mind is one such system that must necessarily work according to the specific rules and procedures governing the processing of input.

The "computational theory of mind" underlying computationalism claims that the long-assumed gap between mind and matter can be closed by grounding the mental in the physical world using the concepts of "information," "computation," and "feedback":

For millennia the gap between physical events, on the one hand, and meaning, content, ideas, reason, and intention, on the other, seemed to cleave the universe in two. . . . But the cognitive revolution unified the world of ideas with the world of matter using a powerful new theory: that mental life can be explained in terms of information, computation, and feedback. Beliefs and memories are collections of information—like facts in a database, but residing in patterns of activity and structure in the brain. Thinking and planning are systematic transformations of these patterns, like the operation of a computer program. Wanting and trying are feedback loops, like the principle behind a thermostat: they receive information about the discrepancy between a goal and the current state of the world, and then they execute operations that tend to reduce the difference. The mind is connected to the world by the sense organs, which transduce physical energy into data structures in the brain, and by motor programs, by which the brain controls the muscles.[26]

A computational approach to education, according to Bruner, does at least three things: It restates classical theories of teaching or learning in a computable form; it comes up with a description or protocol of what actually transpires in the process of problem solving or mastering a particular body of knowledge, and then restates it in "strict computational terms"; it takes students through a process of re-description of the output of a prior operation, to "turn around" on the results of a procedure that has worked locally and to re-describe it in more general, simplified terms. In applying this feature of all "adaptive" computational programs to learning, the student "goes meta," considering how she thinks as well as what she is thinking about.[27] Adaptive here means reducing prior complexities to achieve greater fitness into a criterion. For example, putting an *s* at the end of a noun makes it plural. This operation is then applied to all nouns to achieve the same end, and when the new rule fails to pluralize a noun, say, *woman,* the learner generates additional ones. She continues to do so until she comes up with a relatively "adequate rule for pluralizing, with only a few odd 'exceptions' left over to be handled by rote."[28] The learner, at each step of this process, reflects on what she has done, in order to "re-describe" it in general terms.

There are various aspects of the behavioral objectives model that appear in computationalism in new ways. For example, the centrality of operationalism in the former is akin to the crucial role given to re-describing the "operations" carried out to solve problems in the latter. The language of objectives, to take another example, seeks to be technical and free from interpretation and, as stated before, the behavioral objectives model finds it difficult to embrace the complexity that context introduces in the evaluation of the student's progress. In computationalism, too, input into a device by way of language must be encoded in such a way as to leave no room for ambiguity. Consequently, one of the "strategic" characteristics of the computational model is the deliberate decision to deemphasize certain elements such as "the influence of affective factors or emotions, the contribution of historical and cultural factors, and the role of background context in which particular actions or thoughts occur."[29] But these are elements essential to learning; the meaning of words and concepts cannot be isolated from their contexts.

Bruner himself finds it impossible to accept that rules common to all information systems could cover the "messy, ambiguous, and context-sensitive process of meaning making."[30] The question he poses is how to encode an input according to the context in which it is encountered. Citing the example of the word *cloud* he asks:

> Shall it be taken in its "meteorological" sense, its "mental condition" sense, or in some other way? Now, it is easy (indeed necessary) to provide a computational device with a 'look up' lexicon that provides alternative senses of *cloud*. Any dictionary can do it. But to determine *which* sense is appropriate for a particular context, the computational device would also need a way of encoding and interpreting all contexts in which the word *cloud* might appear. That would then require the computer to have a look-up list for all possible contexts, a "contexticon." But while there are a finite number of words, there are an infinite number of contexts in which the particular words might appear. Encoding the context of Hamlet's little riddle about "yonder cloud" would almost certainly escape the powers of the best "contexticon" one could imagine![31]

Bruner's example helps to clarify things. A prior input of the word *cloud* cannot encode the infinite contexts in which one can encounter it. Before Shakespeare wrote the play, it would have been impossible to determine the context in which Hamlet teases Polonius "with ambiguous banter about 'yonder cloud' shaped like a camel, nay 'tis backed like a weasel,' in the hope that this banter might evoke guilt and some telltale knowledge about the death of Hamlet's father."[32] In language, we can state with a degree of certainty, there will always be contexts not imagined before, in which a nest of new meanings for a word can be found.

Bruner goes on to state that an "educationally interesting" theory of mind should "contain specifications of some kind about the "resources" required for a mind to operate effectively. These include not only instrumental resources (like mental "tools"), but also settings or conditions required for effective operations."[33] Just as the operation of the hand cannot be fully appreciated without taking into account the type of tools with which it is equipped: a screwdriver, a pair of scissors, or a laser-beam gun, the operation of the mind cannot be understood without considering the tools at its disposal. It is for this reason that the systematic mind of a historian, for example, "works differently from the mind of the classic 'teller of tales' with his stock of combinable myth-lie modules."[34] When it comes to identifying settings and conditions that assist the mind to operate more effectively, the computational approach is "bound by the constraints of computability—that is whatever aids are offered to mind must be operable by a computational device."[35] Bruner seeks to overcome these limitations of the computational model by embracing culturalism, although he asks that the disagreements between the two not be exaggerated. Culturalism has no difficulty incorporating the insights offered by the computational approach; what it cannot do is to deny meaning-making processes that do not meet the rules of computability.[36]

Bruner's analysis of culturalism is rich. The proposal that is relevant here as we explore the characteristics of the "subject of understanding" is that education, in initiating the young into a culture should "partake of the spirit of a forum, of negotiation, and of the recreating of meaning."[37] "Although meanings are 'in the mind,' they have their origins and their significance in the culture in which they are created. It is this cultural situatedness of meanings that assures their negotiability and, ultimately, their communicability."[38] Bruner reminds us that the pedagogy that views education as the process through which knowledge and values are transmitted by the more expertly knowledgeable ignores the social production of meaning. The transmission model presupposes that the young are "underprovided not only epistemically but deontically as well—lacking in a sense of value propositions and a sense of the society." They are not only "underequipped with knowledge about the world," which needs to be imparted to them, but are also "'lacking' in values." Such characterization of the child, "whether driven by Original Sin, by primary process,[39] or by egocentricism" implies that there is something that should be "rooted out, replaced, or 'compensated.'" The pedagogy would therefore view teaching as "surgery, suppression, replacement, deficit-filling, or some mix of them all." Bruner further explains that with the emergence of behavioral "learning theory" an additional method was introduced into the teaching process: reinforcement with reward and punishment as the instruments of "a new technology" for accomplishing the intended educational goals. He goes on to suggest that even developmental theories which regard growth of the intelligence mainly from the inside out and the role of environment merely as one of providing nourishment appropriate to the stage of development are not up to the task of creating an enriched pedagogy. Thus, he concludes: "What we lack, in the main, is a reasoned theory of how the negotiation of meaning as socially arrived at is to be interpreted as a pedagogical axiom."[40]

In his presentation of culturalism, Bruner recognizes that he must go back and forth between questions having to do with the nature of the mind and the nature of culture; to look at the interaction between the "powers of individual minds and the means by which the culture aids or thwarts their realization."[41] He, thus, puts forward nine tenets that would guide a psycho-cultural approach to education. One of them, the "constructivism tenet," is particularly relevant to the present argument. Culturalism, Bruner contends, has a double task. At the macro level, it looks at culture as a "system of values, rights, exchanges, obligations, opportunities, power." At the micro level, it concentrates on how the individuals "construct realities and meanings, at what cost, and with what expected outcomes." Culturalism is concerned with "inter-subjectivity" and should be counted among the "sciences of the subjective."[42]

Bruner's culturalism adds new dimensions to computationalism's educational approach, according to which the candidate for the subject of understanding could not be more than a highly complex computer. Two of its accomplishments are of particular importance for our inquiry: it recognizes the significance of context in the process of understanding, and it acknowledges the collective dimension of understanding. In culturalism, Bruner moves away from an exclusive focus on the workings of the brain; the aim of education includes the creation and recreation of culture. Thus the learner—our "subject of understanding"—becomes a participant in forum-like processes of meaning-making in a constantly changing environment. Yet, it seems that the constructivist thread running through his account commits Bruner to models of learning in which the learner is either transforming and manipulating information, processing and codifying the representations of the parts of the environment with which she interacts, or is negotiating meaning in the everyday practices of life. This, one could argue, represents a tenuous relationship between the learner and reality. That such activity contributes to understanding is not denied; it is that total commitment to constructivism causes one to miss the richness of meaning that emerges from acknowledging, to use David Bakhurst's words, "the social dimension of the mind without forsaking a sensible realism in which minded beings inhabit a world which is, to a large extent, not of their making."[43]

Although constructivism can be dressed in appealing forms, its illusions can best be identified in its radical version. Ernst von Glasersfeld, a strong proponent of radical constructivism, for example, rejects "the naïve commonsense perspective" that the elements constituting the complex environment in which knowledge is created "belong to a *real* world of unquestionable objects, as real as the student," and that these objects "have an existence of their own, independent not only of the student but also of the teacher." He argues that there is no basis for believing in an "external reality" apart from our experience, as we are only in contact with the impressions we receive via our sense organs. As learners we subjectively construct sets of beliefs on the basis of sense impressions, but these do not correspond to some aspects of a reality that exists outside of our cognitive functions. "The notion that knowledge is the result of a learner's activity," he states, "rather than that of the passive reception of information and instruction, goes back to Socrates and is today embraced by all who call themselves 'constructivists.'" However, he points out that those whose works constitute the radical wing of the constructivist front have a particular attitude "characterized by the deliberate redefinition of knowledge as an adaptive function. In simple words, this means that the results of our cognitive efforts have the purpose of helping us cope in the world of experience, rather than the traditional goal of furnishing an objective representation of a world as it might 'exist' apart from us and our experience."[44]

D. C. Philips and J. F. Soltis point to the inconsistency in von Glasersfeld's thinking which "problematizes the notion of a 'reality' external to the cognitive apparatus of the individual knower/learner" while allowing for the existence of social influences. They state: "After all, teachers and parents and siblings and so forth—no less than the atoms and molecules and forces of the external physical universe—are part of the realm external to the knower that von Glasersfeld is so skeptical about." They further caution against the "tendency within many forms of constructivist epistemology (despite occasional protestations to the contrary) towards relativism, or towards treating the justification of our knowledge as being entirely a matter of sociopolitical processes or consensus, or toward the jettisoning of any substantial rational justification or warrant at all (as is arguably the case with the radical constructivists)." In their view "any defensible epistemology must recognize—and not just pay lip service to—the fact that nature exerts considerable constraint over our knowledge-constructing activities, and allows us to detect (and eject) our errors about it. This still leaves plenty of room for us to improve the nature and operation of our knowledge-constructing communities, to make them more inclusionary and to empower long-silenced voices."[45]

The criticisms of radical constructivism are suggestive of the care one would have to exercise, were one to incorporate certain characteristics of the "constructivist" in the vision of the subject of understanding. Bakhurst warns us that "willingness to fictionalize the self" defeats the objective of bringing back meaning to the phenomenon of mind. Self is then "as much made by meaning as making it." If we insist that there is no "aboriginal reality," we would have to conclude that "the world as we encounter it is a product of the organizing power of the mind, of the 'narrative construction of reality'" and "where everything 'real' is, in a sense, an artifact of our modes of interpretation and categorization."[46, 47] Bakhurst cautions us to be clear that the "mediational means" of "cultural tools" do not "somehow get between us and reality itself. Rather, their use serves to bring reality within our reach." "Just as the use of a hammer does not remove us from the object on which we are working," he clarifies, "so our concepts, models, theories and so on need not create a barrier beyond which we cannot see. We use them to disclose the world to us, not to obscure it."[48]

Excessive Subjectivism

A major problem with seeing the process of understanding entirely from the perspective of constructivism is the relativism inherent in the knowledge being constructed—a result of undue emphasis on the subjective. This is not to say that aspects of ethical and much of social reality are not constructed by the human mind according to the dynamics of a given culture. Nor do we have to deny that theory influences the way even physical reality is observed. It is just that the subject of understanding as a constructivist is in constant danger of excessive subjectivism, particularly in relation to views of the moral universe. Bernard Williams' argument against moral relativism discourages us from depending too much on Bruner's "sciences of the subjective" in identifying the characteristics of the subject of understanding, the protagonist of moral empowerment. According to Williams, moral judgments do not simply describe the speaker's own attitude since the very possibility that the claims they make can be rejected by someone who utters a contrary moral judgment gives such claims substance stretching beyond the mere "autobiographical" account of tastes, feelings, and preferences. Further, he suggests that moral outlooks could be right or wrong, in so far as they reflect beliefs and convictions about questions of import—for which a certain level of consensus within society should exist—and are not simply expressions of personal likes and dislikes. Even if reasons for holding one set of beliefs as opposed to another were no more than rationalizations for conformity or non-conformity with a particular group, and "our moral attitudes were rarely *determined* by reasons," he goes on to assert, "our model of moral attitudes and moral judgments must at least be complex enough to leave room for the rationalizations. It is only if the position to which a man is led by these forces satisfies some conditions of being the sort of position to which reasons are relevant that we can understand it as a moral position at all."[49]

The subjectivist position has been keenly criticized by MacIntyre as well, his account of its modern embodiment in the "emotivist" self being particularly revealing. MacIntyre charts the emergence and development of emotivism—the doctrine that all evaluative judgments are nothing but the expressions of preference, attitude, or feeling—from the late seventeenth century to the present time. Emotivism has been presented by its advocates as a theory about the meaning of sentences used to make moral judgments. The theory claims to elucidate the meaning of a certain class of sentence by referring to its function of expressing feelings or attitudes. MacIntyre points out that to fulfill such function, the theory would have to identify and characterize these feelings and attitudes. But, in general, it does not expound on this matter, since the unstated assumption seems to be that personal preference is the final arbiter. Thus, the argument offered by emotivism is circular:

> "Moral judgements express feelings or attitudes," it is said. "What kinds of feelings or attitudes?" we ask. "Feelings or attitudes of approval," is the reply. "What kind of approval?" we ask, perhaps remarking that approval is of many kinds. It is in answer to this question that every version of emotivism either remains silent or, by identifying the relevant kind of approval as moral approval—that is, the type of approval expressed by a specifically moral judgement—becomes vacuously circular.[50]

Further, emotivism as a theory does not distinguish between expressions of personal preference and those of an evaluative nature. It regards sentences that are bound by context—for example, when someone in authority speaks to another who recognizes such authority—equivalent to statements that express moral assessment in general. This arises in part from the confusion it perpetuates between the meaning of a sentence and of its use. MacIntyre cites Gilbert Ryle's example of the angry schoolmaster venting his feelings by shouting at a small boy who has just made an arithmetical mistake: "Seven times seven equals forty-nine!" The example makes clear that the use of the sentence to express a feeling has nothing to do with its meaning. Emotivism, MacIntyre concludes, is not a theory about the meaning of a certain class of sentence to make moral judgments but about the use of sentences to express feelings or attitudes and to influence the feelings and attitudes of others. This is particularly evident when factual and moral elements are sharply differentiated by assuming that the criteria for deciding between truth and falsehood is easily agreed upon in the realm of facts, whereas in moral judgments no rational method can perform such function. If agreement is at all to be secured, emotivists would argue, it is through the expressions of feelings and attitude and the force they exert to produce the same effects on others.

Emotivism determines much of our contemporary moral debate and moral utterance. MacIntyre attributes the interminable character of disagreements in the moral sphere to "conceptual incommensurability"—incommensurability pertaining to underlying premises. For example, pacifists would invoke the value of innocent lives to argue that there is no justification for war, another group would summon the ideas of success and survival to argue for the necessity of being prepared for war, yet others would appeal to justice to argue that only wars waged to free the oppressed are warranted. Defenders of such rival positions use rational arguments that take them back from their particular conclusions to their original premises and there is no established way of deciding the superiority of one claim over another. In the end, "argument ceases and the invocation of one premise against another becomes a matter of pure assertion and counter-assertion." This interminability in public moral debates corresponds to a "disquieting private arbitrariness."[51] Yet a "paradoxical air" surrounds these debates as, despite their inherent inability to arrive at consensus, they aspire to be expressed in a language that appeals to some independent and impersonal standard of objectivity—so much pleasure for so many people, unconditional freedom of the rational being, or the intrinsic duty of someone holding one or another position. Another feature of contemporary moral debate is the attempt to sever the premises of rival arguments that are conceptually incommensurate from their original historical contexts. In such circumstances, the only civilized alternative seems to be superficial multiculturalism. As MacIntyre puts it, "the surface rhetoric of our culture is apt to speak complacently of moral pluralism." However, the notion of pluralism is imprecise as it equally applies to "an ordered dialogue of intersecting viewpoints" and "an unharmonious mélange of ill-assorted fragments." That "we simultaneously and inconsistently treat moral argument as an exercise of our rational powers and as mere expressive assertion" is symptomatic of "moral disorder."[52]

MacIntyre views Kierkegaard's *Either/Or* as one of the intellectual sources that has contributed to the rise of the emotivist self. The book describes vividly the characteristics of two individuals embodying the "aesthetic" and the "ethical." Kierkegaard's analysis of the "aesthetic mode of existence," according to Patrick Gardiner, has a "psychological subtlety and an elaborate attention to detail that defy brief summary." Yet Gardiner is able to highlight some of the main traits:

[The] man who lives aesthetically is not really in control, either of himself or his situation . . . he tends to live "for the moment," for whatever the passing instant will bring him in the way of entertainment, excitement, interest. Committed to nothing permanent or definite, dispersed in sensuous "immediacy," he may do or think one thing at a given time, the exact opposite at some other; his life is therefore without "continuity," lacks stability or focus, changes course according to mood or circumstance. . . . Even so, it should not be inferred that such a man is always or necessarily governed by mere impulse; on the contrary, he may be reflective or calculating. . . . If, however, he does adopt long-term goals or decide to follow certain maxims, it is in purely "experimental" spirit: he will continue only for as long as the idea appeals to him, the alternative of giving up if he gets tired or bored, or if some more attractive prospect offers itself, remaining forever open. . . .

The aestheticist "expects everything from without"; his approach to the world is basically a passive one, in that his satisfaction is finally subject to conditions whose presence or fulfilment is independent of his will. This submission to the contingent, the "accidental," to what occurs in the course of events, may take a variety of shapes. Sometimes it is reliance upon "external" factors, like possessions or power or even the prized affection of another human being, but it may also involve ones that are intrinsic to the individual himself, like health or physical beauty . . . it is the mark of the aesthetic individual that he does not seek to impose a coherent pattern of life, having its source in some unitary notion of himself and of what he should be, but rather allows "what happens" to act upon him and to govern his behaviour. Inward reflection can show this to be so, and when it occurs it is liable to produce a pervasive sense of despair in the person concerned; his entire life . . . may be seen to rest upon an uncertain basis and thus appear drained of meaning.[53]

In Gardiner's assessment the "ethical" perspective focuses uncompromisingly upon the individual whose personality is "its own end and purpose":

The ethical subject is portrayed as one who regards himself as a "goal," a "task set." Unlike the aestheticist, who is continually preoccupied with externals, his attention is directed towards his own nature, his substantial reality as a human being with such and such talents, inclinations, and passions, this being something which it constantly lies within his power to order, control, and cultivate. There is thus a sense in which he can be said, consciously or deliberately, to take responsibility for himself; he does not, as the aestheticist is prone to do, treat his personal traits and dispositions as an unalterable fact of nature to which he must tamely submit, but regards them rather as a challenge—his self-knowledge is not "a mere contemplation" but a "reflection upon himself which itself is an action." Moreover, by such inward

understanding and critical self-exploration a man comes to recognize, not only what he empirically is, but what he truly aspires
to become. . . . In other words, the ethical individual's life and
behaviour must be thought of as infused and directed by a deter-
minate conception of himself which is securely founded upon a
realistic grasp of his own potentialities and which is immune to
the vicissitudes of accident and fortune. He is not, as aestheticist
was shown to be, the prey of what happens or befalls, for he has
not surrendered himself to the arbitrary governance of outside
circumstances and incalculable contingencies.

Nor, from the standpoint he adopts, can success and failure be
measured by whether or not his projects in fact find fulfilment in
the world. What finally matters is his total identification of himself with his projects; it is the spirit in which things are done, the
energy and sincerity with which they are undertaken and pursued
that are relevant here—not the observable consequences of the
actions performed.[54]

A plausible reading of *Either/Or* suggests that while it represents two
rival modes of existence, leaving it apparently to the reader to decide
which perspective to adopt, the arguments it offers on behalf of the
ethical perspective unmistakably undermine the aesthetic mode. Mac-
Intyre's interpretation of *Either/Or* is different; it even differs, by his
own admission, from Kierkegaard's retrospective account of the book
as well as from those given by the best Kierkegaard scholars. MacIntyre
considers that the aesthetic and the ethical each submit to a different
set of premises beyond which no criteria can be offered to support their
positions. Therefore, someone presented with a choice between the
two can be given no reason for preferring one to the other. In answer
to those who consider the ethical as the obvious choice because "the
energy, the passion, of serious choice will, so to speak, carry the person who chooses into the ethical," it could be said that "the aesthetic

can be chosen seriously, although the burden of choosing it can be as passion-ridden as that of choosing the ethical." MacIntyre especially thinks of those young men of his father's generation "who watched their own earlier ethical principles die along with the death of their friends in the trenches in the mass murder of Ypres and the Somme; and who returned determined that nothing was ever going to matter to them again and invented the aesthetic triviality of the nineteen-twenties."[55] He points out that in *Either/Or* "the principles which depict the ethical way of life are to be adopted *for no reason*, but for a choice that lies beyond reasons, just because it is the choice of what is to count for us as a reason. Yet the ethical is to have authority over us. But how can that which we adopt for no reason have any authority over us?"[56]

Irrespective of the accuracy of MacIntyre's reading of *Either/Or*, his analysis still serves to provide us with a crucial characteristic of the emotivist self. At first glance, it seems that the aesthetic individual is its embodiment. But we gradually realize that the distinction between external and internal forces determining choices one makes is not sufficient to portray two entirely different modes of existence. The emotivist self seems to be present in both the aesthetic and the ethical because of the primacy given to the subjective choice. This is what MacIntyre helps us to see. For the emotivist self, it is not the choice between good and evil that is significant, but the *choice* of whether or not to choose in terms of good and evil.

MacIntyre further attributes the ascendance of emotivism to the failure of the enlightenment project and the attempts of moral philosophers, particularly Kant and David Hume, to find rational justification for morality outside a teleological framework. This may only be partially true, but it is undeniable that in MacIntyre's description of the emotivist tradition, we can identify numerous features of the dominant culture of our age. We, too, see in our times the prevalence of "the condition of those who see in the social world nothing but the meeting place for the individual wills, each with its own set of attitudes and preferences and who understand that world solely as an arena for the achievement of their own satisfaction, who interpret reality as a series of opportunities for their enjoyment and for whom the last enemy is boredom."[57] MacIntyre argues that we ought to confront emotivism in order to overcome the challenge raised by the claim that "*all* moral, indeed all evaluative, argument is and always must be rationally interminable."[58] For us, his analysis is a warning lest, in a world in which the emotivist self exerts such enormous force, we allow certain of its characteristics to enter our conception of the subject of understanding. In an emotivist culture, the sense of what constitutes candid and non-manipulative social relations is lost because personal preferences and impersonal evaluation are collapsed together. Sentences are used in debates and arguments to persuade others of the superiority of one's own preferences. In such an environment, the individual does not perceive the discrepancy between meaning and use of sentences. Meaning is no longer the property of concepts but a pretense that allows the agent to use sentences, albeit unconsciously, to achieve his goals. He could claim he is appealing to independent criteria while all he is doing is expressing his feelings in a manipulative manner. The emotivist self is a poor choice for the "subject of understanding." On the one hand, lacking the ability to distinguish between statements expressing personal preference and those containing propositional knowledge, it cannot properly connect to an object of understanding, and on the other, its modes of understanding could not be trusted, for it is prone to be influenced in social relations, albeit unconsciously, by manipulative means and to perpetuate such ways. The failure of the once prevalent "values clarification," an offspring of humanist psychology, to achieve moral clarity, a requisite of moral empowerment, is but an indication of the havoc created in the field of education when it is invaded by the culture of emotivism.

Having rejected the emotivist self as a candidate for the subject of understanding, we could explore the extent to which the characteristics of the "self" defined by communitarianism—an apparent opposite to individualism—may enter our vision of the protagonist of moral empowerment. In much of the relevant discourse, the communitarian view of the self takes shape in contrast to how the "liberal self" is conceived. From a liberal perspective, individuals are not defined by their membership in social institutions and social practices; they can at any time stand out and question their loyalty to and participation in them and, if necessary, relinquish them. Self in this perspective is prior to its socially given roles and relationships. Communitarians consider this view untenable. For them the self is "embedded" or "situated" in existing social practices and social roles. Our self-perception, they argue, stems from these roles and practices. Even notions such as freedom and self-determination without "embeddedness" in the community are empty.

The relationship between the individual and the collective is a vast subject in itself; it was touched on in the previous chapter and will be examined to a limited extent in the last. It may be necessary to mention here, however, that the contrast between the communitarian view of self and the liberal outlook with which the emotivist self finds some affinity is not as sharp as it seems at first. According to Will Kymlicka, this contrast proves to be ambiguous once the relevant arguments receive closer scrutiny. The distinction made between the "unencumbered" liberal self which is prior to any end, project or social commitment, no matter how immersed it may be in them, and the "embedded-self" of the communitarian situated in existing social roles and practices, and "constituted by its ends" represents a false dichotomy.[59] Michael Sandel, as a communitarian, for example, admits that the boundaries imposed by ends that are to constitute the self are flexible; they can be redrawn, incorporating new ends and excluding others. He states that "a certain faculty of reflection" and "a certain capacity for self knowledge" are necessary if the subject is to be "empowered to participate in the constitution of its identity." We, therefore, need to regard "the bounds of the self as open" and "the identity of the subject as the product rather than the premise of its agency."[60] On the other hand, as the liberal argues in response to the critics of the concept of unencumbered self, what is essential is not that we perceive in abstract "a self prior to its ends," but that "we understand ourselves to be prior to our ends in the sense that no end or goal is exempt from possible re-examination."[61] Thus, as Kymlicka puts it, the differences between the two positions "hide a more fundamental identity; both accept that the *person* is prior to her ends. They disagree over where, within the person to draw the boundaries of the self . . ."[62]

Once we accept that the self prior to its ends can be understood "in the sense that no end or goal is exempt from possible re-examination," we are able to, and we should, return to subjectivism and look for certain characteristics of the subject of understanding even in Kierkegaard's account. His subjectivity allows one to suspend for a time the ethical—created by finite reason in the form of Kantian or Hegelian universals—in order to make space for a wider rationality. Gardiner's comment on Kierkegaard's description of the religious mode of existence in *Fear and Trembling and Repetition,* where he speaks of the story of Abraham, demonstrates this point:

> From a religious point of view, ethics never possesses more than a 'relative' status; the denial that from that standpoint it could be envisaged as ultimate or supreme was something that [Kierkegaard's] treatment of the Abraham story was expressly designed to bring into sharp focus. But to insist that it only had relative validity was not to assert that it had no validity at all: it did not follow from his account of the story that moral requirements were devoid of all foundation or that they could in a general way be dispensed with. What he did wish to argue was that within a religious perspective they took on an altered aspect, received a "completely different expression." And by this he seems partly to

have meant that the obligation to conform to them finally rests upon a commitment to God, where the latter is conceived to be an infinite or absolute 'other' that transcends human reason and understanding: "the single individual . . . determines his relation to the universal by his relation to the absolute, not his relation to the absolute by his relation to the universal."[63, 64]

Referring to his own time, Kierkegaard expressed concern that the whole tendency of the age "might lie in the fact that, in all this knowledge, one has forgotten what it is to exist, and what inwardness means . . ."[65] He did not deny an objective reality; in fact, he considered extreme subjectivism as madness: "With the solely subjective definition of truth, madness and truth become ultimately indistinguishable."[66] According to Gardiner, he denounced what he considered to be "a propensity to identify with amorphous abstract entities like 'humanity' or the 'public,'" through which people absolve themselves from "individual responsibility for what they thought and said."[67] Yet, we should be reminded that disproportionate emphasis on self in our own times has not diminished the propensity to shirk responsibility for one's words and deeds.

Ironically, Kierkegaard's gloomy prediction for the future of education seems to have been fulfilled at least partially: "In fact there are handbooks for everything, and very soon education, all the world over, will consist in learning a greater or lesser number of comments by heart, and people will excel according to their capacity for singling out the various facts like a printer singling out the letters, but completely ignorant of the meaning of anything."[68] Interestingly, Kierkegaard's view on how *knowing*—of a certain kind—leads to a lost and deserted status of *being* echoes the tension mentioned earlier in this chapter between educational approaches that emphasize content and those that focus on the individual learner. The assertion of a dichotomy between a subjective agent and an objective world does not allow for the type of relationship that must flourish between the two if education is to engender understanding. The "subject of understanding" must engage in a great deal of introspection and reflection in order to understand. But much of what should be understood is found in fields and disciplines of human knowledge with varying degrees of claim to objectivity. Moreover, the subject of the verb "to understand" is not an entity roaming in complete independence; it is situated within the context of an ever-enlarging circle of physical and social relationships.

Our arguments have brought us to a point where we need to pause and examine what we may have achieved in this chapter. Having identified "understanding" as a fundamental concept to be analyzed in our exploration of educational processes concerned with moral empowerment, we looked for insights in the work of several authors to get a glimpse of possible "candidates," some of whose attributes would be incorporated into a vision of the subject of understanding in the discourse to which this book is to contribute. It is clear that our discussion has not led us to a recognizable picture of the protagonist of moral empowerment, nor should we have expected it to do so. What we now have are insights into the kind of characteristics that should or should not enter our conception of the subject of understanding. There are clearly aspects of the mind's capacity to sort and process information that evoke the metaphor of the computer. There is also a good deal of knowledge that can be generated using the tools and resources of culture without resorting to radical constructivism. As to the emotivist self, none of its features can readily enter our picture of the subject of understanding, but appropriate subjectivity is a necessary dimension of that picture. However, our subject of understanding is not simply a combination of these characteristics. It is important that "looking for insights" as an approach adopted in this inquiry does not become a kind of eclecticism. To escape this fate, we must be able to describe, even if vaguely, a protagonist of moral empowerment whose individuality has integrity of its own and who has the capacity to engage in the very complex process of understanding reality in its many dimensions. But it is too early in the inquiry to achieve such a purpose. A number of other key elements have to be examined in the ensuing chapters before the goal can be reasonably met. What is needed now is more clarity on the concept of understanding and how nurturing it involves the fostering of spiritual qualities.

CHAPTER 4

NURTURING UNDERSTANDING AND FOSTERING SPIRITUAL QUALITIES

There is an infinite dimension to understanding. The notion of infinity does not deny the limitations of human understanding; what it suggests is that not in all instances can it be circumscribed, for example, in the way computationalism and culturalism seem to propose. There is a boundlessness to be taken into account both in relation to concept acquisition and when understanding is viewed as an attribute of the human soul with endless potentialities. To explore this infinity, an endeavor such as ours inspired by religious conviction must look deep into its foundations where its conception of the human being has taken shape. Here, the physical universe, no matter how vast, is embedded in a much larger reality to which all religious traditions have referred as spiritual. This larger reality has its own existence and is not merely an emergent set of qualities of the physical universe. The natural scientist, of course, is entitled to choose to ignore spiritual reality and focus entirely on explaining complex webs of causes and effects within the realm of the physical and in terms of emergence. He cannot prove or disprove that certain qualities emerge because they do or do not have independent existence, an existence which, after all, no physical instruments could possibly examine.

Among FUNDAEC's contributions to the discourse of Bahá'í-inspired educational endeavors is an approach that allows adherence to a religious view of existence without trespassing the bounds set by science. In a strictly materialistic paradigm, it has argued, knowledge is, in the final analysis, acquired through the senses, this despite all the complexities introduced by the theory dependence of observation, the role of paradigms and/or research programs in scientific inquiry, and the intricacies of culture. Stimuli are received by the senses and processed by the brain—an entirely material object, a collection of highly specialized cells communicating through physical and chemical interactions. Collective activities of these cells are given names, such as short- and long-term memory, cognition and affective responses, and are studied in depth. Yet, there is nothing to account for mental states but the workings of a huge set of atoms and molecules with an extremely complex web of interactions. So the question of who understands would be reducible in principle to the question of which configuration of atoms and molecules and what set of interactions receive the generic name *understanding*.

The relationship of body and mind is an age-old question in philosophy. Descartes' assertions in this regard have been discredited. The criticisms are incisive. However, the worldviews that seek to replace the mistaken duality of body and mind are not persuasive either. Bakhurst explains that there are "two principal styles of anti-Cartesianism on the contemporary scene": The first includes "varieties of naturalism," which "aspire to explain the relation of mind and world by employing only explanatory resources compatible with the natural sciences." The extreme version of naturalism in the philosophy of mind seeks to replace the "mistaken 'folk psychology'" theory of the mental with a "scientifically more respectable theory cast in neuroscientific terms." The extreme forms of naturalism in epistemology consist of "evolutionary approaches to knowledge that construe matters of justification of belief purely in terms of an organism's strategies for adaptation to its environment." Both extremes are "exercises in revisionary metaphysics in the name of science, in that they seek to engineer fundamental changes in our present conceptions of ourselves." The second style of anti-Cartesianism takes shape in "radical constructivism," whose proponents contend that "it is a mistake to suppose that our representations genuinely depict an objective world."[1] These two worldviews form in part the premises underlying educational thought and, despite strong arguments against explanations of reality that deny the relevance of an objective world as well as those that reduce the mental to the physical, they continue to influence its practice.

Bahá'í scriptures do not support the Cartesian duality of body and mind: "The mind comprehendeth the abstract by the aid of the concrete. . . . It is by the aid of such senses as those of sight, hearing, taste, smell and touch that the mind comprehendeth."[2] But the exercise of the powers of the mind is not limited by the physical senses: "The other mode of the spirit's influence and action is without these bodily instruments and organs. For example, in the state of sleep, it sees without eyes, it hears without ears, it speaks without a tongue, it runs without feet. . . . For the spirit has two modes of travel: without means, or spiritual travel, and with means, or material travel—as birds that fly, or as being carried in a vehicle."[3] The mind, moreover, is regarded as "the power of the human spirit," as "the perfection of the spirit and a necessary attribute thereof, even as the rays of the sun are an essential requirement of the sun itself."[4] The rational soul or the human spirit "encompasses all things and as far as human capacity permits, discovers their realities and becomes aware of the properties and effects, the characteristics and conditions of earthly things."[5] The human soul did not descend into the body,[6] because descent and entrance are characteristic of physical bodies. There is a subtle relationship: "The connection of the spirit with the body is even as the connection of this lamp with a mirror. If the mirror is polished and perfected, the light of the lamp appears therein . . ."[7]

The interpretation of reality couched in the language of neuroscience or of evolutionary biology is rich enough to allow for the most extensive study of the brain and its functioning as well as the examination of the higher-order entity called culture, the latter being no more than the manifestation of interactions among a large number of sets of atoms and molecules over a very long time. Within this paradigm the physical universe and aspects of social reality can certainly be studied. But while the scientist, reluctant to introduce unnecessary elements into the work of science, can engage in numerous fruitful lines of inquiry, as educators we are not bound to naturalism. The assumption that spiritual reality has as much an existence as physical reality may not add anything to the operation of the natural sciences. But what if taking it into account does make a difference in our pedagogical choices? What if the nurturing of understanding in the context of pursuing one's own growth and contributing to the transformation of society—a society that, after all, slides every day deeper into a state of moral confusion—does depend on our assumptions about the nature of spiritual reality and the existence of the human soul? Are we not justified, then, to at least explore these assumptions, taking of course every caution to avoid the close-mindedness and the obscurantism that have historically hampered religion's ability to deal with the ways of science?

Nurturing Understanding

For a Bahá'í-inspired endeavor, exploration of the spiritual dimension of human existence necessarily occurs in the context of the view that the reality of the human being is the soul and that the soul is not a material substance. The duality of body and mind with all its inherent problems is not a necessary consequence of belief in the existence of the soul. Mental faculties are inherent properties of the soul as radiation is an essential property of the sun. It is through the powers of the soul that the mind comprehends, imagines, and exerts influence, while the soul is a power that is free. Such a belief—taken as an article of faith if necessary—can admit that the mind comprehends many an abstract concept with the help of the concrete observed through the physical senses. The computational functions of the brain, as identical as they may be to those of a computer, do not cause difficulty for this viewpoint. The ever-presence of evolving culture is not denied as one seeks explanations for individual and collective thought and experience. What does occur is that the language being used becomes broader, opening space for certain powers—otherwise ignored—to be considered and cultivated. Intelligence ceases to be defined merely as the capacity of the brain, but more broadly as the combined capacity of a number of interacting faculties of the human soul. Objectives of curricula are formulated so as to include the sharpening of these faculties, allowing the powers of the spirit to flow and bring harmony and prosperity to the life of the individual and of humanity. On a practical level, the introduction of such an assumption points to as yet unchartered terrain in the search for solutions to the ever-evasive challenge of motivation in education. When everything is reduced, explicitly or implicitly, to interactions between material entities, one can only seek sources of motivation either externally, in social and economic achievements, or internally, in ill-defined notions such as self-esteem and self-fulfillment. But necessary as these may be in specific situations, motivation to learn is best sought in the realm of the spirit, as an illumination that excites one or more of the faculties of the human soul.

These reflections expand the concept of understanding. In addition to being viewed as a process, and occasionally as an achievement, understanding is also considered an attribute of the human soul. There will continue to be facets of understanding tied to the world of the contingent, such as processing information and negotiating meaning in a cultural context. Yet understanding as a whole will acquire permanence, not in the sense of storing and retaining knowledge in memory, but the kind of permanence that the concept of the soul brings to the contemplation of human existence. Permanence does not mean static state; understanding will be an attribute endowed with its own dynamics of growth fed by the comprehension of concepts and assimilation of facts facilitated by the functioning of the brain.

When understanding is viewed in a broad sense as suggested above, it becomes possible to explore its relationship as an attribute of the human soul with other such attributes, which, in addition to finite manifestations in *doing*, have a more independent existence related to *being*. Underlying this line of reasoning is the conviction that among all the attributes a human being can possess, those in at least one category, to which we refer as "spiritual qualities," should be considered constituents of our being, and that the development of these is of particular significance to moral empowerment. Whereas in popular discourse, an assortment of characteristics such as punctuality, amiability, alertness—as well as some modern creations like assertiveness—are discussed as virtues, spiritual qualities are distinct attributes fundamental to our identity as a human being. In fact, by them, a wide range of virtues gain significance. The sharing of one's resources with others in specific circumstances, for example, is invested with profound meaning when it is intimately connected to generosity as a divine perfection that the soul of the human being is to increasingly acquire. A kindly tongue as a manifestation of a kind heart has far greater value than the mere habit developed in conformity with the rules of etiquette. Tactfulness, to take another example, seems superficial when compared to qualities such as wisdom and humility. The immediate task before us, then, is to explore the nature of this special category of human qualities and establish the reciprocal relationship between fostering them and the nurturing of understanding in education.

Virtues and Practice

The exploration being proposed in the above cannot be carried out without an analysis of the concept of virtue in its most general sense. But the theme has been treated at such great depth in philosophy that trying to address it in any systematic way here would be pretentious. The approach undertaken instead is to select one credible and substantial account, in this case MacIntyre's account of virtues and practice, not as a theoretical framework, but like the works of other authors examined in this inquiry, as a source of insight.

MacIntyre's narrative is well known. There are two concepts crucial to his account: "practice" and "goods." The word practice refers to "any coherent and complex form of socially established cooperative human activity."[8] Tic-tac-toe and throwing a ball around are not considered practices; games such as chess and football are. MacIntyre argues that each practice holds within it a set of internal goods which are realized through the achievement of standards of excellence appropriate to and definitive, albeit partially, of that practice. Personal attitudes and preferences need to submit themselves to the authority of the best standards and rules of practice, even though "the standards are not themselves immune from criticism." Further, a practice has a history. The direction of the stages it passes through is set by "progress towards and beyond a variety of types and modes of excellence."[9]

There are distinctions between internal and external goods. If motivated by an external good such as a candy, a child playing chess, for example, would have every reason to cheat in order to win. However, he could find a whole new set of reasons for playing if he came to recognize goods that are internal to the game. The child would, for instance, become motivated by how the game develops "a certain highly particular kind of analytical skill," "strategic imagination," and "competitive intensity." External goods such as prestige and money are "contingently" attached to practices; one could always obtain them through alternative means. Internal goods, on the other hand, can only be achieved by engaging in a particular practice and are "identified and recognised by the experience of participating in the practice in question."[10] Those who lack the relevant experience are not competent judges of internal goods.

The example of portrait painting as a practice in Western Europe affords MacIntyre the opportunity to make a distinction between two kinds of internal goods. In one line of evolution, the practice is initially concerned with iconography; saints are portrayed as icons and the portrait bears no resemblance to the depicted face. Later, resemblance takes the place of the iconic relationship, for example, in the relative naturalism of certain fifteenth century Flemish and German paintings. With Rembrandt a synthesis is achieved: "the naturalistic portrait is now rendered as an icon, but an icon of a new and hitherto inconceivable kind." The first kind of internal good in this example is "the excellence of the products, both the excellence in performance by the painters and that of each portrait itself." The second is to be found in "participation in the attempts to sustain progress and to respond creatively to moments"—it is "the painter's living out a greater or lesser part of his or her life *as a painter* that is the second kind of good internal to painting."[11]

Through discussion of internal goods and standards of excellence, MacIntyre presents a notion of virtue which wraps it in practices: "A virtue is an acquired human quality the possession and exercise of which tends to enable us to achieve those goods which are internal to practices and the lack of which effectively prevents us from achieving any such goods."[12] Christopher Higgins points out that, while for MacIntyre virtues are primarily "dispositions" or "excellences" of persons to achieve goods, they also constitute goods in themselves, since they are partly constitutive of our well-being.[13]

Although practices are vital to the development of virtues at a fundamental level, MacIntyre emphasizes that they are not the only context within which the concept takes shape. Virtues are rendered "intelligible" against a background of social and moral life. It is only in a particular historical milieu that a virtue assumes its meaning. The list of virtues and their rankings are not constant across eras and traditions. For example, physical strength is ranked high for Homer; it is the hallmark of a warrior king, whereas for Aristotle the prerequisite of all other virtues is practical wisdom (phronesis). A certain virtue considered significant within one tradition can be nonexistent in another and sometimes even seen as a vice. Love, faith, and hope—central virtues in the New Testament—are not found in Aristotle's account of virtues. Humility—a virtue praiseworthy in Christian tradition—is actually considered a vice by Aristotle relative to magnanimity. In this sense, there are "too many different and incompatible conceptions of a virtue for there to be any real unity to the concept."[14]

MacIntyre tries to resolve this difficulty by suggesting that a core conception of a virtue does emerge if one considers three contexts within which the virtue develops: "practice," "the narrative order of a single human life," and "moral tradition." Higgins identifies these contexts as three levels of valuation, and explains how the virtue of patience, for example, moves through the first two of these three levels. Its exercise would allow the practitioner to draw out the goods internal to a practice and to preserve its integrity. In considering the patience required in each instance, one has to ask "waiting for what?" This question can only be answered in the context of a practice—a teacher is patient with the students and a politician in negotiation. Higgins suggests that the concept of patience is saved from rupturing as varieties of "patience" are multiplied within different practices through the individual life narrative. A parent, a potter, and a politician would each have to find out what role the virtue of patience would play in life outside their own specific practices and synthesize different understandings of patience.[15]

In the third level, virtues are seen as those qualities the exercise of which lead to the human *telos*. Here "the moral horizons of a tradition," in Higgins' analysis, provides the broadest structure within which virtues can be evaluated in terms of the inquiry into good *qua* human beings. Virtues acquire specific significance and are graded differently across various traditions and within a particular age or cultural ethos.

At this level, the virtue of patience, taking Higgins' line of reasoning, would mean something quite different in a modern industrial culture where it can easily be seen as an obstacle to success and in many ancient cultures where it was among the most venerated qualities.

Higgins points out that "MacIntyre's three moral domains are ultimately complementary, indeed interdependent." There is both "an upward and a downward dependence among the three levels." The "upward dependence can be seen as one moves from the level of practices, where goods and virtues are specific and multifarious, through the level of the individual, where some work of synthesis and hierarchisation is already necessary, to the level of the community where fewer, more general goods and virtues are endorsed by all." There is also a downward dependence. Communities rely on practices "to pursue their communal goods"; these goods are structured in terms of the goods internal to particular practices; and the work of integrating them into individual and communal lives is itself a practice.[16]

MacIntyre's account of virtue and practice provides a language and a valuable set of concepts with the help of which we can explore the notion of spiritual qualities. Virtues, whether analyzed in philosophical discourse or addressed in a program of moral education, refer to an undifferentiated mixture of attributes including attitudes, intellectual abilities, habits, and mental as well as physical skills. To tie the development of a number of such virtues to particular practices may be highly useful for specific educational programs. But is the conception of every category of virtue, one must ask, to be so fundamentally bound to practice? There is no doubt that engagement in a given practice does require the development of certain virtues and that these virtues are the means to the achievement of goods internal to the practice in question. And conversely, every virtue will find some expression in one or another practice. Yet, are there not categories of virtues for which the relationship with practices is not so fundamental a feature, but of secondary importance?

MacIntyre himself appears to be cognizant of this problem when, as mentioned above, he incorporates into his account two other contexts within which the concept of virtues becomes intelligible. Beyond this, he feels obliged to identify virtues of justice, courage, and honesty "as necessary components of any practice with internal goods and standards of excellence,"[17] without which they will only be instruments for achieving external goods. But, even when the various dimensions of MacIntyre's narrative are taken into account, something fundamental seems to be missing: the possibility that certain virtues, apart from being instrumental in achieving internal goods in one or more practices, may be essential components of being human. Take, for example, Anscombe's statement that the human being "regarded not just biologically, but from the point of view of the activity of thought and choice in regard to the various departments of life—powers and faculties and use of things needed—'has' such-and-such virtues: and this 'man' with the complete set of virtues is the 'norm,' as 'man' with, e.g., a complete set of teeth is a norm."[18]

There are other problems with the tendency to overemphasize the concept of practice in the exploration of human qualities. One difficulty arises in relation to motivation. Achieving internal goods can be a source of motivation for participants in a practice. But what is it in the child that would recognize the value of the internal goods as opposed to the candy he may receive if he performs well? From the point of view of an educator, at least, being motivated by internal goods is highly desirable. Yet, no matter how much consideration is given to goods internal to a practice, the conditions internal to the learner that give rise to motivation cannot be sidestepped. In the case of the child learning to play chess, "competitive intensity" is one of the internal goods mentioned by MacIntyre. But what correspondence is there, one may ask, between competitive intensity in playing chess and competitiveness as an inner quality? Should competitiveness be nurtured within the child irrespective of how it could undermine certain other highly valued qualities—say generosity and selfless love—only because it is considered an indispensable good to a practice?

The intention here is not to argue that educational processes would not be concerned with practices per se. But in doing so, they would have to explore a number of questions that are not immediately answered, at least by MacIntyre's account of virtues. For example, how is the integrity of a practice ensured? The apparent answer is that the authority and standards of excellence in a practice, albeit themselves susceptible to criticism, are to provide the framework. Attitudes, choices, preferences, and tastes have to be subordinated to these standards. But other factors such as profound moral convictions, principles, and beliefs, which could be considered goods in themselves, also affect the way a practice unfolds. How are these to be treated in helping an individual adopt the required standards of excellence while being initiated into a practice?

It is also necessary to ask how an educational process should deal with sets of internal goods that either conflict or compete with each other. MacIntyre suggests that individuals engaged in various practices each with their own sets of goods could ask themselves "what is my good?" This would involve the ability to put in order the various goods they acknowledge and find for each a place among other goods, presumably in the context of the narrative of their own lives. And they would succeed in this undertaking only if they do it "in company with those others who participate with them and with each other in various practices and who also participate with them in the common life of their whole community."[19] What is being suggested is the formulation of a scheme whereby individuals and communities can determine their own goods and organize the structure of goods internal to and between practices. Assuming that such an undertaking is possible, what would be the standard against which competing goods as well as the relative worth of goods in various practices can be evaluated? It is doubtful that "participation in the common life of the community" alone can, in the climate of our modern culture, provide the solution to this problem.

MacIntyre's own description of the concept of "character" helps illustrate some of the difficulty. He refers to character as "the object of regard" by the majority of the people belonging to a culture, as morally legitimizing "a mode of social existence" by which the members of the general population come "to understand and to evaluate themselves."[20] A number of "characters" define the culture of a particular period and place. The culture of England in the Victorian era, for example, was largely defined by the characters of the Public School Headmaster, the Explorer, and the Engineer, and that of Wilhelmine Germany by the characters of the Prussian Officer and the Professor. Let us consider, then, the bureaucratic manager who according to MacIntyre together with the therapist, represent the characters of the present emotivist culture: as one which legitimizes a mode of existence and by which people in general come to evaluate themselves. MacIntyre points to Max Weber's insistence that "the rationality of adjusting means to ends in the most economical and efficient way is the central task of the bureaucrat." And the justification of his activity lies in the appeal to his ability "to deploy a body of scientific and above all social scientific knowledge, organized in terms of and understood as comprising a set of universal law-like generalizations."[21] What we see today is that these generalizations are applied to almost all practices, even those with widely different aims from bureaucratic management per se. The authority assumed by the managerial practice has dominated the standards of excellence in almost every practice and its goods, among which efficiency and technocratic expertise rank high, have transformed internal goods across many a practice. MacIntyre traces the rise of the technocratic expert from the search for a social science in the enlightenment era to the goals that inspired social reformers, and from the aspiration of social reformers to the ideals of practice and justification of civil servants and managers, and from "the practices of management" to the "theoretical codification of these practices and of the norms governing them by sociologists and organizational theorists." Finally, "textbooks written by those theorists in schools of management and business schools" were used to shape "the managerial practice of the contemporary technocratic expert."[22] Let us now consider the field of education and ask, how did so many of its own ideals and standards of excellence become subordinated to those of another practice? Why did not "participation in the common life of the community" help educators "order the various goods" so as to preserve the integrity of their own practice? It is not that one practice should not incorporate the goods of another. But did this borrowing have to be so extensive to plant technique rather than profound content at the heart of education?

In short, while presenting a highly valuable narrative on virtue, MacIntyre walks too closely to the borders of relativism. Others cross the border with no hesitation. Todd May, for example, who considers practice to lie at the intersection of the individual and the social, defines practices as constitutive of "who we are." It is the personal style one develops while engaging in practices and not an illusory secret self, according to May, that explains the uniqueness in each of us. Moreover, any reference to our being, whether religious or philosophical, that does not fall within the purview of practices would equally be an illusion: "*the illusion of metaphysical depth.*"[23] It is ironic to note that a concept common in the phenomenon of religion across all traditions is that of self-sacrifice. Yet, the concept is intelligible only when *being* is understood in relation to *doing* and the exercise of such qualities as love, justice, and humility, qualities that have the power to transform conventional relationships both within and across practices, and in communities. Achievement of goods within practices as the main motivator for action does not pay sufficient attention to such qualities as essential constituents of human beings.

Acknowledging the great value of MacIntyre's account, but allowing for other accounts that treat certain virtues like justice and honesty at a much more fundamental level, increases our ability to resist moral relativism. David Carr, for example, speaks of the danger of attaching virtues to rival moral traditions and points out that the language of virtues is "the cross-cultural ethical currency of humankind."[24] Nussbaum also speaks of the non-relativity of Aristotelian virtues in the way they correspond to universal spheres of human experience. Appropriate functioning in each sphere defines virtuous action. This objective morality when further developed will retain the grounding in actual human experiences without losing "the ability to criticize local and traditional moralities."[25]

It is not that avoiding all relativism is possible, or even desirable, if one is to stay away from rigid orthodoxy. A relativism established in time, for example, helps one to overcome rigidity. One such relativity is discernable in the doctrine of progressive Revelation as expounded in the Bahá'í Faith. In another context, Williams, who differentiates between various forms of ethical relativism recognizes a "relativism of distance." Here "distance" does not refer to the exotic or to what is elsewhere, but to the distant past or to the future. He perceives two types of confrontation between different moral outlooks: real and notional. In the case of the notional, the contrasting outlook belonging to the past does not represent a real option for us. While reflection on bygone value systems might inspire some thought relevant to modern life, we do not live the life of a "Bronze Age chief" or a "medieval samurai" and cannot take on their outlooks. However, confrontations among cultures of today are real, as we are all within the "causal reach" of one another. Williams criticizes the kind of viewpoint standardly called relativism that regards the language of appraisal—good, bad, right, wrong, and so on—as culture specific in today's world.[26] "Standard relativism says simply that if in culture A, X is favoured, and in culture B, Y is favoured, then X is right for A and Y is right for B; in particular, if 'we' think X right and 'they' think X wrong, then each party is right 'for itself.'" The distinction between "we" and "they" in this form of relativism is not merely given; it is the result of "a political decision or recognition." Williams claims that standard relativism arose first in the Western world in the fifth century B.C. when the Greeks "reflected on their encounters" with people who were not identified as Greeks. "It was in part, perhaps, a reaction against the sense of superiority that the Greeks typically brought to that distinction." And, "it is no accident that the paradigm expression of the distinction between nature and culture, which contributed to relativism, referred to the despised enemy: 'fire burns the same in Persia as it does here, but what counts as right and wrong is different.'"[27] He goes on to explain that modern relativism is in some complex way related to colonialism. Some colonialists believed that native peoples should all be forced or encouraged to adopt European outlooks completely; others thought in this strict manner only about certain populations. And there were places in which specific practices were suppressed while others were not. Anti-colonialists later rejected all these perspectives and advocated that "European powers should leave everyone alone." Williams suggests that, now, after colonialism, we all have to work out our relations with various societies and "standard relativism still cannot help us." In our interactions with another society, "we cannot just count them as them and us as us: we may well have reason to count its members as already some of 'us.'"[28]

Fostering Spiritual Qualities

The various observations made in the above seem to justify the search for an account—of at least a subset of all virtues—which would overcome some of the difficulties associated with the narrative of virtues wrapped in practices, this in a way that the value of the narrative is not entirely lost. But how would Bahá'í-inspired educational efforts go about such a search? Once again, we may look to FUNDAEC, which seems to have taken a few initial steps in this direction. FUNDAEC begins its search by trying to identify some of the forces that motivate a person to pursue a twofold moral purpose. Two forces stand out as of paramount importance. The first is "attraction to beauty" manifesting itself in myriad ways: in love for the majesty and diversity of nature; in the impulse to express beauty through the visual arts, music, and crafts; in the pleasure of beholding the fruits of these creative endeavors; in the stirrings within the human heart of noble emotions in response to the beauty of an idea, the elegance of a scientific theory, and the perfection of character in one's fellow human beings; and in longing for order and meaning in the universe and in social relations. Many have elaborated on different aspects of the notion of beauty. Iris Murdoch, for example, refers to occasions in our surrounding for "unselfing" as beauty: Beauty is something that nature and good art share; it gives a "fairly clear sense to the idea of quality of experience and change of consciousness." There is a difference between forced self-directed enjoyment of nature and a "self-forgetful pleasure in the sheer alien pointless independent existence of animals, birds, stones, and trees. 'Not how the world is, but that it is, is the mystical.'" Good art, not self-consoling fantasy art, "both in its genesis and its enjoyment" is opposed to "selfish obsession." "It invigorates our best faculties and . . . inspires love in the highest part of the soul."[29]

The world's great religious traditions see this vital force of attraction as directed toward the Beauty of the Creator. By acknowledging it, their scriptures awaken and sustain the qualities that are inherent in the human soul. This they accomplish "not only by the standard of behaviour they uphold, the vision of human perfection they disclose, and the laws they promulgate, but also through the beauty of the language in which they express profound truths."[30] FUNDAEC cites the following passage in order to illustrate the sentiments this language can evoke in the human heart:

O Ye People that Have Minds to Know and Ears to Hear! The first call of the Beloved is this: O mystic nightingale! Abide not but in the rose-garden of the spirit. O messenger of the Solomon of love! Seek thou no shelter except in the Sheba of the well-beloved, and O immortal phoenix! dwell not save on the mount of faithfulness. Therein is thy habitation, if on the wings of thy soul thou soarest to the realm of the infinite and seekest to attain thy goal.[31]

The second force that together with attraction to beauty, according to Fundaec, impels moral purpose is "thirst for knowledge." This force motivates "every human being to gain an understanding of the mysteries of the universe and its infinitely diverse phenomena, both on the visible and on the invisible planes. It also directs the mind to seek a fuller understanding of the mysteries within one's own self. Oriented by a vision of beauty and perfection, an individual who is motivated by a thirst for knowledge approaches life as an investigator of reality and a seeker after truth."[32]

Only when the lamp of search, of earnest striving, of longing desire, of passionate devotion, of fervid love, of rapture, and ecstasy, is kindled within the seeker's heart, and the breeze of His loving-kindness is wafted upon his soul, will the darkness of error be dispelled, the mists of doubts and misgivings be dissipated, and the lights of knowledge and certitude envelop his being.[33]

Before we continue with this line of reasoning, we should pause and mention a danger inherent in the language to be used in relation to the two forces being considered. Overemphasis on the powers of the individual is a disquieting characteristic of the so-called positive pedagogy. It is easy to confuse convictions about human nobility and potential powers of the human spirit with exaggerated notions of self. Beliefs centered on these powers, if not scrutinized with care, can lead to unwarranted romanticism about the individual. This romanticism dressed as faith in human potential makes it easy to believe in an array of fashionable grandiose statements—"our program provides tools for genuine long range success"; "we cultivate imagination"; "get daily educational practice as an adventure in self-discovery." We all find it difficult to weed out ideas presented in bite-size slogans and wrapped in beautiful packages whose pretentions mask their meaninglessness. Yet this is a capability we need to acquire if we aim to focus on the true manifestations of human nobility.

With this cautionary note in mind, let us see if this brief examination of the two forces given such prominence in FUNDAEC's thinking can shed some light on the nature of spiritual qualities as a category of attributes education would need to address. The task is not to define spiritual qualities but to point to some of the characteristics that would make it possible to distinguish them with sufficient clarity from other categories of virtues. One statement suggests itself: Spiritual qualities are those attributes of the individual that are intimately involved in the operation of the two motivating forces, and without them the forces could be misdirected. Understanding, the way it is being approached in this inquiry, is like the water that satisfies one's thirst for knowledge and the light that guides one's attraction to beauty. Therefore, nurturing understanding and fostering spiritual qualities need to be considered inseparable goals of education as moral empowerment. There is a clear implication here that one needs to continually develop certain spiritual qualities in order to advance in understanding, and simultaneously, the development of spiritual qualities requires continual advancement in understanding. But the connection between the two processes runs deeper.

The Bahá'í writings consider certain qualities such as justice, love, generosity, and truthfulness to be reflections of divine attributes in the mirror of the human heart. In fact, a fundamental purpose of earthly existence is taught to be the acquisition of these qualities, which, as do physical organs developed in the womb of the mother for life after birth, define the capacity of the human soul in its infinite journey toward the source of all beauty and knowledge. Understanding, too, is a crucial determining factor of this capacity in the soul's eternal evolution. It is in this relationship with the divine that the deeper connection between understanding and spiritual qualities would be sought by a Bahá'í-inspired educational endeavor.

It is beyond the scope of this inquiry to explore the mystical components of Bahá'í belief, and we have only touched on a few propositions here to illustrate how a Bahá'í-inspired discourse on education must draw on them. But emphasis on certain qualities as essential constituents of the human being would not depend entirely on mystical arguments. A brief reference to the way FUNDAEC introduces and discusses the concept of spiritual qualities in a first-level text—remembering that it is to guide a philosophical discussion among youth—may prove useful. The textbook in question is called *Properties* and is the first in a series dedicated to the enhancement of capabilities related to the power of expression, beginning with the examination of words and concepts that help us describe the world around us with a certain degree of precision. The unit opens with a discussion of concepts and associated words that enable us to distinguish and describe the objects we see: shape, size, position, and color. It goes on to introduce the concept of properties of matter, both general—for example, that it can exist in the three phases: solid, liquid, and gas, each with its own general properties—and specific to a given substance—for example, specific heat and melting and boiling points. Having explored the concept of property in some detail through simple readings and language exercises, the text turns to the human being by asking whether the concept also applies in this context. Do human beings have general and specific properties that we can use to describe them? Do they have properties in common with animals, plants, and minerals and do they have their own unique properties? It explains to the students that although in describing a person we do not use the word "property," we do employ terms like "attribute" and "quality," which convey the same kind of meaning. Having examined briefly attributes such as honesty, courage, and generosity, the text asks students whether honesty or dishonesty, truthfulness or deceit, kindness or cruelty, generosity or greed, are properties of the human being. It then proposes that human beings possess a higher and a lower nature. When the attributes of the higher are not present, then the characteristics of the lower dominate. "The higher nature must control the lower nature in order for a person to be noble. Nobility is the true property of a human being who is to be characterized by such qualities as honesty, truthfulness, kindness and generosity."[34]

It is not necessary to go into the details of the lessons in question. Being a unit on language, it has ample scope to introduce concepts and words, facilitating, thereby, a rich discussion of spiritual qualities without entering into a particular religious discourse. In relation to truthfulness as a "property of the human being," for example, it becomes possible to discuss the difference between lies and errors, the dangers of propagating falsehood unintentionally and of not recognizing one's own prejudice, the possibility of lying to oneself, and how truthfulness, in the final analysis, demands dedication to the investigation of reality. The lesson on justice as another property of the human being returns to the question of prejudice. "The habit of making decisions without investigating reality breeds prejudice. Prejudices flourish because people spend their lives blindly imitating others. With the help of justice, we can see with our own eyes and not through the eyes of others. Justice is the quality that allows us to distinguish between truth and falsehood."[35] The lesson on love, reminds the students of how the concept is misused in today's society, confusing it with physical desire. "The basest forms of behaviour are said to be caused by love, and in its name, acts of revenge, jealousy, and infidelity are justified."[36] The lesson then goes on to examine how certain other spiritual qualities such as sincerity, forgiveness, generosity, and patience are intimately connected with love.

The idea of transcendence, so closely associated with religious experience, has also been introduced in this unit. To get a glimpse of that which lies beyond what is seen and known at a given time is a yearning of the human soul. Didier Maleuvre points out that as human beings we are conscious of the distinction between "mental representations and their objects," the finiteness of what we know, and the inexhaustible nature of the object of our quest. This awareness spurs us to modify our representations continuously, but the dividing line never disappears; it affords us the possibility to continue in our search. The horizon of human understanding, although requiring "a ground-level immanent viewpoint on reality," cannot exclude the "beyond," the "unseen," and the "transcendent"; it "arises from the action of casting an internal perspective on the faraway," but is a "groundling's view of a world rife with transcendental openness." In transcendence the human soul takes part in the dialectic at play between the "finite" and the "infinite":

> Transcendence is the mental experience that consists in regarding the plane of known reality as open-ended . . . the horizon beckons toward transcendence but does not fulfil it. . . . In philosophical terms, we may say that the horizon is the creation of a diligently immanent observer possessed by an unrequited longing for the unseen. It is this love that keeps him gazing upward and outward; and it is perhaps the love of his own gazing, and the humble acknowledgement of his finiteness, that keeps him from claiming to know or possess the other side—if an other side there be. Put otherwise, the horizon arises from a religious longing that chooses not to avail itself of the available answers—those by which the satisfied longing settles into dogma.[37]

In the unit under consideration thoughts such as the above are in the background and students are not required to deliberate on philosophical questions. Rather, they are asked to explore the capacity to overcome the limitations imposed on the human being by nature. Understanding the laws that govern nature is essential to the exercise of this capacity; so is the understanding of our nobility, which, for example, helps us to control anger and conquer disappointment. But the wish to rise above one's circumstances can be misdirected, say, in attempts to become wealthy by oppressing others. The desire to transcend perceived or real limits imposed on us by society leads us to abase ourselves if it is not ruled by the principles of justice.

Seeking an Account of Spiritual Qualities

With this brief reference to the content of a few lessons in one of FUNDAEC's texts to illustrate the possibility of raising the students' consciousness of spiritual qualities as properties of the human soul, we can now explore certain characteristics of an account of spiritual qualities to which Bahá'í-inspired educational programs could readily relate.

APPROPRIATE LANGUAGE

Clearly a large number of concepts are connected to each spiritual quality. Nurturing the understanding of these concepts is part of fostering spiritual qualities. In this sense, they constitute "objects of understanding." Nurturing the necessary understanding involves the elaboration of the appropriate language, in this case inspired by insights from religion, a theme that will be discussed in chapter 6 in the section on the complementarity of the languages of science and religion. As it will be argued there, the language in question will have to embrace an expanded rationality in order to tap the roots of motivation in students. What, one may ask, are some of the features of the appropriate language?

The language would have to involve the student in an exploration of moral issues but stay away from the relativism of approaches such as values clarification. To achieve this, it has to set a direction—a higher and a lower—but avoid moralizing. In this context, Taylor's account of languages of qualitative contrast offers valuable insight. These, although marginalized by utilitarianism and Kantian formalism, acknowledge the "qualitative distinctions we make between different actions, or feelings, or modes of life, as being in some way morally higher or lower, noble or base, admirable or contemptible."[38] Sensitivity to these qualitative contrasts, which, borrowing Bahá'í terminology, arises from "spiritual susceptibility," motivates us to aspire toward higher goals, be less concerned with inferior ones, and completely stay away from certain others. According to Taylor, those for example who hold integrity, liberation, and charity as worthy of pursuit in a special way, incommensurate with pursuit of wealth, position or comfort, are often ready to sacrifice these lesser goods for the higher ones. Qualitative contrast can be expressed in a number of ways, through admiration for that which is higher and contempt for the base, through a sensibility to the higher good that commands our "awe" and respect, and through an instrumental obligation toward ordinary goals and a profound commitment to higher ones. Ordinary goals such as wealth or comfort require one to do a number of "instrumental" things, but they are dispensable in the sense that no one should be condemned for not having them, whereas higher goals such as integrity are indispensable—"those who lack them are not just free of some additional instrumental obligations which weigh with the rest of us; they are open to censure."[39] The languages of qualitative contrast are not restricted to the moral sphere; they are also used, for example, in the aesthetic domain. Although in the case of the former the boundary around what constitutes moral cannot always be neatly drawn, there are instances when indifference toward a certain good is blameworthy and a relatively firm dividing line can be discerned. Someone may be insensitive to the difference between the music of Mozart and Boieldieu, but he will not be morally condemned on that account. We would, however, blame a person who saw no difference between his concern for the flowers in his garden and the lives of refugees faced with starvation. To those who discredit languages of qualitative contrast on the basis that the kind of human activities designated by them as higher and lower are subject-related and that they correspond to nothing in reality, Taylor responds:

> Purging subject-related properties makes a lot of sense in an account of inanimate things. It cannot be taken as *a priori* self-evident that it will be similarly helpful in an account of human beings. We would have to establish *a posteriori* that such an absolute account of human life was possible and illuminating before we could draw conclusions about what is real, or know even how to set up the distinction objective/subjective.[40]

He goes on to say that "it may well be that much of human behaviour will be understandable and explicable only in a language which characterises motivation in a fashion which marks qualitative contrasts and which is therefore not morally neutral."[41]

Another feature of the language which is to serve as a vehicle for understanding spiritual qualities is that it should convey a vision of human existence extending beyond the requirements of day-to-day life. The understanding achieved is to enable the student to distinguish between superficial and lasting results of one's words and actions, directing moral purpose toward that which has permanence. Aspiring toward the "lasting" has too often led to contempt for the world. The understanding of spiritual qualities as vital elements of human existence, it is assumed, can be nurtured in such a way that it leads not to asceticism but to a coherent approach to one's own spiritual growth and to one's contribution to the processes that transform society.

EVOLUTION OF MEANING

In addition to making explicit the need to nurture, with the aid of an appropriate language, the understanding of concepts associated with each spiritual quality, our account—of which these paragraphs are only an initial outline and which has to be elaborated through action and reflection by the network of Bahá'í-inspired educational endeavors—should address simultaneously the autonomous and permanent nature of spiritual qualities and the evolutionary changes in their meanings according to historical context. This would be congruent with the Bahá'í belief that religious truth is relative and revealed progressively. The human heart, for example, is prone to love. In the language used by FUNDAEC, to love is one of the "properties" of the human being. On what we focus our love varies from occasion to occasion, and how we go about choosing one or another focus is determined by numerous social and cultural factors. In one sequence, for example, love can be expressed in larger and larger contexts, a friend, the family, the clan, the tribe, and the nation. At a given historical moment, love for one's country may be the largest of these contexts and patriotism the highest expression of love, even demanding the sacrifice of some of its other manifestations. But if the hallmark of the age of maturity of the human race is the realization of the oneness of humankind, the potential for a much wider expression of love, a kind of universal love, must be emerging and the fostering of this spiritual quality has to be a concern of education. Other loyalties are not necessarily to be forgotten, but they are to take new meaning in the context of this larger loyalty. Yet, all such expressions of love, even for the entire human race, are limited. In a certain sense, they are finite manifestations of something that is infinite. The account being explored here would consider the consciousness of an infinite love essential to the fostering of love as it expresses itself in changing finite contexts:

Know thou of a certainty that Love is the secret of God's holy Dispensation, the manifestation of the All-Merciful, the fountain of spiritual outpourings. Love is heaven's kindly light, the Holy Spirit's eternal breath that vivifieth the human soul. Love is the cause of God's revelation unto man, the vital bond inherent, in accordance with the divine creation, in the realities of things. Love is the one means that ensureth true felicity both in this world and the next. Love is the light that guideth in darkness, the living link that uniteth God with man, that assureth the progress of every illumined soul. Love is the most great law that ruleth this mighty and heavenly cycle, the unique power that bindeth together the divers elements of this material world, the supreme magnetic force that directeth the movements of the spheres in the celestial realms. Love revealeth with unfailing and limitless power the mysteries latent in the universe. Love is the spirit of life unto the adorned body of mankind, the establisher of true civilization in this mortal world, and the shedder of imperishable glory upon every high-aiming race and nation.[42]

Those elaborating educational programs concerned with moral empowerment would have to nurture the student's perception of the infinite dimension of love, indeed of all spiritual qualities. They cannot focus exclusively on the finite expressions of each quality in individual and social life. Otherwise, fostering spiritual qualities will be finally reduced to inducing change in behavior in certain predetermined situations.

JUSTICE: AN EXAMPLE OF A SPIRITUAL QUALITY

So important is the task of analyzing spiritual qualities in the context of humanity's movement toward its maturity that a more detailed examination of another quality seems warranted. Given the centrality of justice to moral empowerment, we will dedicate several pages to one narrative of its historical evolution that suggests seeking its roots in the concept of reciprocity. This is not the only narrative possible, but it will serve to point to directions in which one can advance. In his book *A Brief History of Justice*, David Johnston states:

The oldest and probably most widely endorsed understanding of justice focuses neither on an overarching goal from which the principles and rules of justice are allegedly to be derived, nor on a conception of the right and a set of unyielding duties that flow from it—but on the characteristics of relations among persons. This understanding is rooted in the concept of reciprocity, a concept which is malleable enough to have shaped and embellished over the centuries into a considerable range of elaborated conceptions of justice, but which retains a core meaning that ties together all those conceptions as members of a single family of ideas.[43]

In Johnston's view, reciprocity in the classical era reflected the nature of relationships among people in a hierarchical society. Crime in Mesopotamia, for instance, was punished according to the Babylonian law; when the perpetuator and the victim were both free men the sentence was proportional to the severity of the offence, but a free man who put out the eye of a serf was only fined one mina of silver. The Hebrew law demanded a balanced reciprocity: life for life, an eye for an eye, and so on. Aristotle divided justice into two forms—distributive and corrective—both of which were based on the concept of reciprocity, albeit differently manifested. Distributive justice was applied in the context of participation in a shared enterprise, particularly political association, instituted by human beings belonging to a common society and contributing in diverse ways to the attainment of the good life. Reciprocity demanded, among other things, that distribution from the public funds be dispensed in proportion to the contribution made by each member. The aim of corrective justice was to restore the equilibrium that the commission of a wrong had disturbed and Aristotle's articulation of the principle of reciprocity in this respect, though intricate, was nevertheless close in meaning to that of "an eye for an eye." Reciprocity in both its manifestations helps bind together the members of the political community. The classical formulations of justice and the Aristotelian conception of it shared the underlying belief in an order—natural or divine—from which rules and laws of justice could not deviate.

Johnston argues that from the time of the Sophists a tension began to emerge between this view and the outlook that the social world is susceptible to being fashioned by human intention and design. The former view prevailed over the latter until well into the second millennium; the latter consolidated in mid and late eighteenth century in the work of thinkers like David Hume and Adam Smith. Hume, who found inspiration in Newton's grasp of the laws of motion, believed that it is within humanity's reach to similarly grasp the laws of motion that apply to human societies. Thus institutions of society, namely those of private property, exchange of goods, and contractual agreement could be reshaped in such a way as to serve the needs of the people. The institution of private property, in particular, allowed people to have rights to the goods they produced or the land they occupied, and by its means they could be assured of receiving benefits for their labors. In this formulation, the virtue of justice is defined by respect for such rights and "the inclination to be just" is cultivated in order to "secure the advantages of a society that will generate ample wealth through commerce for the purpose of enhancing human beings' enjoyment of life."[44] Hume considered justice an inclination "contrary to nature" and stated that "public utility is the *sole* origin of justice."[45]

Smith likewise emphasized the creation of wealth in augmenting human happiness, but differed from Hume in that he saw the sense of justice as inherent to human constitution, and not as something that is gradually learned after people become aware of its usefulness. In addition to the tendency to "protect the weak," "curb the violent," and "chastise the guilty," Smith identifies another propensity in human nature, which ought to be incorporated into the idea of justice. Central to his theory of wealth generation is the conception of "division of labor"—people producing specialized goods that are demanded by others and exchanging them for other types of goods they desire. Division of labor, he stated, "is not originally the effect of any human wisdom," it is "the necessary, though slow and gradual, consequence of a certain propensity in human nature . . . the propensity to truck, to barter, and exchange one thing for another."[46] According to Johnston, this group of eighteenth-century utilitarian thinkers, by focusing on human happiness, "redefined justice as an instrument in the service of utility," thus pushing "reciprocity to the margin of the idea of justice." He points out that Kant subsequently criticized this way of thinking and placed reciprocity more at the center of the question of justice. He conceded that all human beings are of equal worth, but rejected the idea that justice could be built on the basis of human happiness, given that its causes are so varied. He proposed that justice is founded on the human capacity for freedom. The exercise of this capacity allows us not to be slaves to our physical desires and instincts—aspects of our empirical self—but to subject our decisions and actions to the laws we give ourselves either singly or collectively by the self that transcends these inclinations: the "super-sensible" self. This capacity for freedom is the foundation of human rights and gives substance to another understanding of reciprocity:

Man's freedom as a human being, as a principle for the constitution of a commonwealth, can be expressed in the following formula. No-one can compel me to be happy in accordance with his conception of the welfare of others, for each may seek his happiness in whatever way he sees fit, so long as he does not infringe upon the freedom of others to pursue a similar end which can be reconciled with the freedom of everyone else within a workable general law—i.e., he must accord to others the same right as he enjoys himself.[47]

Kant integrated this formula for the expression of human freedom in his idea of an "original contract"—a contract conceivable by human reason comprised of terms that protect the rights of each individual member of the state and to which the "super-sensible" self gives consent. Johnston points out that for Kant the idea of the original contract is the means through which it can be determined whether or not laws are just: "A set of laws that would allow some members of a state to be deprived of the means required in order to meet their needs is a set of laws from which at least some people would have withheld their consent in an original contract. Such a set of laws would therefore be unjust." "If, on the other hand, a law is such that it could have been the object of such an agreement—an agreement to which an entire people could have given its assent—then it is at least arguably just."[48] In relation to corrective justice, Kant proposes strict and balanced reciprocity: "whatever undeserved evil you inflict upon another within the people, that you inflict upon yourself [. . .] only the *law of retribution* [. . .] can specify definitely the quality and the quantity of punishment."[49]

Johnston continues his narrative by stating that in the nineteenth century the idea of social justice, the seeds of which were sown a century earlier, became the focus of attention of prominent thinkers. That humanity was now able to reconstruct its institutions, conventions, and practices in order to alleviate human suffering was based on the unprecedented advance in science and technology as well as the great social transformations to which the French Revolution gave rise. Social justice implied that a set of principles could be worked out to be deployed in order "to assess a society's institutions as a whole and to argue for a transformation of those institutions if they are found wanting."[50] The question posed by Henry Sidgwick captured the spirit of search for social justice at the time: "Are there any clear principles from which we may work out an ideally just distribution of rights and privileges, burdens and pains, among human beings as such?"[51]

Two sets of responses were offered to such questions. The first centered on the principle of desert "according to which what people deserve to receive is based on what they contribute to society."[52] Socialists and defenders of free markets both agreed that "social justice is achieved when contributions are rewarded in accordance with the principle of desert," but they "parted ways over the questions about the manner in which the notion of a 'contribution' should be conceived, and a fortiori over the institutional means for achieving social justice."[53] As a socialist principle, the principle of desert is realized when "competent and unbiased authorities allocate rewards according to some collectively defined conception of desert"; as a liberal principle, it is realized when "individuals are as free as possible to enter into transactions with others and to reap the returns those others, taken individually, are willing to bestow."[54] The second set of responses centered on the principle of need summarized in the phrase: "from each according to his ability, to each according to his need."[55] This principle recognizes not only the differences in native abilities and talents, but also the lack of opportunity to develop them. Over the years many objections have been raised to both points of view and the debate on the priority that should be given to the principle of desert or of need continues today.

In the twentieth century John Rawls formulated his theory of "justice as fairness." He argued that the utilitarian framework, at the heart of which is the greatest happiness principle, does not offer sufficient protection for liberty. "If the aggregate gains in happiness to the majority are greater than the loss of happiness suffered by the minority, then the greatest happiness principle would justify the minority's loss of liberty."[56] However "justice denies that the loss of freedom for some is made right by a greater good shared by others."[57] Rawls also criticized utilitarianism for its "monistic conception of good." Human happiness is only one of the ends human beings pursue. He, too, like Kant believed that human capacity for freedom, rather than pursuit of happiness should be the focus of our ideas about justice. Rawls considered justice as the most important feature of social institutions: "[j]ustice is the first virtue of social institutions [. . .] laws and institutions no matter how efficient and well-arranged must be reformed and abolished if they are unjust."[58]

Rawls' theory of justice, Johnston mentions, focuses on society's basic structure as the "primary subject of justice" and not on the kind of rules that regulate interactions and transactions among private persons, or on what constitutes just action for individuals. He considers the effects of basic structure—social institutions and arrangements, political constitution, and economic structure—"profound and present from the start."[59] Society's basic structure not only determines the inequalities of opportunities people face, but also shapes their expectations of what they can achieve in life from the very beginning. And since we have no say over our native endowments or the circumstances in which we are born, the notion of desert cannot serve as a sound principle for the just distribution of social goods. Thus Rawls centers his attention on the distribution of the benefits of society. The premise is that all would derive more advantage from participating in a scheme of social cooperation than they would if each were to live solely by his own efforts. Therefore, benefits—both those belonging to the category of material and economic goods and the kind that are non-economic in nature such as the enjoyment one derives from friendship—and not burdens are the significant outcomes of social cooperation.

Rawls decides on a method partly borrowed from Kant's idea of original contract. But, as Johnston points out, while the idea of a hypothetical contract was used by Kant to test the justice or injustice of laws and policies, Rawls employs it in a more ambitious and more elaborate fashion in order to identify a set of principles of social justice. He asks that we imagine an ideal society in which an agreement has been reached among its members determining the terms of their association. We are to imagine that each member of this society is represented in a condition called "original position" by someone who will safeguard his rights and privileges. The original position is an ideal theoretical situation in which the representatives of the members of society, the "parties" as he names them, come together in order to achieve consensus on a set of principles for the just distribution of the advantages and benefits of society. These principles form the basis for selecting the structure of society among the alternatives available. This basic structure will then provide the framework within which laws will be adopted, policies developed, and specific decisions reached. Rawls stresses that the parties in the original position are rational; they will strive to gain a greater rather than a lesser share of social benefits for the members of society whom they represent. To ensure that they can reach agreement with their counterparts on fair grounds, he places them behind a "veil of ignorance," a veil that prevents them from having any knowledge of the skills, the abilities, the social status, and even the identity of those on whose behalf they speak. Rawls assumes that this kind of knowledge would impel the parties to negotiate for principles that would largely benefit the people they represent, without due regard for fairness. For example, a party would demand principles in favor of those who are intellectually gifted, if he were to know that the member he represents is exceptionally intelligent. The rationality behind the veil of ignorance does not presuppose that members of society are egoistic. They could, for example, choose to dedicate part of their portion of social goods to promote causes that benefit others. Finally, the parties in the original position would have to "adopt a distinctive measure to determine how well-off the members they represent are in comparison to others." The utilitarian metrics of happiness calculated by material wealth is too narrow. "The appropriate measure would be made up of several diverse elements, including certain rights and liberties, income and wealth and the social bases of self-respect," that Rawls called "social primary goods."[60]

Rawls believes that two principles of justice would be chosen in the original position:

a) Each person has the same indefeasible claim to a fully adequate scheme of equal basic liberties, which scheme is compatible with the same scheme of liberties for all; and

b) Social and economic inequalities are to satisfy two conditions: first, they are to be attached to offices and positions open to all under conditions of fair equality of opportunity; and second, they are to be to the greatest benefit of the least-advantaged members of society (the difference principle).[61]

Regarding the first principle, the basic liberties of citizenship consist of "freedom of thought and liberty of conscience; political liberties (for example, the right to vote and to participate in politics) and freedom of association, as well as the rights and liberties specified by the liberty and integrity (physical and psychological) of the person; and finally, the rights and liberties covered by the rule of law."[62]

Regarding the second principle, Rawls argues that while, the distribution of wealth and income need not be equal, it must be to everyone's advantage, and at the same time, positions of authority and offices of command must be accessible to all. One applies the second principle by holding positions open, and then, subject to this constraint, arranges social and economic inequalities so that everyone benefits.

Besides a set of principles of social justice that facilitate the identification of the basic structure of a just society, Rawls' theory also prescribes a set of attributes that such a society should cultivate in its members. These attributes are intertwined with the two above-mentioned principles of social justice; they are the attributes that parties in the original position would want the citizens of a just society to develop in order to "understand and consent to the terms of social cooperation by which they are governed," and "to form, to revise, and rationally to pursue a conception of the good, a conception that would form the basis of a member's plan of life."[63]

Johnston observes that Rawls' theory makes three distinct claims. The first is the "causal claim" that the institutions and practices comprising a society's basic structure "determine how well the members of a society are able to do in life." The second is the "conceptual claim" that the principles of justice governing this basic structure "may be quite different in character from the rules and criteria that apply to other problems of justice." The third claim is that "we can best address the wide range of questions that arise about justice by first developing a sound theory of social justice. This theory can then constitute the foundation for defensible ideas about justice with regard to other subjects." Johnston argues that the first two claims are largely defensible, but finds the last one problematic. There is no ground to presuppose that principles of social justice are "intellectually prior to, or serve as a foundation for" justice in the context of relationships and actions. In his view "nothing is more central to the way in which human beings think about fairness among relative equals than the norm of balanced reciprocity." The complexity of social institutions and practices requires principles governing their operations that help create conditions of greater equality, for example, by giving the employees in a company the power of collective bargaining. And if these principles are to be acceptable to human beings "they must be rooted in the sense of justice—a sense that is best expressed through the concepts of reciprocity and desert."[64]

With this overview of Johnston's historical account let us return to our original purpose. We have proposed that to foster spiritual qualities an educational process must nurture the understanding of certain concepts closely connected to them. This, we have said, entails the elaboration of the appropriate language inspired by insights from religion. In the example of justice we are looking for some of the concepts that need to be understood by the students as they progressively learn to manifest it not only as a social imperative, but also as a spiritual quality with ever expanding and non-exhaustible meaning and implication.

Let us suppose that justice as a spiritual quality has a certain affinity with what Johnston calls a "sense of justice." Then to say that the sensibility of reciprocity is in some way fundamental to the operation of justice is an acceptable statement. Difficulties arise when reciprocity is considered as the central idea around which a conception of justice is shaped, overlooking the vitality of other equally significant concepts such as impartiality, truth, moderation, and power.

It is, for example, universally acknowledged that impartiality is integral to the operation of justice. But only a certain version of the concept has been popularized. We are told that to be impartial we must be objective, not allowing emotions, personal opinions, and preferences to cloud our judgment. It is emphasized further that impartiality requires the rejection of deeply rooted prejudicial outlooks prevalent in a particular society. The synthesis of these two demands—one related to one's own inner state and the other concerned with influence from without—leads to the commonly held, but faulty, view that there is a neutral position, attainable by all, from which true judgments can be made. To be impartial is to think and act from this advantageous point. Yet, the impossibility of divesting ourselves entirely of our own perspectives is evident. Such a simplistic view of impartiality, then, needs to be adjusted, which forces us to deal with the question of justice at a higher level of complexity.

In analyzing one of the units of Fundaec, we have already described how it has treated spiritual qualities such as truthfulness, justice, and love as properties of the human soul. With regard to justice, it has encouraged students to explore it as a spiritual quality by the aid of which one can see with one's own eyes and know through one's own knowledge, drawing on a particular admonition in the Bahá'í writings: "The best beloved of all things in My sight is Justice; turn not away therefrom if thou desirest Me, and neglect it not that I may confide in thee. By its aid thou shalt see with thine own eyes and not through the eyes of others, and shalt know of thine own knowledge and not through the knowledge of thy neighbor. . . ."[65] Justice viewed in this way, as the faculty of the human soul that guides each of us to comprehend reality and its subtleties, compels us to strive for impartiality, not as a fictitious neutral state, but as the requirement of independent investigation of truth. But then if impartiality is something justice cultivates in us, "seeing with our own eyes" cannot mean the kind of seeing that is colored with our lower passions, with envy and a narrow self-interest. It is a seeking after truth that demands the abandonment of these inclinations. It is a freeing of oneself of idle fancy and imitation that creates the possibility to "look into all things with a searching eye."

A sophisticated theory of justice such as Rawls' places those deliberating on justice in an ideal state behind a veil of ignorance, shutting them off from certain knowledge and information, so that they can choose the just social arrangements among available alternatives. He believes that such knowledge makes the parties in the original position partial and unfair. There is the assumption here that the dominant impulse in a human being is that of seeking one's own benefits, and that in order to reach consensus on the principles of justice, it is necessary to curtail this impulse by denying access to certain knowledge. But, one can ask, is not the considerable advance achieved by Rawls in the discourse on justice attributable to a faculty of his, a faculty undistorted by self-interest, which impels him to search for principles that would shape the structure of a just society? Why would he, then, ignore the existence of this same selfless propensity in human beings in general? And does not justice itself require that we, in full knowledge of ourselves and of our conditions, transcend self-interests and our own limited perspectives? Can justice be cultivated in individuals and in social institutions without a clear perception of the moral dimension of existence? One can further ask if pursuit of truth called for by the faculty of justice is not a motivating force stronger than pursuit of self-interest? And should not the educational process under consideration draw on this force to tap the roots of motivation in the student?

Moderation is another principle closely connected to justice. That much of the injustice in society is due to a lack of moderation—extreme disparity in riches, fortunes, and opportunities—is abundantly clear. What is not so obvious is how justice as a spiritual quality is the power that enables individuals to observe the proper limits in all things and to see the harm inherent in excess. "Whoso cleaveth to justice, can, under no circumstances, transgress the limits of moderation. . . . The civilization, so often vaunted by the learned exponents of arts and sciences, will, if allowed to overleap the bounds of moderation, bring great evil upon men."[66] Theories of justice that focus merely on distribution of social and economic goods according to poorly defined notions of desert or need, inevitably lose sight of the significance of the principle of moderation. So many who speak of desert assume that justice is served when each person receives a due share of the overall social benefits, corresponding as accurately as possible to the contributions he or she has made to the prosperity of society. This posture finds support in individualistic worldviews. Yet, in all domains of human endeavor progress is achieved when different abilities, talents, and performances complement each other. And even if it were possible to compensate each individual for his or her single contributions to society, would we not still need criteria that would assist us in determining which activities are to be considered as a contribution and in gauging the value of one relative to another?

Contributions are often defined in relation to the goals and objectives of social practices, and the worth of one's labors is measured according to the norms and institutional arrangements already in place. Johnston gives the example of a soccer game to illustrate this point. A productive striker deserves more praise than an average player, because the objective of the game is to win within a set of rules that specify the ways it can be pursued. If, for instance, the objective of the game were to promote comity among the members of both teams then actions other than striking a goal would be counted as contribution deserving praise. Moreover, as Johnston points out, societies value different objectives; "some are more interested in glory, while others are more interested in luxury, and these two objectives are far from exhausting the universe of available alternatives."[67]

It is important to note that the values people hold cannot be hidden behind a veil of ignorance. How markedly different would the vision of a just society be if the predominant value were to be expressed as "Man's merit lieth in service and virtue and not in the pageantry of wealth and riches"![68] Will not justice as a spiritual quality to be fostered in education assist humanity to advance toward an understanding of the principle of moderation that places values in their proper spaces in relation to one another?

Defining justice solely on the basis of need has its own problems. Many proponents of this approach point out that the notion of desert does not take into consideration the deprivation of those who either lack natural endowments or are denied access to opportunities in the existing social structure. However, as dictated by the prevalent world-view within which the debate between desert and need takes place, the contributions of individuals and populations are measured mostly in terms of growth in productivity and wealth. Honesty, generosity, love, and justice itself as a spiritual quality, do not make contributions to the social order on their own; they do so only when used instrumentally. An appropriate vision of the vast potentials with which every human being is endowed, potentials that proper education can release, is held hostage to societal aims defined narrowly in terms of material output. Under these circumstances, it is easy to view individuals who do not seem to make notable contributions to such aims as bundles of need. This is not to say that deprivations do not exist and justice should not demand that proper social structure be created to address them. But even on a purely material plane, needs are perceived differently according to what level of prosperity is expected. Johnston mentions that needs are fairly minimal when mere survival is concerned, more extensive when one is to lead a healthy and long life, and still larger when one is to live in dignity. In a society that constantly appeals to greed, the attraction to luxury and love of extravagance dull the senses. Consequently, the notion of need is invoked equally on behalf of people who struggle for their very survival and by those whose greed, constantly fanned by propaganda, is without limit. Thus, as is the case with desert, to employ the notion of need properly in the practice of justice, an educational process has to be in place that helps students appreciate the dictates of moderation and recognize the evils of excess.

Another set of issues arises when we acknowledge that justice conceived primarily as a characteristic of social institutions cannot be contemplated without reference to power and the way it is to be exercised. We have already examined briefly the discourse on power in chapter 2 and pointed out how often it is centered on domination and conflict. It could be argued that justice requires the exercise of power, in the form analyzed by theorists such as Lukes, in order to fight tyranny and oppression. But confining the connection of the two concepts to this particular context leads to an incomplete understanding of justice. Force will not be made the servant of justice, if such attributes as impartiality, truth seeking and moderation, inherent to justice as "a property of the human soul," were not to play their proper role in public life. A process of moral empowerment should seek an expanded notion of power that helps reshape the essential relationships of social existence—among individuals and groups; between the individual, the community, and the institutions of society; and between these and the natural environment—according to the principle of the oneness of humankind, the establishment of which is the hallmark of the maturity of the human race. Fostering justice as a spiritual quality is an integral part of this process of empowerment, for the "purpose of justice is the appearance of unity among men."[69]

Since unity, among other things, implies reciprocity, we should consider once again Johnston's historical narrative. As mentioned before, he argues that "sensibility for reciprocity"—presumably what Rawls calls a "tendency to answer in kind"—is central to the sense of justice. He observes that it is commonplace for "people who have received significant benefits from others" to feel an obligation "to requite those benefits in some fashion, if they are able to do so." And conversely "people will often go to great lengths to retaliate against others who have inflicted harm, if they are able to do so." Further he remarks that it is not "unusual for people to retaliate against perpetuators of harm even if they are not the victims and the act of retaliation is costly to themselves."[70] Johnston concedes that the ancient notion of reciprocity, a mutuality respecting the hierarchical order, is incompatible with "the postulate that all human beings are equal in worth," and proposes a revision of the "notion of justice as reciprocity" in order to take into account inequalities in talents and abilities, this "in a way that inverts the priorities evident in ancient ideas about justice." Kantian formulation is "blind to the fact that human beings who are considered equal in *worth* commonly are not also equal in *capabilities*." Johnston affirms that "justice is done when less is required or expected from those with lesser capabilities and more is expected of those with more capabilities."[71]

An important question before us is whether Johnston's revision of the ancient concept of reciprocity goes far enough. We can argue that consciousness of the oneness of humankind as it develops endows the notion of reciprocity with greater meaning than what has been suggested by him. Once again the metaphor of the human body mentioned in chapter 1 is instructive. "In the body of man . . . the spirit, when in ideal control of all the lesser parts of the organism, finds the utmost harmony throughout the whole body—each part is in perfect reciprocity with the other parts. The commands and impulses of the spirit are obeyed by the body and the body in turn in its actions and functions identifies and determines the expression the spiritual impulses shall take."[72] The interconnectedness of organs in the human body has its parallel in the body of humankind, the members of which are held together by bonds of reciprocity. These bonds in the body of humankind are sustained by the spiritual impulse released through Divine Revelation. It is not reciprocity in the sense that "people who have received benefits from others" feel an obligation "to requite those benefits in some fashion" supplemented by consideration of differences in initial talents and capabilities, it is reciprocity generated through the power of a host of spiritual qualities such as love, generosity, compassion, forgiveness, humility, and justice itself, all stirred by the consciousness of the oneness of humankind. And, one expression of divine justice in creation is that the soul of every human being has been endowed with these qualities in potential to be developed on this earthly plane of existence.

INTERACTIONS AMONG SPIRITUAL QUALITIES

The earlier reference to the evolution of the concept of love and this lengthier analysis of justice demonstrate that a great deal of groundwork has to be done if we are to gain sufficient insight into the nature of each spiritual quality. Yet, it is essential that spiritual qualities not be considered as isolated entities: their autonomous character indicates independence of the entire category from the ephemeral. Bahá'í-inspired educational efforts, then, need to give attention to interactions among spiritual qualities. But this cannot be done if one focuses only on behavior. Examining qualities at the level of their expression through behavior gives rise to certain flawed questions: Can the exercise of one spiritual quality require the exclusion of some other in specific situations? Can courage, for example, sometimes require the absence of wisdom? Can one spiritual quality in a particular instance be in conflict with another? Can justice be at times in conflict with kindness? Similar questions have been asked in relation to the exercise of virtues. In that context, the notion of "minimal requirement" has been employed to argue for the way virtues operate together to produce effective result and avoid harm.[73] Accordingly, one should always

117

weigh the minimal requirements of justice, for example, in expressing kindness. Yet, it is difficult to see how such a minimal requirement can be established for each virtue without further narrowing behavior to recognized codes. On the other hand, it has also been argued that to overcome the apparent conflict between virtues requires the avoidance of excess in their exercise, which suggests a maximum beyond which one should not go. However, in the case of spiritual qualities, to speak in such terms sounds contradictory. What is too much justice or a minimal requirement of love, if these are the properties of the human soul? These spiritual qualities as reflections of the attributes of God have infinite manifestations. Would it not, therefore, be more consistent to say that the exercise of one requires the presence of all the other spiritual qualities? Justice is not in conflict with compassion; without the power of compassion the exercise of justice can take on the characteristics of cruelty. The notion of excessive love seems to oppose its nature as a property of the human soul; it is more accurate to say that love interacts with a host of other qualities such as purity, detachment, wisdom, and generosity and that the expression of love loses its vigor when it becomes mingled with passion, jealousy, and possessiveness.

SERVICE

Finally, an important feature of the account of spiritual qualities we are seeking is that they are to be understood and developed in service to humanity. The term "service" is commonly used to imply activity for the benefit of others and embraces a variety of undertakings. The conception that constitutes an element of the framework being explored in this inquiry refers to acts that are directed by the twofold moral purpose and seek the transformation of one or another aspect of the essential relationships that define human existence. Acts of service are characterized by continuity and by growing complexity; they are not disconnected events. They may initially be simple and easily accomplished, but as knowledge grows and capacity develops, the protagonists of moral empowerment are able to take on more demanding challenges. As with understanding, the image of a path captures important features of the conception of service. In fact, it is often used in the Bahá'í community to visualize effort and movement as well as resilience to overcome difficulties. A path of service invites participation, and participants advance along it at different paces and strides. One does not walk the path alone; there is faith in the capacity of others and joy in their accomplishments. Walking the path of service is contingent on one's state of being. The efficacy of service is not evaluated only by the perceived success or failure of an enterprise, but also by the extent to which understanding has advanced and the necessary spiritual qualities have been developed. This is not an evaluation carried out from outside, but by every single participant. The path of service is experienced and known not by one or two, but by a growing number of people; an entire population comes to assume ownership of it.

The relationship between spiritual qualities and acts of service seems to have features in common with the way practice and virtues are linked in MacIntyre's account. For example, virtues as internal goods are essential to a practice, just as spiritual qualities are indispensable to the integrity of acts of service. But there is a fundamental difference. Standards that are to guide the evolution of practices are usually thought to be within them; acts of service, on the other hand, are not merely regulated by the rules and standards of the specific practices with which they are associated, but more significantly by the moral values that inspire them. Further, the reality of service is not confined to specific actions; it pervades the environment with the potency to transform the relationships that shape that environment. Service changes selfish grumble to selfless joy in giving, greedy exploitation to reciprocity and fairness, and arrogant knowing to a humble posture of learning. Although, service is manifested through action, it is inseparable from one's state of being. It unites doing and being. At a most fundamental level, it is a requirement of what it is to be human: "That one indeed is a man who, today, dedicateth himself to the service of the entire human race."[74]

CHAPTER 5

OBJECT OF UNDERSTANDING: THE CONTEXT

If an educational process is to seek the moral empowerment of the student, nurturing understanding cannot be confined to what happens in the mind of the "subject of understanding." She is to act on many an "object of understanding," although not all, and contribute to a collective effort to transform them. Understanding physical reality allows for transformations in the physical world, not least through the creation and application of technology as fundamental aspects of human culture. In transforming the physical, the human agent breaks certain laws of nature only in appearance; in reality the laws are such that they permit the transformation in question. That large solid inert objects do not fly in the earth's atmosphere is a feature of the way the physical world works only at a certain level; there are more fundamental laws that make possible the flight of the airplane. If they exist, the laws that govern the evolution of social reality—or of culture—should also allow for transformation to occur in this dimension of existence. Comprehending an object of understanding and acting upon it, then, requires of the subject of understanding a certain posture with respect to reality. What is the proper posture and how does an educational process help the student to assume it? It seems clear that some way of looking at reality itself is required before one tries to answer this question; the conceptual framework guiding the educational process must include elements that at least suggest some view of reality, no matter how vague and incomplete. Of course, not every view of reality will do. To insist on empowering the students to actively participate in the transformation of society and at the same time transmit to them a picture of culture as the predetermined outcome of the imposition of the physical environment on human beings, for example, is bound to lead to a host of contradictions. What we need to do, then, is to find an approach to physical, social, and spiritual reality that could inform Bahá'í-inspired education, knowing that its framework will evolve through a process of action and reflection on action.

As far as physical reality is concerned, the framework being sought in this inquiry is based on the premise that the physical universe exists and evolves according to an order, the patterns and laws of which, in principle, lend themselves to being comprehended by the human mind. Bahá'ís would hold to this fundamental conviction upon which the edifice of science is built, and would find it supported by the tenets of their Faith. But they would also assume the existence of a larger reality in which the physical universe is embedded. There are dimensions of this reality that have to be explored in the context of moral empowerment. The discussion in the previous chapter of spiritual qualities not as mere excellences attached to a practice, but as attributes of the human being with their own permanent existence, is one example of such an exploration.

In social reality we see the operation of forces originating in both the physical and the spiritual realms of existence. The subject of understanding draws on these forces to act on this reality and to transform it. To analyze this process we need to gain insights from theories that try to describe social reality and its evolution. One such account is presented by John R. Searle in *The Construction of Social Reality*. In the first section of this chapter, we examine briefly some of Searle's views but, important as these may be for our inquiry, certain features of his thought prove problematic. To go beyond them, we explore in the

122

section that follows several ideas advanced by Thomas Nagel in *The View from Nowhere,* an invaluable source of insight for any discussion of reality. Our exploration is enriched by a brief reference to the notion of "absolute conception" as set forth by Bernard Williams.

The relationship between the subject and object of understanding is a theme that is also addressed in a somewhat different discourse, one that addresses problems arising from the fragmentation of the knowledge of reality. Fragmentation of knowledge and its ill effects on education have been a source of anxiety for FUNDAEC since its inception, and a few of its arguments—philosophically less rigorous than Nagel's or Williams'—but insightful nevertheless—are presented in the next section. The chapter ends with a section on "Thought and Reality" in which we discuss briefly some of John McDowell's ideas, suggesting that they speak to FUNDAEC's concerns at a fundamental level.

Constructing Social Reality

Searle provides a description of social reality the structures of which, though invisible, are deeply rooted and emerge from the physical stuff of the universe. He employs examples such as money, marriage, property, and the like, to show that social reality is constructed, while physical reality, or what he calls its "brute facts"—mountains, rivers, and planets—exists independently of the human mind. Reality embraces brute facts, as well as facts whose existence is *"relative to the intentionality of observers, users, etc."*[1] Items belonging to this latter category are either fabricated to perform a certain function or are naturally occurring objects to which an aesthetic, a practical, or some other function is assigned. A chair and a screwdriver are examples of the first, while swimming in the river and using specific types of tree as lumber are examples of the other.

The assignment of functions lifts brute facts out of the world of matter and gives them a social status not built into their molecular structure. Searle argues that nature is devoid of any intrinsic function.

It is all about causal relations. There is a normative component in function that cannot be reduced to causation. It is, for example, intrinsic to nature that the heart pumps blood and causes it to circulate through the body, a movement that is related to other causal processes having to do with the survival of the organism. But this brute fact is transformed into a different category of facts when we assign a function to it and place it relative to a system of values such as life, reproduction, and health, supported by a vocabulary that includes malfunction, heart disease, and heart failure: "We do not speak of better or worse stones, unless of course we have assigned a function to the stone."[2]

Functions are either "agentive" or "nonagentive." Agentive functions are assigned to fabricated and naturally occurring objects relative to the interests—practical, aesthetic, educational, and so on—of conscious agents. Nonagentive functions are "assigned to naturally occurring objects and processes as part of a theoretical account of the phenomena in question."[3] The functions given to a screwdriver and to a stone that we use as a paperweight are cases of the former, while the function assigned to a heart is an example of the latter. Searle goes on to identify a special class of agentive functions that stand for objects and states of affairs independent of themselves. These representations of activities and objects which are part of the institutional system of language are called "symbolism" and "meaning." We do not need to go into Searle's description of the relationship between language and social reality here. Suffice it to say that he sees linguistic forms as partly constitutive of social facts.

In order to give a more complete description of the construction of social reality, Searle adds two other features to his account: collective intentionality and agreement. Collective intentionality, he argues, should not be equated with individual intentionality coupled with mutual beliefs. He argues that those philosophers who thus reduce it misconstrue collective intentionality as a commitment to a view that "there exists some Hegelian world spirit, a collective consciousness, or something equally implausible."[4] According to him, while it is true that mental life is inside each individual brain, it does not follow that all mental life has to refer to individual intention. The intentionality inside one's head can be individual as well as collective. The violinist playing in an orchestra is doing her part in performing a symphony. There is a collective intentionality, although it is contained in the head of each performer separately. Therefore, "we intend" is an entity that is real.[5]

If collective intentionality exists, Searle argues, so does the collective imposition of agentive function on objects. When the function imposed on objects is by virtue of their physical features, say when two or more people would naturally use a log as a bench, it would not be difficult to see collective intentionality at work. However, when the function is not dictated by the intrinsic physical features of the object, then its imposition requires an additional element: collective agreement.[6] Using the example of territorial boundary, Searle asks us to imagine how the concept with its rules and conventions could have evolved from a stone wall built by a primitive tribe to keep intruders out, into a boundary marker—say, the remnant of a wall—performing the same function by the way of collective agreement. The marker, now acting symbolically, is given a function extending beyond its physical features. That a piece of paper is considered to be, say, a twenty-dollar bill is another example. Here is a social fact belonging to a whole category of facts to which Searle refers as institutional. Institutional facts require special human institutions such as language and systems of constitutive rules. Constitutive rules, in contrast to regulative rules which "regulate antecedently existing activities," not only regulate but also "create the very possibility of certain activities."[7] Rules of driving, for example, are regulative and those of chess are constitutive; they create the very possibility of playing chess.

With examples such as the above, Searle argues that the "key element in the move from the collective imposition of function to the creation of institutional facts is the imposition of a collectively recognized *status* to which a function is attached."[8] There is a collective status attached, for instance, to the territorial marker or the piece of paper demanding a whole set of institutional arrangements.

In his description of social reality Searle is clearly trying to establish the logical priority of brute facts over institutional facts. He states that his aim is "to assimilate social reality to our basic ontology of physics, chemistry, and biology," "to show the continuous line that goes from molecules and mountains to screwdrivers, levers, and beautiful sunsets, and then to legislatures, money, and nation-states."[9] To develop "a hierarchical taxonomy of social and institutional reality"[10] is an objective based on the assumption that "social facts in general, and institutional facts especially, are hierarchically structured. Institutional facts exist, so to speak, on top of brute physical facts." "What is true of money is true of chess games, elections, and universities. All these can take different forms, but for each there must be some physical realization."[11] Social reality—in Searle's account—is rooted in the brute facts of an external reality. This external reality is composed of particles in fields of force, some of which form systems. The systems are divided into living and non-living. Some living systems have evolved consciousness to various degrees and human beings are included in this category. According to this ontology, just as the human mind represents a set of higher-level features of the brain, features that are at once "mental" and "physical," culture signifies the culminating point of human beings' collective physical evolution. He states that he uses "the 'mental' so construed, to show how 'culture' is constructed out of 'nature.'"[12]

This brief description of Searle's conception of social reality points to a few elements of the philosophical framework being sought here. To understand that much of social reality is actually constructed during a long historical process confirms the subject of understanding in her intention to transform it. That we assign function to objects through collective intentionality and agreement and that "we intend" has a reality of its own—irrespective of whether this collective intentionality resides in each individual's mind or has an existence akin to "Hegelian world spirit"—bring to light the nature of certain interactions between the subject of understanding and reality. But we need not reconcile the totality of Searle's account with the narrative of moral empowerment that is gradually being developed. Insights, in the way we are using the concept here, do not arise from espousing a theory in its entirety. Disagreements also help achieve clarity. Searle seems inclined to reduce purpose in all its dimensions to function, and the worldview that emerges from his analysis is largely materialistic. He appears to be proposing a kind of physicalism, perhaps as a solution to the mind-body duality, when better solutions are available. Nagel's views, to which we now turn, expose the unacceptable features of physicalism and establish a relationship between the external and the internal that helps us see more clearly the posture to be assumed by the subject of understanding toward physical as well as social reality.

Positioning the Subject of Understanding

The internal/external tension can, to a certain degree, be attributed to the claim of objectivity to unadulterated truth, on the one hand, and an equally extreme assertion—as in radical constructivism—that there is no knowledge to be found beyond individual experience, on the other.[13] Nagel analyzes the notion of objectivity and shows its limitations. He reminds us that objectivity is a method of understanding rather than a standard or test of reality. He then explores the nature of an objectivity that is broader than what he calls "*physical* conception of objectivity." This conception, he remarks, "is not the same thing as our idea of what the physical reality is actually like, but it has developed as part of our method of arriving at a truer understanding of the physical world, a world that is presented to us initially but somewhat inaccurately through sensory perception."[14] It is this physical conception of objectivity that is challenged when it is brought to bear on certain features of the mind.

Nagel describes the stages through which we gain an objective picture of reality in the physical sense. The first stage involves those perceptions which "are caused by the action of things on us, through their effects on our bodies, which are themselves parts of the physical world." The next stage entails the realization that perceptual appearances do not resemble objects accurately and are thus detachable from their true nature of objects. This awareness comes about as we perceive that "the same physical properties that cause perceptions in us through our bodies also produce different effects on other physical things and can exist without causing any perceptions at all."[15] The third stage has to do with forming a conception of the nature of things independent of their perceptual appearance. Our particular as well as the more general human perceptual points of view are left out. Models, theories, and concepts that are not tied to the human perceptual point of view help us advance our understanding of the physical world.

Nagel notes that the world so conceived is centerless, but he also considers it featureless. He argues that this bleached-out physical conception of reality, though powerful, cannot give rise to a method for seeking "a complete understanding of reality." For the process began with how things appear to us as a result of the effect of the action of things on our bodies. In the course of getting closer and closer to an objective understanding of the world, perceptions and specific viewpoints were omitted as irrelevant. However, they continue to exist along with "the mental activity of forming an objective conception of the physical world, which seems not itself capable of physical analysis." Nagel holds that there is more to reality than what the "physical conception of objectivity" allows for. Yet, "the physical has been so irresistibly attractive, and has so dominated ideas of what there is, that attempts have been made to beat everything into its shape and deny the reality of anything that cannot be so reduced."[16]

There is an underlying "epistemological criterion of reality" in all forms of reductionism—behaviorist, causal, or functionalist—"that only what can be understood in a certain way exists." But, unlike the physical aspect of the mental, "the subjective features of conscious mental processes" cannot be understood by the methods employed for understanding "the physical world that underlies the appearances."[17] The question Nagel poses, therefore, is how to include the subjective "in the world as it really is,"[18] and whether there is a better way in which objectivity can be understood. To put it in the language being used here, a better conception of objectivity entails a continuously enlarging process involving the subject and object of understanding.

> To acquire a more objective understanding of some aspect of life or the world, we step back from our initial view of it and form a new conception which has that view and its relation to the world as its object. In other words, we place ourselves in the world that is to be understood. The old view then comes to be regarded as an appearance, more subjective than the new view, and correctable and confirmable by reference to it. The process can be repeated, yielding a still more objective conception.[19]

Nagel's analysis of objectivity resonates with Bernard Williams' notion of "absolute conception of reality" as the ideal of objectivity in science. A key idea in Williams' philosophical investigation is the possibility of convergence. He argues that "discussions of objectivity often start from considerations about disagreement."[20] While there are disagreements, which, for example, arising from purely incompatible personal desires, do not show any failure of knowledge or understanding on the part of individuals involved, there are other kinds of disagreements which do reveal lack of understanding of certain shared concepts. Such disagreements are often discussed in terms of how they fall on the opposite sides of such contrasts as practical and theoretical, evaluative and factual, ought and is; much work goes into classifying them accordingly. Efforts to go beyond these contrasts tend to reduce the evaluative to the practical—say, considerations of justice to the practical allocation of goods—and to extend the factual to the theoretical. Williams expresses doubts about such exercises and believes them to be of "positivist inspiration." In examining how disagreements are dealt with, he introduces the idea of convergence as the best explanation of the end of disagreement under the most favorable conditions. He does not limit the scope of explanation to dealing with disagreements. Agreements, too, are in need of explanation but in a different context and with different practical implications.

Williams argues that convergence does not mean the same thing in science and in ethics, which he considers two sharply differentiated areas of inquiry. He urges us not to only acknowledge the distinction but to understand it in the context of convergence. "In a scientific inquiry there should ideally be convergence on an answer, where the best explanation of the convergence involves the idea that the answer represents how things are."[21] In the realm of ethics there is not such "coherent hope," at least at a high level of generality. He points out that the distinction does not have any bearing on the possibility of convergence. Human beings can reach convergence on ethical issues. However, it is important to realize that such convergence, unlike convergence in science, does not come about as a result of being guided by how things actually are. "This means, among other things, that we understand differently in the two cases the existence of convergence or, alternatively, its failure to come about."[22]

Williams refutes claims made by relativists who suggest that convergence in science is insignificant. They argue that the notion of the "world" either as one which confirms our beliefs and judgments, or as one which is prior to our descriptions of it and which all systems of belief are trying to represent, is empty. In the case of the former, it is said, the concept of the world does nothing more than to repeat our beliefs, and in the case of the latter it refers to something "unspecified" and "unspecifiable." Williams mentions that there is a third option: a conception of the world already there "in terms of some but not all of our beliefs and theories." When reflecting on the external world, which exists independent of our experience, we must first concentrate not on our beliefs about it, but on how they represent aspects of that world:

> We can select among our beliefs and features of our world picture some that we can reasonably claim to represent the world in a way to the maximum degree independent of our perspective and its peculiarities. The resultant picture of things, if we can carry through this task, can be called the "absolute conception" of the world. In terms of that conception, we may hope to explain the possibility of our attaining the conception itself, and also the possibility of other, perspectival, representations.[23]

Williams' notion of "an absolute conception" seems to be at once both the ideal of an objective reality that becomes more and more accessible to us and the method through which we can distinguish between "the world as it is independent of our experience" and "the world as it seems to us." Our perspectival views and those that are different from ours can be explained in relation to the conception itself. This conception, Williams states, does not provide an account of knowledge, but "the possibility of a convergence characteristic of science."[24]

The purpose of this brief reference to Williams has been to enhance Nagel's picture of objectivity through a conception for which Nagel himself has ample respect. There is a certain feature of this kind of approach to reality and to the process of understanding that is of particular relevance to a Bahá'í-inspired framework for education. By freeing the notion of objectivity from its limited physical conception, it becomes possible to include the subject of understanding in the reality it seeks to understand, but not at the center of it, and as Nagel puts it, "without reducing the mental to the physical."[25] Nagel argues, and we can assume Williams would have agreed with him, that we are not part of the world as it appears to us, but as it is in itself, and in this sense we should be able to include ourselves in a conception that is not tied exclusively to our point of view. We are able to "think of ourselves from outside—but in mental and not physical terms."[26] As we place ourselves in the world as it is, we include the existence of appearance in an extended reality. And this reality, like physical reality, is center-less. In order to imagine this extended reality, we need to consider our own minds as instances of something more general. "We must think of mind as a phenomenon to which the human case is not necessarily central, even though our minds are the center of our world." Further, as Nagel insists, even in its extended version, objective understanding of reality will always be incomplete. "This means that the pursuit of an objective conception of reality comes up against limits that are not merely practical, limits that could not be overcome by any merely objective intelligence, however powerful." Nagel does not find this to be a cause of alarm because "there is no reason to assume that the world as it is in itself must be objectively comprehensible, even in an extended sense." That reality extends beyond the physical does not mean that "all of it is available to some transcendent perspective that we can reach from here."[27]

An important feature of Nagel's argument is that he removes the dichotomy between the subjective and the objective; the distinction between the two becomes more a matter of degree and covers a wide spectrum. It becomes possible to think of reality as "a set of concentric spheres, progressively revealed as we detach gradually from the contingencies of the self."[28] We can pursue an objective conception of the world, including the mind, as long as we do not assume that everything real can be reached by such a conception. "Reality is not just objective reality, and any objective conception of reality must include an acknowledgment of its own incompleteness."[29]

Nagel presents a significant criticism of physicalism: ". . . physicalism is based ultimately on a form of idealism: an idealism of restricted objectivity. Objectivity of whatever kind is not the test of reality. It is just one way of understanding reality."[30] This insight into the nature of physicalism is important as we try to discover the elements of a philosophical framework for Bahá'í-inspired educational processes. As mentioned in the brief description of Searle's argument, recognizing that many aspects of social reality are built by collective intentionality and agreement and are therefore amenable to transformation is relevant to education seen in terms of moral empowerment. That underneath these constructions one will invariably find brute facts of the physical world does not present any problems either. But the question that has to be asked is whether there are other powers working in human existence, as real as the physical ones, which also play a fundamental part in the construction of social reality. Physicalism would try to explain the existence of these other powers, some of which were explored in the context of fostering spiritual qualities in the previous chapter, on the basis of the physical world as well; it would not be content with explaining "some" or even "many" observed phenomena in terms of the physical, its ambitious project would be to explain "all." That is the reductionism, and the idealism, that Nagel seems to reject:

> The realism I am defending says that the world may be inconceivable to *our* minds, and the idealism I am opposing says it could not be. There are more radical forms of idealism than this, such as the view that to exist is to be perceived, or that what exists must be an object of possible experience for us, or that what exists or is the case must be an object of possible knowledge for us, or must be verifiable by us, or that it must be something about which we could have evidence . . . I believe that they all depend finally on the more general form of idealism.[31]

The immediate question the kind of reductionism discussed by Nagel raises for us is whether the twofold moral purpose of pursuing one's own spiritual and intellectual growth and contributing to the transformation of society—a purpose that provides the impulse for the educational process being investigated here—arises solely from physical evolution; in the final analysis, from the forces that physics believes govern the operation of the physical universe. To be hesitant to take such a leap of faith is not to deny that the theory of evolution is one of the greatest achievements of science, or to suggest the need to introduce into it woolly ideas that would reduce its scientific value. What is at stake is simply this: are the students to be convinced that the extraordinary effort the pursuit of this twofold purpose will demand from them is a mere requirement of the "selfish gene"? Our answer to this question is a clear "no."

Fragmentation

As mentioned at the beginning of this chapter, some of the issues discussed in the above also present themselves when one looks at the problems caused by the fragmentation of knowledge in education. FUNDAEC's concern with the question originates in observations related to social action. Social action, it reminds its students, does not mean frenetic activism, participation in every project that seems to address one or another social ill. Its main purpose is to transform existing social reality into a higher one and as such depends on an ever deepening knowledge of that reality based on an increasingly more accurate reading of society. But what is the nature of such knowledge and how are we to gain it?

In trying to answer this question in a chapter of a text called *Constructing a Conceptual Framework for Social Action*, it offers a mixture of its own thoughts and those of David Bohm in *Wholeness and the Implicate Order*. Actually FUNDAEC's affinity with Bohm is limited; its founders are clearly at home with his expressions as a scientist, but wary of the way he introduces a certain brand of mysticism into science. As far as the question of fragmentation of knowledge is concerned, the chapter in question does rely heavily on Bohm's analysis of the subject. The summary of arguments presented below, although not a direct quote from FUNDAEC, is entirely based on its ideas.

According to Bohm, in today's society, the human mind is struggling with a state of confusion arising from a fragmentation that interferes with its clarity of perception and creates an endless series of problems without the ability to solve most of them. Society has been broken up into separate and conflicting parts, and the environment, viewed as an aggregate of separately existing parts, is exploited by different groups of people. Further, each individual human being "has been fragmented into a large number of separate and conflicting compartments, according to his different desires, aims, ambitions, loyalties, psychological characteristics, etc., to such an extent that it is generally accepted that some degree of neurosis is inevitable . . ."[32] That these fragments exist separately is but an illusion. While one may consider fragmentation—of cities, religions, political systems, and so on—to be reality, and wholeness only an ideal toward which we should strive, in Bohm's view, "wholeness is what is real, and . . . fragmentation is the response of this whole to man's action, guided by illusory perception, which is shaped by fragmentary thought."[33]

Bohm admits that in practice it is not possible to deal with the whole of reality at once. It is necessary for the human mind to divide things up in order to reduce problems to manageable sizes. The process of division is a way of thinking that is useful mainly in the practical, technical, and functional domains. When this mode of thinking is carried to how a person thinks of himself and the world in which he lives—what Bohm calls his "self-world view," then he no longer considers the divisions as mere constructs of his mind that are useful

135

or convenient, but rather begins to see and experience himself and his world as actually constituted of separately existent fragments. The fragments assume an autonomous and independent existence:

> Being guided by a fragmentary self-world view, man then acts in such a way as to try to break himself and the world up, so that all seems to correspond to his way of thinking. Man thus obtains an apparent proof of the correctness of his fragmentary self-world view though, of course, he overlooks the fact that it is he himself, acting according to his mode of thought, who has brought about the fragmentation that now seems to have an autonomous existence, independent of his will and of his desire.[34]

In considering Bohm's description of self-world view, one has to acknowledge that human beings have a deep longing for wholeness. How does humanity, despite this longing for wholeness, it has to be asked, end up in the throes of fragmentation? Bohm appears to be seeking the roots of the problem of fragmentation in our habits of thought:

> [F]ragmentation is continually being brought about by the almost universal habit of taking the content of our thought for a 'description of the world as it is.' Or we could say that, in this habit, our thought is regarded as in direct correspondence with objective reality. Since our thought is pervaded with differences and distinctions, it follows that such a habit leads us to look on these as real divisions, so that the world is then seen and experienced as actually broken up into fragments.[35]

It should be mentioned here that the ideas discussed in the above resonate with a statement found in Bahá'í scriptures that the human mind cannot know the essence of things. This idea is fundamental to Bahá'í belief in relation to the "spiritual world," and particularly to the concept of God, referred to as the "Unknowable Essence." It is also applied to the physical world: what is knowable is only the attributes of things. This is clear when one tries to think of such entities as time, space, matter, and energy. But the idea is applicable to social reality as well: No matter how precise and eloquent our descriptions of social systems and processes may be, they are models of reality, not reality itself.

Bohm states that in scientific research "a great deal of our thinking is in terms of *theories*," and looks into the roots of the meaning of the word in Greek to support his notion that "theory is primarily a form of *insight*, i.e. a way of looking at the world, and not a form of *knowledge* of how the world is."[36] That Newtonian theory, which explained so many phenomena with such accuracy, he reminds us, was superseded later by relativity and quantum mechanics does not mean that it was wrong. It means that a theory works in a certain domain, that is, for a certain range of phenomena, and ceases to work outside this range. Bohm uses the words "clear" and "unclear" to express this idea. "The Newtonian form of insight worked very well for several centuries but ultimately (like the ancient Greek insights that came before it) led to unclear results when extended into new domains."[37] In these new domains, relativity and quantum mechanics give new forms of insight and a radically different picture of the world from that of Newton.

> If we supposed that theories gave true knowledge, corresponding to 'reality as it is,' then we would have to conclude that Newtonian theory was true until around 1900, after which it suddenly became false, while relativity and quantum theory suddenly became the truth. Such an absurd conclusion does not rise, however, if we say that all theories are insights, which are neither true nor false but, rather, clear in certain domains, and unclear when extended beyond these domains.[38]

Further, Bohm rules out the possibility of a final form of insight corresponding to absolute truth or even a steady series of approximations to it. Rather, he argues that "one may expect the unending development of new forms of insight (which will, however, assimilate certain key features of the older forms as simplifications, in the way that relativity theory does with Newtonian theory)." This requires, however, that our theories be regarded "primarily as ways of looking at the world as a whole (i.e. world views) rather than as 'absolutely true knowledge of how things are' (or as a steady approach toward the latter)."[39]

The understanding that theory is a series of insights into reality, and not absolute knowledge of how things are, constitutes an important element of FUNDAEC's conceptual framework, and, we could argue, a Bahá'í-inspired discourse on education could easily identify with it. But this is only half of the story. It also has to be accepted that the models and theories we carry in our mind, whether elaborate or rudimentary, influence the way we observe things, what we see, and what we accept as indisputable facts.[40] This does not deny the existence of reality independent of us. What it does is to bring to the fore the distinction between reality as one interconnected whole, and our own models of reality—models that are necessarily concerned with describing fragments of it.

Thought and Reality

The notion that our theories about reality are not exact representations of reality as it is, although highly attractive, could also lead to unwanted fragmentation. It could be misinterpreted to imply that we are separating our mind and our thoughts from what we may call objective reality, including the physical universe and its diverse phenomena. In arguing that this danger can be avoided, FUNDAEC resorts to a speculative reflection. In one of its texts it invites students to engage in an exercise of imagination, knowing that the images employed do not represent a model of the mind or the world in any way. Having explained the nature of some of the challenges that phenomena at the quantum level present to science, it asks the students to imagine, as Bohm has done, the possibility that physical reality at its most fundamental level does not consist of particles but actually of a flow—of a movement. What are some of the images that come to mind, for example, in thinking about the flow of a river? As the river flows, numerous structures appear; they last for a certain period of time—some longer than others—and eventually disappear. Small vortices come into existence and then vanish. There are other patterns such as ripples and waves.

All these structures have their own identity but are also connected to each other in a fundamental way. Their existence and behaviour emerges in the flow of the river. They are "abstracted from the flowing movement, arising and vanishing in the total process of the flow."[41] They only possess relative independence or autonomy of behaviour, for the transitory subsistence of each one of them in the flow of the stream is very much dependent on the transitory subsistence of the others. Could it be, then, that the particles of matter, for example, are like the vortices that appear in the flow of reality?[42]

The text then asks the students to take one further step and imagine that thoughts, such things as theories and models, could also be various kinds of structure in this same flow. Through this flow, they too would be intrinsically connected with each other and with the particles of physical reality and the sharp distinction between the mind and objective reality would disappear.

This brief account indicates that Fundaec has identified the relationship between thought and reality as a significant question in need of clarification. A valuable source of insight in this respect is McDowell's *Mind and World;* to analyze his ideas is not an easy task, but an outline of a few elements of his thought, no matter how inadequately expressed, can point to a promising direction of inquiry. It may be helpful to begin with the way Marie McGinn introduces McDowell's project. According to her, he "sets out to diagnose and overcome the philosophical tradition that has emerged in the context of the rise of modern science." This "post-Cartesian" tradition is committed "to a certain form of naturalism, one which identifies the natural world with what can be treated within the conceptual resources of natural sciences," and at the same time is preoccupied with such problems as "the mind-body problem, skepticism about the external world, skepticism about other minds, and the problem of freedom and determinism." These are aspects of the fundamental difficulty of understanding "how conscious, sapient, rational, active subjects fit into nature" within the framework of that tradition. The question is "how sentience, sapience, rationality and agency are possible in a world that is conceived as physical in nature."[43]

As McGinn puts it, although McDowell seeks to "deliver a philosophical understanding within which skeptical doubts no longer appear pressing," he does not begin his arguments by focusing directly on epistemological questions. The doubt expressed in "the idea that we cannot explain how knowledge of the world is possible" has its roots in a deeper problem, which McDowell identifies as the perceived threat presented by a way of thinking that leaves our minds out of touch with the world:

> The deeper problem, McDowell believes, is the problem of understanding how our thoughts can be about a mind-independent world. How are we to make sense of our thoughts having a content such that their truth or falsity depends upon how things are in a mind-independent world? How the mind makes contact with the objective world is not in the first instance, McDowell argues, a question about how we can *know* about the world, but of how we can *think* about it: how does thought "catch reality in its nets"?[44]

McGinn turns next to what McDowell has called "minimal empiricism": the idea that experience must constitute a tribunal, mediating the way our thinking is answerable to the world. That our thinking is answerable to the world, McGinn points out, implies that it is answerable to something outside thought; it is the idea that whether our thoughts are true or false "depends on something that is independent of thought." There must, therefore, be "some tribunal that is independent of our system of beliefs against which we can judge our beliefs for correctness or incorrectness."[45] The only candidate that can act as an external constraint on our system of belief is experience—"impressions" and "impingements by the world on a possessor of sensory capacities."[46] It follows that "our beliefs must be *rationally responsive* to what is given in experience. Experience must be the final test of whether a belief ought to be accepted as true." But the post-Cartesian tradition is unable to achieve this aim. As a result it is "faced with an antinomy: on the one hand, it seems that experience *must* function as a tribunal if thought is to bear on reality (minimal empiricism); on the other, with the presuppositions of the tradition in place, we cannot see *how* experience can function as a tribunal."[47]

The above explanation offers a picture of the "philosophical anxiety," the presuppositions of which McDowell wishes to expose. The following paragraph from Crispin Wright gives further insight into what *Mind and World* tries to achieve:

McDowell believes that there is no hope of a satisfying vision of our place as rational, enquiring beings within the natural world if the latter is conceived in the currently dominant fashion. That conception elevates the sort of description of the world offered by modern physical science into a metaphysics of what the natural world essentially is: a "Realm of Law"—a domain of causal-nomological connection from which purpose and meaning are absent and whose complete description has no need of any of the vocabulary distinctive of minds and their activity. The modern "naturalism" in philosophy which attends this conception of Nature thus finds itself with a problem—that of finding space for the categories whereby we express our *Spontaneity*[48]—categories of meaning, intentionality, and normativity—in a world whose fundamentals are thought to be amenable to fully adequate description by modern natural science.[49]

Wright further explains McDowell's line of thought:

It begins with an epistemological dilemma: a problem about the relation between experience and our most basic empirical beliefs. The problem . . . is to attain a conception of the nature of experience which lets its relation to our empirical beliefs be a *rational* one and at the same time allows experience to emerge as a *real worldly constraint* on our thought. McDowell claims that when experience is conceived as by modern naturalism, there is an irreconcilable tension between these desiderata, and that only a radical refashioning of the concept of experience can provide for their simultaneous satisfaction—a refashioning whose availability has typically been quite overlooked by philosophers. It is in order for us to understand how the necessary refashioning *is* intelligible, and satisfactory, that a revised conception of what should count as natural is called for. What we need to make space for is precisely a conception of experience which opens the world up to us and thereby allows it to give us *reasons for* our beliefs. But the world of modern science can exert only *causal* constraints; and experience, for modern naturalism, can only be an *effect* of our interaction with it. Modern science treats of Nature in a disenchanted form, as it were. So, according to McDowell, experience, as a natural process, is likewise disenchanted—divested of content—and thus disabled from playing the reason-giving role we need it to play.[50]

In seeking to overcome "the Kantian legacy of minds' alienation from an unknowable noumenal reality,"[51] McDowell calls attention to Wilfred Sellars' formulation of the "logical space of reasons." Sellars states that "in characterizing an episode or a state as that of *knowing*, we are not giving an empirical description of that episode or state; we are placing it in the logical space of reasons, of justifying and being able to justify what one says."[52] According to McDowell, Sellars is identifying the natural "with the subject matter of a mode of discourse that is to be contrasted with placing something in the normative framework constituted by the logical space of reasons." This means separating "concepts that are intelligible only in terms of how they serve to place things in the logical space of reasons, such as the concept of knowledge," from "concepts that can be employed in 'empirical description'"[53]—description understood, in McDowell's view, as placing things in the logical space of nature. The division leads one, he argues, to the conclusion that the relations that make up each logical space are inevitably different in kind. Those of the logical space of nature "do not include relations such as one thing's being warranted, or . . . correct, in the light of another."[54] To accept this dichotomy is to place experience conceived as "impressions" and "impingements by the world on a possessor of sensory capacities"[55] in a logical space other than the logical space of reasons. Experience, in the context of such a sharp division, cannot serve as a tribunal mediating a way of thinking that is answerable to the world. Wright explains the difficulty with an example:

[I]t would, seemingly, be one thing to make a case that the beliefs and desires which rationalize a particular performance of an agent may be identified with certain neural items which are involved in the aetiology of the associated behaviour; quite another to maintain that the *rational* explanation they provide is thereby reduced to the associated *causal* explanation.[56]

Two prevalent resolutions of the tension between the "logical spaces" are both rejected by McDowell. The first is to renounce even minimal empiricism. McDowell sees Sellars' solution in this category, forcing us to abandon empiricism "in the relevant sense." This is because Sellars considers the logical space of reasons to be essentially different from the logical space to which "empirical descriptions" belong. A second way in which the dichotomy between the two logical spaces could be resolved is to consider the logical space of reasons as just part of the logical space of nature. McDowell labels the outlook shaped by this approach "bald naturalism." Bald naturalism refuses to accept that relations comprising the logical space of reasons are anything but natural, and sets out to reconstruct the normative relations out of the materials belonging to the space of nature. McDowell proposes an alternative by stating that it is not "philosophically threatening to suppose there is insight in the thought that reason is not natural," only if "natural" is conceived the way "countenanced by bald naturalism."[57] He "holds on to the thought" that the "structure of the logical space of reasons is *sui generis*, as compared with the structure of the logical space within which natural-scientific description situates things." Yet, he argues that accepting "the idea of experience" as "the idea of something natural," does not necessarily have to mean that the idea has no place in the logical space of reason. This becomes possible if we do not identify "the dichotomy of logical spaces with a dichotomy between the *natural* and the normative."[58]

McDowell suggests that we should not view experience merely as non-conceptual input from the world via our senses, but as a kind of occurrence or state that already has conceptual content. In experience, we sustain causal as well as rational relations to those parts of reality with which we come into contact. For McDowell "openness to reality" captures this relationship:

This image of openness to reality is at our disposal because of how we place the reality that makes its impression on a subject in experience. Although reality is independent of our thinking, it is not to be pictured as outside an outer boundary that encloses the conceptual sphere. *That things are thus and so* is the conceptual content of an experience, but if the subject of the experience is not misled, that very same thing, *that things are thus and so*, is also a perceptible fact, an aspect of the perceptible world."[59]

And according to Wright if McDowell is right,

> . . . not just experience, as a potential justifier of empirical beliefs, but the *real world* in turn, as that which is to be capable of imping-ing upon us in a way which induces experiences of determinate content, must be thought of as *conceptual*. We arrive at a concep-tion of experience not merely as something which is intrinsically content-bearing, . . . but as also essentially an "openness to the layout of reality," where this openness is a matter of conceptual fit between the experience and the situation experienced. . . . Conceptual content . . . belongs to the very fabric of the world.[60]

Further, our experiences constitute only "glimpses" of the world that extends beyond "what is manifest in the experiences themselves."[61] The potential to achieve higher and higher levels of conscious thought, then, must exist in advance and be constituted by the natural capac-ity to achieve what Nagel has called "harmony with the world far beyond the range of our particular experiences and surroundings."[62] The world, in its broadest sense, possesses that which allows for the exercise of our conceptual powers; it admits the space of reasons, not the "pre-scientific superstitious" space of beliefs, but one in which the boundary between the normative and the natural is not so severely drawn. In this way McDowell seeks "to reconcile reason and nature." Another idea of value in McDowell's line of thinking as he tries to reconcile reason and nature is his version of the notion of "second nature." Human beings already in possession of a first nature with its root in the biological world acquire a second nature "in part by being initiated into conceptual capacities, whose interrelations belong in the logical space of reasons."[63] McDowell borrows Hans-Georg Gadamer's description of the difference between a merely animal mode of life and one that is uniquely human. A mere animal life, what we share with brutes, is "led not in the world, but only in an environment" which is nothing more than a "succession of problems and opportunities, constituted as such by those biological imperatives."[64] In acquiring conceptual capacities through enculturation we "rise above the pressure of what impinges on us from the world";[65] we become inhabitants of the space of reasons, able to deal with meaning, intentionality, and normativity. McDowell draws on Aristotle's insight that "rational demands of ethics are autonomous" in the sense that they do not require validation "from outside an already ethical way of thinking." Yet he points out that "this autonomy does not distance the demands from anything specifically human," as long as we do not think in the context of "a naturalism of disenchanted nature." McDowell suggests that recapturing the idea of second nature, "can keep nature as it were partially enchanted." Second nature brings into full view the potential that exists in our human make-up; it "could not float free of potentialities that belong to a normal human organism."[66] On the one hand, these potentialities are non-reducible to materials that can be contained in the space of nature as conceived by bald naturalism. On the other hand, second nature is immune to magical supernaturalism, since ethical upbringing and transmission of tradition—activities that are unique to human beings—draw on conceptual capacities present in our organism.

In ascribing normativity to nature and experience, and in explaining the workings of the second nature, McDowell eschews the "supernatural." From a Bahá'í perspective, the idea of the supernatural as a collection of powers totally outside the realm of the natural, intervening to break the laws of nature, is not robust enough to describe reality either. Nature is embedded in and connected to a larger world with a spiritual dimension. As Baha'u'llah states:

Nature in its essence is the embodiment of My Name, the Maker, the Creator. Its manifestations are diversified by varying causes, and in this diversity there are signs for men of discernment. Nature is God's Will and is its expression in and through the contingent world.[67]

The following statement of Baha'u'llah offers further insight into this complex relationship between the physical and the spiritual:

Whatever is in the heavens and whatever is on the earth is a direct evidence of the revelation within it of the attributes and names of God, inasmuch as within every atom are enshrined the signs that bear eloquent testimony to the revelation of that Most Great Light. . . . How resplendent the luminaries of knowledge that shine in an atom, and how vast the oceans of wisdom that surge within a drop! To a supreme degree is this true of man, who, among all created things, hath been invested with the robe of such gifts, and hath been singled out for the glory of such distinction. For in him are potentially revealed all the attributes and names of God to a degree that no other created being hath excelled or surpassed.[68]

That everything in nature manifests to some degree the names of God endows all parts of it with meaning. Beauty, truth, generosity, and mercy, among other attributes, are reflections of the divine in the world of creation. Moreover, there is an underlying educational purpose: "every atom in existence and the essence of all created things" have been intended for the "training" of the human being.[69] Openness to the world is openness to a much larger reality than what McDowell is ready to accept.

McDowell, in his treatment of second nature, clearly acknowledges the potential that exists in human species, but Bahá'í teachings recognize a far greater arena for the realization of this potential, an arena in

147

which operate spiritual qualities as reflections of divine attributes in the mirror of the human heart. Human beings possess two *interacting* natures. First is the biological, influenced by the struggle for survival during a long evolutionary process. The second is spiritual with a capacity to reflect qualities, such as love, mercy, kindness, justice, and understanding, as described in the previous chapter. Our interaction with nature has a sensible component, but viewed from the higher human perspective, "nature" itself is an intellectual reality, not the disenchanted world of bald naturalism divested of meaning. McDowell states that if "we acquiesce in the disenchantment of nature, if we let meaning be expelled from . . . 'the merely natural,' we shall certainly need to work at bringing meaning back into the picture when we come to consider human interactions."[70] It seems that despite the brilliant account he provides, McDowell falls short in showing us how the "movement of the planets" or "the fall of a sparrow" can be "rightly approached in the sort of way we approach a text or an utterance or some other kind of action."[71] There would have to be threads of meaning, as it were, that connect nature with human intellect and human activity. The conceptual implanted in the very fabric of nature is an expression of God's will, and this is the source in which a Bahá'í-inspired account will search for meaning. But to explore intelligible reality, including nature itself as an embodiment of that reality, we have to refer to our sensory experience. In 'Abdu'l-Bahá's words:

> The other kind of human knowledge is that of intelligible things; that is, it consists of intelligible realities which have no outward form or place and which are not sensible. For example, the power of the mind is not sensible, nor are any of the human attributes: These are intelligible realities. Love, likewise, is an intelligible and not a sensible reality. For the ear does not hear these realities, the eye does not see them, the smell does not sense them, the taste does not detect them, the touch does not perceive them. . . .

Likewise, nature itself is an intelligible and not a sensible reality; the human spirit is an intelligible and not a sensible reality.

But when you undertake to express these intelligible realities, you have no recourse but to cast them in the mould of the sensible, for outwardly there is nothing beyond the sensible."[72]

Here we get an inkling of the continuity of the physical, the intellectual, and the spiritual dimensions of one reality, not fragmented, but closely interrelated and intermingling. Just as the powers of human souls allow us to reach the shores of true understanding, physical senses themselves become a metaphor for spiritual susceptibilities and perceptions, so we speak of how we can see with our spiritual eyes and hear with our spiritual ears.

Let us bring this chapter to an end with a summary of what we have tried to achieve. In the beginning of this chapter, we set ourselves two tasks: to explore in general terms an all embracing reality, which in the final analysis is not only the ultimate object of understanding but also the largest context within which every object of understanding is situated; and to make explicit the presuppositions inherent in a few different views of reality, presuppositions that would influence how the subject of understanding would interact with any aspect of reality she is trying to transform. To accomplish these tasks, we looked briefly at the work of a number of thinkers in succession in order to enhance our awareness of the complexity of issues involved. Our exploration began with an analysis of Searle's narrative. While we acknowledged that a narrative such as his could admit the role the subject of understanding should play in the construction of a society moving ever closer to its maturity, we found his description of social reality emerging from the brute fact of nature to be too restrictive. Nagel helped us advance in our exploration by showing the limitations of the physical conception of objectivity, thereby allowing us to position the subject of understanding in an extended reality. For us, however, it is not only the physical and the mental aspects of the subject of understanding that are part of this reality, but also the spiritual. William's notion of "absolute conception" as a counter argument to the proposals set forth by relativists demonstrated the possibility of ever getting closer to a conception of the world independent of our particular beliefs and representations. Next we looked at the way FUNDAEC had drawn on Bohm's notion of fragmentation and his attitude toward theory as a source of insight in order to help its students move away from naïve descriptions of reality. Finally, we discussed a few insights gained from McDowell's rather complex set of arguments. Our intention was not to delve into his profound exploration of *Mind and World*. We tried to show how McDowell's ideas help address the anxiety about the relationship between thought and reality at a profound philosophical level. But there is an immediate question we can now pose in the context of a more sophisticated view of reality: Why would a process of moral empowerment place so much emphasis, as FUNDAEC does, on the development of capabilities in the realm of science, particularly the natural sciences? One of the underlying assumptions of the arguments presented in this inquiry is that many intellectual and spiritual qualities and attitudes are common to capabilities in both the scientific and moral domains. McDowell's statement that "the conceptual sphere does not exclude the world," in other words, "what we experience is not external to the realm of the kind of intelligibility that is proper to meaning," reveals a fundamental relationship between the empirical and the normative. What is an exciting prospect is that, in nurturing understanding, education need not be confined by the boundaries created around the natural and the normative, realizing that "conceptual capacities, capacities for the kind of understanding whose correlate is the kind of intelligibility that is proper to meaning, are operative also in our perception of the world" in itself, the world "apart from human beings."[73]

CHAPTER 6

COMPLEMENTARITY

The previous three chapters were dedicated to an exploration of the nature of the subject of the verb "to understand," the object of the verb "to understand," and the process of understanding itself. These themes, it was suggested, cannot be studied in isolation from each other, and in our analysis we have tried to take into account their interconnection. The discussion of the object of understanding up to now has been at the most general level of reality in its physical, social, moral, and spiritual dimensions. Unless extreme constructivism—in which the only aim is to offer students tools to construct their own knowledge—is to be adopted, education has to draw upon the universe of knowledge that humanity continually gathers, evaluates, and organizes about the various aspects of reality. This chapter is meant to bring us a step closer to addressing the challenge of integrating knowledge in the content of educational programs seeking moral empowerment. How are "objects of understanding" selected, organized, and treated in a curriculum that aims to build capacity in students to pursue their own intellectual and moral growth and to contribute to the transformation of society? And, what are the sources of the relevant knowledge and the "virtues" with which students are to be endowed?

A starting point for exploring these questions is Paul Hirst's analysis of such concepts as disciplines and forms of knowledge. In the next chapter, we will examine his ideas in more detail; for now, it is sufficient to refer to the classification he proposed of forms of knowledge—mathematics, physical and biological sciences, human and social sciences, history, moral understanding, literature and the fine arts, philosophy and religion—as well as his designation of fields of knowledge as theoretical and practical. Hirst used this classification to examine the planning and practical conduct of liberal education.[1] But educational programs with other aims would also look into these disciplines and forms as sources of knowledge from which elements would be selected for the elaboration of content. The criteria used to determine which elements should be chosen, and in what combination, would depend on the specific aims and the philosophical framework of the program. When moral empowerment is a major concern, the role of religion as a source of knowledge needs to be carefully analyzed.

A number of issues immediately present themselves in this connection. Hirst simply lists religion along with the other forms of knowledge. Yet, although disagreements about the specific contribution each discipline makes to education do exist among educators, the divergence of views on the value and the possible role of religion is of a different nature. Is the study of religion to be carried out in the broad context of "humanities" as is done in many liberal arts programs? Is it to be examined as a social phenomenon and studied within the disciplines of human and social sciences? What is to be done about the kind of religious instruction bent on shaping the mind according to dogmas that do contradict the logic and truth criteria of the other forms of knowledge in the above list? An option, one that is followed by a number of programs, is to leave the inculcation of religious belief to religious communities, incorporate ethical issues in various areas of secular education as needed, and offer "moral education" separately, drawing on different moral systems as sources. Hirst himself argues for the autonomy of moral knowledge based on rational judgment; at the same time he admits that understanding ourselves as moral beings allows for the establishment of a positive relationship between morals and religion. He claims that while there exists a domain of religious belief, there is not as yet a "domain of publicly justifiable religious knowledge."[2] As advances are made toward establishing such a domain, the content of education will need to include the corresponding knowledge. What is important is that schools teach "about" religion—not necessarily its history or psychology, but its concepts and truth criteria. The purpose is for the students to understand as fully as possible about religion, but this "does not imply belief in or acceptance of, what is understood."[3]

A Bahá'í-inspired educational process would not deny the fruitfulness of appropriate avenues "to teach about religion," but would strive to find a proper place in its curricula for spiritual concepts and religious insights—from the major religions of the world in general and the Bahá'í Faith in particular—as expressed by religion itself and not through the lens of other disciplines. Such an aim, however, is worthy of pursuit only if religion does not stand in opposition to science. This implies a fresh examination of the relation between science and religion. The historical development of the two led to the widespread view that they intrinsically contradict each other. The problem here is not simply between religion and the natural sciences. All the other disciplines mentioned by Hirst are accepted to be in accord with human reason in one way or another, but religion, even when deemed reasonable, is often considered qualitatively different, fundamentally built on faith as opposed to reason. Religion, of course, is not the same as faith, and science is not the same as reason, yet disagreements between science and religion are closely associated with an assumed dichotomy between reason and faith. In this chapter we question this dichotomy, suggesting that it is based on a narrow definition of rationality, and argue for complementarity between religion and science—a claim that goes further than the assertion that they are not necessarily incompatible with each other.

That in so many schools of thought science and religion have been held in opposition has enormously influenced the ethical and social environment in which "modern man" lives. In the process of moral empowerment, students are to learn to contribute to the transformation of the very society in the building of which this modern man has played such a major role. In most societies in which Bahá'í-inspired endeavors are exploring education as moral empowerment, the project of modernization—with all its vicissitudes—was promoted by a worldwide enterprise called development which set out to save the masses of humanity from the throes of poverty and, in the process, managed to impose a particular rationality on these societies. M.P. Cowen and R.W. Shenton speak of the motivation behind this rationality when describing how "the positivists' faith in the potential contained within industrial society for the reconciliation of progress and order was only to be actualised, or so they believed, through trusteeship. . . . Trust that industrial society would confer social benefit, rather than, promote self-development of the few, had to be made active through the agency of trusteeship. Thus, the trusteeship of the few who possessed the knowledge to understand why development could be constructive, and were accepted as trustees because they were understood to be already developed, became integral to the intention to develop those who remained undeveloped."[4]

It seems reasonable, then, to begin the discussion of this chapter with a cursory look at the nature of the global development enterprise, the kind of rationality that initially shaped it and the way it saw—or rather ignored—the spiritual dimension of the life of the populations it was intent on modernizing. The fact that "development" was the starting point for the work of FUNDAEC will also allow us to continue drawing on its experience, which was shaped to a great extent by its view of complementarity between science and religion.

The Modernization Project

Contributing to the transformation of society as discussed here is associated with the larger process of humanity's transition to the age of maturity and the advance in both material and spiritual civilization that is envisioned to accompany it. The social and economic development of nations, with substantial reduction in the gap that separates the rich and the poor, is a significant component of this process. Cultivating the capacity of people to become participants in development, rather than mere recipients of technological packages and targets of political agendas prepared in centers of power, is an important component of the empowerment process being examined in this inquiry.

The concept of progress is not new, and words such as "advanced," "cultured," "backward," and "uncivilized" have existed in human vocabulary for a long time. Yet, the set of activities through which governments and international organizations would collaborate to "modernize" the entire world took shape in the early 1950s, particularly in light of the successes of the reconstruction of war-torn Europe. Modernization implied rapid and far reaching changes. Institutions had to change in order to allow rational planning and execution of plans; the nation as a whole had to develop the capacity to apply modern technology to augment production, increase mobility, achieve equality of opportunities, and make possible higher standards of living. Out of this process, the "modern man" was to emerge in every country of the world as it had in the industrialized nations. His outstanding attributes were efficiency, diligence, orderliness, punctuality, frugality, scrupulous honesty, rationality, preparedness for change, alertness to opportunities, integrity and self-reliance, and—although it may seem contradictory in light of how most people behave in the industrial world today—willingness to take the long view rather than seeking short-term gains.

The first two decades of development strategy focused almost exclusively on "modernization through economic growth": capital formation, technological transfer, production stimulated by foreign aid, the building of infrastructure including the construction of schools, emphasizing planning at every step of the way. Once the World Bank declared in the early 1970s that the goals of development had hardly been achieved and that the number of people living in absolute poverty had risen to 800 million, confidence in the project was shaken.

The critical examination by the renowned development thinker Mahbub ul Haq in his book, *The Poverty Curtain*, of the character of the "development planners"—including himself—who worked in the forefront of the enterprise to bring economic growth to their nations, illustrates the soul searching that ensued. Referring mostly to the highly motivated technocrats laboring in developing nations, he stated: These were "men who had tremendous confidence in themselves but little confidence in their own societies which they all wanted to transform in a hurry. . . . They were generally men of good intentions, often products of Western liberal education, who played the game of development with deadly seriousness."[5] He characterized the beliefs to which these men held with great conviction in statements such as the following:

> . . . it is well to recognize that economic growth is a brutal, sordid process . . . The essence of it lies in making the labourer produce more than he is allowed to consume for his immediate needs. . . . It is immaterial what one chooses to call this surplus—whether "surplus value" as Marx usually did; or "savings" or "capital formation," in the terminology of modern economic analysis. . . . It would be wrong to dub the consequent emergence of surplus value as "exploitation": its justification is economic growth.[6]

These expressions were considered without question as the obvious products of rational thinking. Many of the modified sets of statements that were expressed with equal confidence in the next decades shared this same underlying rationality. And today, as the financial sector firms its grip on the economic life of the world, every effort is being made to convince the modern man of the efficacy of a tough, "bottom line" approach to the future of humanity, ostensibly a product of the proper use of reason.

It is not necessary to mention in any detail the many changes that the field of development went through in the period following the years to which Mahbub ul Haq refers. Suffice it to say that a great deal of knowledge was accumulated. A number of essential concepts were introduced into development theory and practice. Basic needs, appropriate technology, participative planning, people-centered development, participation of women, environmental protection, and human rights, are a few examples. Slogans like "development is not a package to be delivered by the so-called developed to the underdeveloped" or "it is better to teach a man how to fish than to give him one" became commonplace. Yet, despite all the sophistication in planning and execution, the number of those living in absolute poverty rose steadily.

This inquiry is being carried out at a time when "development" is not as much a central issue in global discourse as it used to be. The reason is not that gross injustices have been overcome. The crisis of civilization has taken such dimensions that the failure of development is considered only one of the many ills humanity is facing. It is, however, instructive to look into the possible causes of such an evident failure; for example, how the literature of development during its early years dealt with people's religious convictions, deemed useful only if they promoted some of the abovementioned characteristics of the modern man, but more often considered as obstacles in the path of modernization. Even the notion of solidarity so central to traditional value systems was suspicious, as were the ties of the extended family which interfered with the logic of the market. But although the ideals of modernization have penetrated every society on earth, the transition from traditional to modern has generated so many negative forces that the stability of the entire world is being threatened. Particularly, religion has not gone away. Its reassertion among both the prosperous and the materially poor is an undeniable fact in the early years of the twenty-first century. That so much of it seeks a particular kind of change with narrowly focused and, at times, fanatical passion has to be a major concern of

157

educational processes that seek to empower students to contribute to social transformation. Is the answer to misdirected religious devotion, the rationality of the modern man with "science," "philosophy," and "the humanities" at its center? Or does the experience of the past decades point to the need for another modernity, one in which faith and reason are not held in opposition?

To explore these questions, we adopt and expand in this chapter on a conception initially introduced into the discussion of Bahá'í-inspired education by FUNDAEC according to which science and religion are examined as complementary systems of knowledge and practice. In a world where religious fanaticism and extreme relativism are simultaneously on the rise, drawing parallels between science and religion is not an easy task. In fact, even talking about religion as a single phenomenon, the way one does of science, is usually frowned upon. "Religions not religion" is the immediate objection raised. The discussion of this chapter should help to justify treating religion, at least the totality of the major religions of the world, as a system of knowledge with a diversity of communities of practice. As mentioned earlier, the Bahá'í teachings point to a kind of relativism of religious truth in time. We do not need to draw on the specific narrative of "progressive revelation" expounded in these teachings. All we need is to suggest that, through whatever means, the expression and understanding of religious truth advances, as do science, technology, and the organization of human society.

Inherence of Metaphysical Convictions

The proposition that science can be viewed as a system of knowledge and practice is a general statement about science that does not require commitment to any specific demarcation criteria separating science from pseudo-science or to theoretical stances on how scientific knowledge advances—as discussed, for example, by Karl Popper, Thomas Kuhn, and Imre Lakatos. The question is whether there are parallels between some of the characteristics of this system of knowledge and religion considered as such. Once the existence of such parallels is successfully argued and it is accepted that religion can also be examined as a system of knowledge and practice in its own right, then it becomes easier to explore the question of the complementarity of the two systems.

The first task, that of looking into parallel—but by no means identical—characteristics of science and religion as systems of knowledge and practice, involves a number of steps, some of which have to do with the clarification of the nature of science. This is not a matter to be addressed here in any length; a few points should suffice to demonstrate the plausibility of the relevant arguments. To begin, naïve descriptions of science that adhere to some rigid conceptions of the "scientific method" make it difficult to consider religion a rational system. In a rather simplistic summary, such conceptions would consist of the claim that science, the occupation of people who have been trained to use their senses, begins with objective observation of phenomena. Repeated observations make possible general conclusions reached by minds educated to apply carefully the principle of induction. Once universal statements are discovered, deduction is used to explain other observed facts and to predict consequences that can then be checked through experimentation. The power of science to make predictions that can be tested is one of its essential characteristics that helps establish its authority. The application of such proven method leads to proven knowledge.

Evidently decades of advance in the philosophy of science have rendered this naïve view obsolete. It is, however, possible to argue that more sophisticated explanations of science are not as yet widespread. Too often, even those who must be fully aware of the demise of positivism seem to employ rigid notions of scientific knowledge in opposition to religious belief. One of the main causes of the confusion is the false dichotomy that has been created between knowledge and faith. Arguments in favor of the dichotomy, however, seem to be based on an assumption about the nature of faith that defines it as lack of knowledge. But can knowledge and faith be so easily separated from each other? The conviction in science that there is order in the universe and that this order allows itself to be understood by the human mind points to the complexity of the relationship between knowledge and faith. Although such a conviction can be the object of philosophical scrutiny and there are even ways of thinking that doubt its validity, it holds such a foundational position in science that without it scientific practice seems meaningless. No one can, of course, claim that it arises from blind faith. For one thing, scientific investigation confirms it at every step. But to attribute its origins to empirical observation would be to contradict human experience. In fact, the universe, despite the regularity of numerous cycles, does not present itself to the human being in daily life as an ordered entity. The conclusion of the primitive man to assign willful spirits to everything around him is a more immediate response to what we experience in our interactions with the physical universe. That there is order susceptible to discovery is a conviction that humanity acquires collectively; it seems to be driven by something intrinsic to the human spirit, confirmed in well-designed experimental arrangements and refined by elaborate theoretical explanations.

Belief in the existence of a certain kind of order in the universe is only one example of the convictions upheld by science the acceptance of which involves some degree of faith. That the scientific enterprise at any given time cherishes beliefs not open to negotiation is a statement which finds support in current philosophical discourse. The following passage from a commentary by Laudan is one example:

> . . . historical and sociological researches on science strongly suggest that the scientists of any epoch . . . regard some of their beliefs as so fundamental as not to be open to repudiation or negotiation. Would Newton, for instance, have been tentative

about the claim that there were forces in the world? Are quantum mechanicians willing to contemplate giving up the uncertainty relation? Are physicists willing to specify circumstances under which they would give up energy conservation? Numerous historians and philosophers of science (e.g., Kuhn, Mitroff, Feyerabend, Lakatos) have documented the existence of a certain degree of dogmatism about core commitments to scientific research and have argued that such dogmatism plays a constructive role in promoting the aims of science.[7]

Examples cited by Laudan are of non-negotiable convictions underlying mega theories of nature. But there are also convictions that, when altered, change the nature of the way science as a whole looks at the universe. Today, a basic premise of science, for example, is that the laws of physics are the same throughout the known universe. This is not provable, and indeed before Newton, it was generally accepted that laws governing heavenly bodies and earthly objects were different.[8] In a collection of articles published under the title *New Metaphysical Foundations of Modern Science*, the contributors try to look into the nature of the metaphysical commitments of science, a term covering assumptions and convictions of the kind mentioned above. The few statements cited below are simply to demonstrate how different the view of modern science has to be from positivist versions of it. Willis Harman, for example, points to what he calls "an ontological assumption of separateness" at the heart of science, modified somewhat with the advent of quantum mechanics:

. . . separability of observer from observed, subjective from objective, causes from effects; separateness of organism from environment, man from nature, mind from matter, science from religion; separateness of "fundamental particles" from one another, of things in general unless there is some "mechanism" to connect them ("action at a distance" precluded); separability of the parts of a system or organism to understand how it "really" works; separateness of scientific disciplines, of investigators, competing over who was first discoverer.[9]

How this "ontological assumption" should change is not our concern here; mere awareness of its existence helps one move away from naïve representations of scientific truth. A highly insightful article in the collection is by Lynn H. Nelson. She argues that "metaphysical commitments are incorporated in theories, methodologies, research questions, and hypotheses—indeed in everything we say about that world; that such commitments constitute part of the evidence for particular theories, research projects, models, and methods, and are themselves subject to empirical constraint; and that attention to the metaphysical commitments incorporated in models, methods, and theories needs to become part of the doing of science."[10] Nelson examines the feminist critique of the "Man the Hunter" theories in various fields to illustrate her arguments. She writes:

The example on which I focus involves an organizing principle that feminist research has exposed as shaping methods, observations, and theories in primatology, anthropology, animal sociology and evolutionary theory, as well as other fields. This is the principle that males are socially oriented; that is, that their activities are skilled and determining of social organization and, in the case of humans, of culture as well; and that females are biologically oriented; that is, that their activities are largely reproductive (assumed, in turn, to be "natural" and unskilled), and without consequence for the most important (and, in the case of humans, the "distinctly human") features of social dynamics. In models and theories incorporating this organizing principle, feminist scientists and critics note, females are satellites to male actors who dominate and determine social dynamics.[11]

162

As feminist critics have shown, this organizing principle proves wrong in face of abundant evidence. Once male-centered assumptions are set aside, it is easy to see, for example, that for hunter/gatherer groups food gathering, in which women played a major role, actually provided as much as 80% of the sustenance, and that this activity of the women, a fundamentally social activity, was "highly skilled, requiring knowledge of hundreds of plants and other ecological factors."[12] What Nelson shows is that the male-centered organizing principle did far more than simply leading some of the advocates of the "Man the Hunter" theory to declare "that only males hunted, that males were dominant over females and children, and that hunting was the most important source of food."[13] She points out that, "feminists in anthropology, primatology, and animal sociology have showed that a similar organizing principle has shaped observations and accounts of social dynamics and behavior in primate groups and in contemporary hunter/gatherer societies." Further, she refers to the convergence between the reconstruction of early human life in the "Man the Hunter" theory and "contemporary (Western) gender stereotypes and social relations." The proponents of this theory, then, were not merely led astray by a set of unwarranted assumptions; their ideas were supported by a "vast feedback system across disciplines and fields,"[14] some of the statements of which were used as evidence to confirm their theory. And this, according to Nelson, is an example of how science is constrained by evidence. "The over-arching constraint on theories and beliefs is coherence, which is understood as a dual constraint." Individual theories, claims, and beliefs "must be coherent with experience." But they must also be coherent with a "larger system of current theory and practice,"[15] which covers various disciplines. This system has its own metaphysical commitments which end up being used by an individual theory as evidence in a particular field—not in bad science but as a necessary aspect of doing good science. Thus, metaphysical commitments cannot be done away with; examining them should be part of the activity we call science.

Transcending the Perceived Dichotomy between Faith and Reason
What has been suggested so far in this chapter is that the notion of
complementarity between science and religion takes on special significance when an educational process intends to use the two as sources
of knowledge from which appropriate objects of understanding could
be identified and explored in the teaching-learning experience. Before
contemplating this notion, we have to accept that religion too can be
seen as a system of knowledge and practice. To do so, we have to stay
away from rigid definitions of science that, although rejected by rigorous scrutiny in philosophy, history, and sociology of science, continue
to govern much of the thinking in many fields including education.
An essential step to embracing more accurate descriptions of science is
to move beyond the false dichotomy between faith and reason. A brief
analysis of Simon Blackburn's rendering of the debate between William Clifford and William James will help us in this respect.[16] Not only
does it illustrate the difficulties one faces when one holds to a strict
duality between faith and reason, but it also shows how deep-rooted
certain attitudes toward convictions of a religious temperament are in
philosophical discourse.[17]

According to Blackburn, Clifford begins the debate with the story of
a ship-owner who convinced himself, despite the doubts he entertained,
that an old ship was seaworthy. He told himself that the ship had been
on many a voyage and returned safely. He dismissed his suspicions
and put his trust in Providence to protect the emigrant families on
board. The ship took to the sea and it sank. The ship owner received
his insurance-money and "told no tales." The story is to demonstrate
the danger that lies in faith. Clifford remarks that the "sacred tradition
of humanity" consists not in "propositions or statements which are
to be accepted and believed on the authority of the tradition," but in
"questions rightly asked, in conceptions which enable us to ask further
questions, and in methods of answering questions."[18] The rigor of
reason lies in its capacity to test things "day by day."

The counterargument offered by James, Blackburn contends, suggests the promptings of the "passional nature" fed by faith. In his response, James identifies belief as the choice between options. At a particular time, we are faced with a "live hypothesis," a belief that has some chance of being true. We have two alternatives—either to believe it or to avoid believing—and leaving the question open is in itself a "passional decision," with the same risk of losing truth.

> To preach skepticism to us as a duty until 'sufficient evidence' for religion be found, is tantamount therefore to telling us, when in presence of the religious hypothesis, that to yield to our fear of its being error is wiser and better than to yield to our hope that it may be true. It is not intellect against all passions, then; it is only intellect with one passion laying down its law. And by what, forsooth, is the supreme wisdom of this passion warranted? Dupery for dupery, what proof is there that dupery through hope is so much worse than dupery through fear?[19]

Blackburn criticizes James for deploying rhetorical devices and accuses him of objectifying and privatizing belief. He scorns the supposition that when an issue cannot be decided by other means it is a leap of faith that gives us the "blessings of real knowledge." Suppose, he argues, it occurs to you that the oak tree in your garden might contain the spirit of Napoleon and you convince yourself of it. Where, he asks, does "real knowledge" come in? Further, he reminds us that "against the alleged blessing" of such convictions, we have to lay a "train of social and practical disasters, ready to explode. If the oak tree contains the spirit of Napoleon, perhaps the child contains the spirit of the devil, and the people next door are all creatures of Satan, and need dealing with accordingly."[20] The intensity of faith—Blackburn agrees with Clifford—is hazardous as it leads to actions that would be disastrous. He sees James playing the battle between faith and reason as if it were a question of the costs and benefits of each. "Refusal to believe in something," he observes, "is not a kind of faith." He is concerned with the consequences of dogmatic conviction and the habit of taking risks in the name of faith.

> The more such faiths you absorb, the more your risks fail to pay off. You make an expensive partner, but is it any worse than that? Clifford, of course, tells us that it is. Your habit is dangerous. Your disrespect for caution, for evidence, for plausibility may lead anywhere. "Those who can make you believe absurdities," said Voltaire, "can make you commit atrocities." By contrast, my caution cannot do any such thing.[21]

Blackburn is analyzing and commenting on a sophisticated debate between reason and faith based on the assumption that the link between faith and action begins with faith, a faith that is blind; it is private; it operates independently of truth;[22] and it easily leads to irrational action with disastrous consequences. Knowledge is given its own space outside faith, and it is attained through "caution," "evidence," and "plausibility." However, this and similar debates about faith and reason do not give us much insight into articles of faith indispensable to knowledge—not the superstitious belief that Napoleon's spirit resides in a given tree or the dishonest belief of the ship owner in Clifford's story, but articles of faith without which humanity would not have made it through its tortuous evolutionary path. Nor are we given a conception of reason expansive enough to include "reasonable" convictions present in both science and religion. Faith is reduced to wishful, fanciful thinking, while reason is presented as an endless process of questioning. To callously identify faith with superstition can be viewed as the expression of a passion. Would it be unreasonable to argue that, in fact, knowledge leads to faith and faith to knowledge?

The answer to this question can be positive if one agrees to let go of conceptions of rationality that identify it with narrowly defined

methods of the "verification of truth." Joseph Dunne's discussion of
J. H. Newman's critique of such definitions of rationality is relevant
here. Dunne reminds his reader that the significance of Newman's
work[23] "lies precisely in his diagnosis of the problem [of rationalism]
as a generic one that required less a defense of religion than a challenge
to the paradigm of rationality which would so summarily discredit
it—and in his consequent articulation of a rationality which would
not only leave room for religious belief but, while doing so, would also
do justice to the many ways of being reasonable that are embedded
in our social practices."[24] Elasticity is required in the processes of reasoning that lead to assent, as Dunne calls to mind Newman's words:
"the processes of reasoning which legitimately lead to assent . . . are
in fact too multiform, subtle, omnigenous, too implicit, to allow of
being measured by rule."[25] The concept of assent has been the object
of profound philosophical investigation by Newman in his book *An
Essay in Aid of A Grammar of Assent*. He defines religious faith as "a
certain, non-evident assent of the *intellect* given to divine truth."[26] The
believers' faith may begin from a simple assent or belief in religious
doctrines—an assent that "they barely recognize, or bring home to
their consciousness or reflect upon, as being assent"—to a complex
one which Newman calls certitude, corresponding to a condition of
mind "which may be said to be possessed of invincible knowledge."
This he identifies as "the highest quality of religious faith."[27]

The proposition that education needs to embrace a broad conception of rationality is relevant when we consider the role various sources
of knowledge are to play in the elaboration of educational content. But
it also affects our vision of the subject of understanding that inspires
the process of moral empowerment. Earlier in this chapter, reference
was made to the modern man in the context of development. A certain
kind of rationality is to characterize this individual, the nurturance of
which, as the early literature of the field shows, was deemed to be a
requirement of progress. Over the years, repeated failure resulted in
the questioning of development strategies, but it is not clear wheth-

er the inadequacies of this rationality have ever been seriously taken into account. There are so many indications that this conception of a rational human being distorts our view of human nature, imposing on society the image of the modern man as a soulless entity set on fulfilling its many self-interests and desires. The moral shortcomings of this entity are becoming increasingly apparent as the crisis of the kind of modernity that has dominated thought for decades deepens. The subject of understanding that we seek here is as different from this "modern man" as it is from the "emotivist self," the "computer," and the "radical constructivist"—the candidates we have already found inadequate. If education were able to overcome the dichotomy between faith and reason, a clearer picture of the desired subject of understanding would emerge. It is reasonable to hope that such a picture would not be fragmented. Mind would not be so separated from heart and the relationship between the cognitive and the normative, between intelligence and morals would not be distorted. Dunne points out that "in human affairs a merely calculative intelligence is no more capable of truth than it is of goodness—or, rather, that without goodness even the most subtle intelligence will find truth itself beyond its reach."[28] He draws on Newman's assertion that the rays of truth "stream in upon us through the medium of our moral as well as our intellectual being; and that in consequence that perception of its first principles which is natural to us is enfeebled, obstructed, perverted, by allurements of sense and the supremacy of the self."[29] Dunne further focuses our attention on Aristotle's words: "this eye of the soul acquires its formed state not without the aid of excellence . . . for inferences which deal with acts to be done are things which involve a starting-point . . . and this is not evident except to the good man; for wickedness perverts us and causes us to be deceived about the starting-points of action."[30] These thoughts bring us to the following words of 'Abdu'l-Bahá:

First must the stream bed be cleansed, then may the sweet river waters be led into it. Chaste eyes enjoy the beatific vision of the

Lord and know what this encounter meaneth; a pure sense inhaleth the fragrances that blow from the rose gardens of His grace; a burnished heart will mirror forth the comely face of truth.[31]

Processes and Methods in Science and Religion

The demonstration, no matter how convincing, that science has its own metaphysical commitments and unprovable premises does not imply by itself that religion can be seen as a compatible, and somehow comparable, system of knowledge. One has to go beyond questions of faith and conviction to examine the processes and the methods through which both science and religion produce, validate, apply, and diffuse knowledge. Even when the existence of spiritual reality is accepted, it would still be hard to claim that the knowledge making up the two systems is of the same kind; the knowledge of the existence of an even "unseen" elementary particle is unlike the knowledge a believer confesses to have of the soul and its existence. But apart from our relationship with the divine, religion is concerned with human life on earth—a life, it asserts, should be imbued with spirituality and thus qualitatively different from a mere physical existence. As Peters puts it "religious experience does not suggest a special kind of experience, akin to telepathy or clairvoyance; rather, it suggests a different level of experience made possible by concepts which enable us to understand the facts of a more mundane level of experience in a new light."[32] In this perspective, religion is a source of profound knowledge about the essential relationships—the transformation of which is the focus of the process of moral empowerment. It can be argued that with respect to this kind of knowledge, religion too is characterized by processes and methods that correspond in some degree to certain features of science.

To be open to the possibility of certain similarities between the way the two systems deal with knowledge is to be aware that while generalization, the formulation of hypotheses, deduction, the testing of predictions and falsification are vital components of scientific methods, they are not carried out mechanically by programed entities but by scientific communities that work within certain worldviews and theoretical frameworks. These determine the kinds of questions to be asked and the possible answers to be explored. The way Kuhn employed the concept of paradigm may not be universally valid, but it cannot be denied that notable advances in science have occurred through pronounced shifts in paradigm.[33] No community of scientists sets out to answer all the questions in the world; much work goes on to extend the range of validity of theories that have already proven their capacity to explain a significant set of interrelated phenomena. During this process, the main statements of the overall theory are hardly questioned. Finally, however, the range of validity of any theory proves to be finite and new theories arise to explain new phenomena which have caught the attention of the scientific community. More advanced theories do not necessarily prove previous ones wrong but clarify the limits within which they operate and provide an understanding of why they work inside those limits.

How does religion, we need to ask, deal with the knowledge it acquires—from both the reading of what it considers revealed truth and the articulation of what it learns in its day to day practice—about individual and collective human flourishing on earth? To see if there are any similarities between its processes and methods in relation to knowledge generation—albeit according to different dynamics—and those of science, one has to be able to separate religious knowledge from widespread superstition and fanaticism propagated in the name of religion. This is by no means an easy task, but nor is the identification of demarcation criteria that separate science from pseudoscience. The task becomes more difficult when one considers the sensitivity with which it has to be approached; one has to be acutely aware of the requirements of freedom of belief and avoid unwarranted judgments of people's cherished convictions. In what follows, we will limit ourselves, to the expression of what Bahá'ís would be willing to demand of religion.

Induction, deduction, and falsification represent certain aspects of the human faculty of reason; religion, as opposed to fanaticism, can and should employ them in the generation, application, and diffusion of the knowledge with which it deals. The principle of the equality of women and men provides a useful example in this respect. Having embraced as an article of faith the existence of the human soul with no sex, color, or ethnicity, Bahá'ís adhere to this principle as part of their core religious belief. Yet, for such a conviction to become firmly established in their own lives, in their communities, and in their efforts to contribute to the transformation of society, it must be scrutinized by reason. Numerous observations followed by generalizations and deductions, rational argumentation on the various applications of the principle, and struggle against ongoing efforts by forces of tradition set out to falsify the principle are all necessary for a belief instilled in a Bahá'í child to become a veritable element of her or his religious knowledge.

This example of the principle of equality of women and men allows us to go further in our analysis of the way religion deals with its knowledge about life here on earth. In broadening our understanding of this principle and the way it has to be established in human society, how would we deal with contrary religious beliefs that consider women inferior to men? Can we explain disagreements on such a fundamental issue without rejecting the validity of all the teachings of such religions? This we can do precisely if, rather than reducing religion to an assortment of creeds in conflict, we view it as a system of knowledge in evolution. What is necessary is the ability to step back and look at the phenomenon of religion from a historic perspective, as has been done with science, not by people who are determined to explain it away but by those who have accepted its existence as a valid system of knowledge. The picture of science that emerges from such an examination includes the coexistence at any given time of scientific communities each working within a given research program. It is even possible at a given moment to identify coexisting scientific communities with different worldviews and paradigms, a condition that is quite prevalent in the social sciences.[34] Such communities show signs of conflict, particularly at the time of the appearance of a new paradigm, although animosity seldom reaches the severity of the persecutions that occur when the founder of a new religion appears and organizes the perception of spiritual reality in new terms.

The repeated appearance of Originators of new religious movements, the circumstances under which They proclaim Their mission, and the way Their religion flourishes and influences the advancement of civilization, as well as the crises that beset the community of Their followers with the passage of time, are historical facts that, when interpreted in a certain way, make possible a vision of religion as a system of knowledge with its own dynamics of progress. In one way or another, these Founders of major religions all claim to "reveal" aspects of spiritual reality, and once revealed, Their utterances "become the subject of exploration, not only by the individual . . . but also by entire populations." In this way, a series of "Revealed Texts," or "Chapters of the same Text," define the "paradigms" within which religious communities carry out their practices. Without them "spirituality would be an expression of personal experience, never to be validated by the intellectual interactions that create social knowledge."[35] What religious communities have historically done cannot be reduced to the practice of a set of rituals; they have created and applied knowledge that has influenced the advancement of civilization. Moreover, the process through which they have dealt with knowledge as they have read their revealed texts, applied what they have read, and generated new knowledge is not totally unlike what scientific communities have done in their efforts to read the "Book of the Universe." Modern secularism has insistently tried to devalue the former process in relation to the latter. Taylor explains that "increasing interest in nature . . . for its own sake, not simply as a manifestation of God" contributed to several historical developments including the emergence of modern scientific outlook. In one narrative, as interest in "nature-for-its-own-sake" grows, "reference to the divine atrophies," and such a posture emerges as the "'natural' stance" and the correct one. Taylor disagrees with this narrative, for, the perfection in nature which elicits in the language of religion the "dimension of grace" does not "cancel or set aside" the perfection inherent in nature sought by science. The two go together. The "autonomy of nature" does not need to deny the "symbolic or allegorical meanings of things": one "focuses on God's speech acts, the other on the marvelous systematic language which makes these acts possible."[36]

An excellent source of insight into the way knowledge is dealt with in both science and religion is Ludwik Fleck's *Genesis and Development of a Scientific Fact*, in which he examines in detail the emergence and establishment of the following fact: Wassermann reaction, which is a serodiagnostic procedure developed in the 1920s, indicates, within acceptable statistical limits, the presence of syphilis in a patient. In analyzing the history of a "completely 'empirical' finding," he explains:

Thoughts pass from one individual to another, each time a little transformed, for each individual can attach to them somewhat different associations. . . . Whether an individual construes it as truth or error, understands it correctly or not, a set of findings meanders throughout the community, becoming polished, transformed, reinforced, or attenuated, while influencing other findings, concept formation, opinions, and habits of thought . . .[37]

Fleck's emphatic statement that "cognition is the most socially-conditioned activity of man, and knowledge is the paramount social creation"[38]—unfortunately misinterpreted by some as supporting radical constructivism—has relevance to both scientific and religious knowledge. In the same way that scientific knowledge is not the simple imposition of "nature" on the human mind, religion as a system of knowledge is not a straightforward reading of "revelation"; it is based on revelation but elaborated through a continual process of learning through social interaction.

The parallels drawn here between some of the processes of science and religion in relation to knowledge do not go far enough particularly when the ultimate purpose is to find a way for certain educational programs to draw on religion as a source of knowledge complementary to science. To evoke the image of paradigms or coexisting research programs in science in order to explain the existence of the variety of religious beliefs has its own dangers. For one thing, left alone it makes it too easy for fanaticism to operate in the name of religion. In science, not every research program is believed by the community of scientists to lead to valid scientific knowledge. The way Lakatos describes such programs gives an indication of the kind of criteria that exist to sort through processes that claim to be scientific.[39] A "research programme is the sum of various stages through which a leading scientific idea passes." At the heart of every research program is a "hard core"—"a set of commitments which cannot be abandoned without abandoning the research programme altogether."[40] There is also "a 'protective belt' of auxiliary hypotheses which shields the hard core from falsification."[41] This protective belt changes in response to new empirical facts and criticism, allowing the program to continue extending the central idea. Further, each research program has its own collection of characteristic problem-solving techniques referred to as its *heuristic*. Lakatos considered the history of science as one of "extended wars of attrition" between research programs that are "progressing" and those that are "degenerating." In the former, change comes from its own inner logic, from the use of its own heuristic. In the latter, change occurs in response to external criticism. "A discipline is scientific so long as progressive programs triumph over degenerating ones."[42] In looking for demarcation criteria between religion as a source of knowledge for moral empowerment and pseudo-religion as a promoter of fanaticism—ironically also empowering—one would have to put further demands on religion than those implied by the use of reason; one could, for example, look into a given religion to see if, at the historical stage in which it finds itself, it has the capacity to allow progressive programs to win over degenerating ones.

One last comment seems necessary to end this section. In presenting the arguments in the previous paragraphs—to justify calling religion a system of knowledge in its own right—we have focused on knowledge about life on earth, and have not advanced any claims about the reasonableness of more mystical teachings including belief in the existence of a Higher Power significant to that life and its relationship to the world. This, however, does not imply that such fundamental aspects of religion do not admit the use of reason. But knowledge of these aspects of reality, however inadequate, demands an expanded rationality, a rationality possessing dimensions that come into play even in science to make sense of a range of empirical observations which is always limited. As Nagel points out:

> Even empirical knowledge, or empirical belief, must rest on an a priori base, and if large conclusions are derived from limited empirical evidence a large burden must be carried by direct a priori formulation and selection of hypotheses if knowledge is to be possible at all.
>
> This accounts for the extremely high ratio of rational to empirical grounds for great theoretical advances like Newton's theory of gravitation or the special and general theories of relativity: even though the empirical predictions of those theories are enormous, they were arrived at on the basis of relatively limited observational data, from which they could not be deduced. And I would maintain that even induction, that staple of empiricism, makes sense only with a rationalist basis. Observed regularities provide

reason to believe that they will be repeated only to the extent that they provide evidence of hidden *necessary* connections, which hold timelessly. It is not a matter of assuming that the contingent future will be like the contingent past.[43]

He further explains:

Although the procedures of thought by which we progress are not self-guaranteeing, they make sense only if we have a natural capacity for achieving harmony with the world far beyond the range of our particular experiences and surroundings. When we use our minds to think about reality, we are not [. . .] performing an impossible leap from inside ourselves to the world outside. We are developing a relation to the world that is implicit in our mental and physical makeup, and we can do this only if there are facts we do not know which account for the possibility. Our position is problematic so long as we have not even a candidate for such an account.[44]

Nagel reminds us that Descartes tried to give us this candidate by "proving the existence of the right sort of God." Of course, he did not succeed, but according to Nagel, "the problem remains. To go on un-ambivalently holding our beliefs once this has been recognized requires that we believe that something—we know not what—is true that plays the role in our relation to the world that Descartes thought was played by God."[45] Although he has no idea what "unheard-of property of the natural order"[46] that something might be, Nagel upholds that the sup-position of the need for a basis for our beliefs in something global—even if we are not able to discover it—is vital for human knowledge to be intelligible. Nagel, of course, having committed himself to a secular project, is looking outside religion for an explanation. One can readily agree with Nagel that Descartes' solution was problematic. But not being bound by a secular worldview, a Bahá'í-inspired program seeks in religion an explanation of the foundations of its beliefs as well. The Bahá'í writings describe God as an unknowable essence "Who, however much we extol the divinity of His Manifestations on earth, can in no wise incarnate His infinite, His unknowable, His incorruptible and all-embracing Reality in the concrete and limited frame of a mortal being. Indeed, the God Who could so incarnate His own reality would, in the light of the teachings of Bahá'u'lláh, cease immediately to be God."[47] Bahá'u'lláh states:

> To every discerning and illumined heart it is evident that God, the unknowable Essence, the divine Being, is immensely exalted beyond every human attribute, such as corporeal existence, ascent and descent, egress and regress. Far be it from His glory that human tongue should adequately recount His praise, or that human heart comprehend His fathomless mystery. He is and hath ever been veiled in the ancient eternity of His Essence, and will remain in His Reality everlastingly hidden from the sight of men. "No vision taketh in Him, but He taketh in all vision; He is the Subtile, the All-Perceiving."[48]

The concept of an unknowable essence implies the impossibility of holding the infinite within the finite mind, and the utter powerlessness of human vision to reach the essence of any part of creation, let alone of His Reality that "takes in all vision." Ironically insight into this inevitable limitation, what Hans-Georg Gadamer calls the religious "insight into the limitations of humanity, into the absoluteness of the barrier that separates man from the divine,"[49] widens the scope of rationality and facilitates the discovery of inherent potentialities in all of creation. This from a Bahá'í perspective is not dogma but a promising beginning.

Complementary Systems of Knowledge

If the argument so far in favor of the comparability of science and religion in certain of their features is plausible, then the stage is set to explore the question of complementarity between them at various levels, beginning with the knowledge of reality itself. Referring back to Nagel's discussion of an extended reality, to what degree can science in its broad sense—ways of knowing that try to depend primarily on the senses and reasoning—lead to an adequate knowledge of such reality? Particularly, if there is a spiritual dimension to human existence and not just one that is constructed from the physical, is not religion a necessary system of knowledge that complements science? This is not a question that admits a simple answer; the following argument based on ideas proposed by FUNDAEC offers insights into the nature of the kind of inquiry that may be undertaken in this respect.

Although the application of ideas from physics to other areas of thought is fraught with difficulties, the way the notion of complementarity is employed in certain interpretations of quantum mechanics can serve as a metaphor that sheds light on the relationship between the two systems. The concepts of "particle" and "wave" in ordinary physics refer to two entirely distinct phenomena. In explaining these phenomena, two different sets of concepts and vocabulary, inseparable from theoretical constructs and experimental arrangements, are used. Position and momentum are examples of concepts related to particles, and wavelength and intensity examples of those pertaining to waves. Particles need a path available to them and a finite amount of time to go from one point to another; two particles cannot be in the same place at the same time. Waves are not restricted in this way; rays of light can interfere with each other at various points of space producing patterns of light and darkness. In this sense two distinct languages are used, one of waves and one of particles, to describe and explain two distinct phenomena. One would never think of something being both a particle and a wave. Yet, experiments that observe the behavior of extremely small constituents of matter, say electrons, show that these exhibit both characteristics. However, the situation is not chaotic; if one sets up one's instruments to look for a wave, electrons behave only as waves and under another experimental arrangement they behave like particles. The answer to this apparently bizarre behavior of nature, at least according to the most prevalent interpretation, is to abandon the notion of "either/or" as well as the notion of "both" and use the concept of complementarity instead. The fundamental constituents of matter are too complex to be described in either the language of waves or the language of particles. The question is not "what electrons really are," but simply that under certain conditions we can explain their behavior in the language of particles and under other conditions in the language of waves. Thus, at a basic level, nature seems to require complementary sets of measurements and descriptions. Underlying the arrangement of instruments in experimental setups are theoretical models. Complementarity as applied to particles and waves seems to be saying something fundamental about reality and the way humanity can know it. It appears to be an indication of the complexity of nature and the inability of the human mind to comprehend it in its entirety. But if this is true for the physical universe, FUNDAEC asks:

Is it unreasonable to assume that when the object of exploration is the sum of both spiritual and physical reality, an object far more complex than the material universe, a single description would also prove to be inadequate? Is it not possible that to understand and explain this reality, humanity needs at least two languages, that of science and that of religion, which together enable it to penetrate its mysteries?[50]

Complementarity in Conviction and Action

Complementarity between science and religion can be examined at another level. Moral empowerment demands action on the part of the subject of understanding as an active protagonist of social transformation. In this context, one may ask: is the connection between understanding and action in the process of empowerment immediate?

It seems that in most cases, if not all, understanding must be transformed into conviction in order to empower a person to act. Let us examine briefly what this proposition may mean in relation to both religion and science.

In chapter 4, we discussed briefly the content of a few lessons in one of FUNDAEC's texts called *Properties* concerned with the enhancement of capabilities related to the power of expression, beginning with the examination of words and concepts that help students describe the world around them with clarity. Among the concepts that are introduced in these lessons is truthfulness as a "property of the human soul," and we used this example in order to demonstrate how "spiritual qualities" could be examined without entering a religious discourse. What we need to query now is the extent to which this type of analysis, say, of truthfulness in terms of related concepts such as truth and lie, accuracy and error, investigation of reality, honesty, and sincerity, actually convinces the student that he should be truthful. The immediate response is that one must go beyond cognition and face the challenge of developing attributes which include appropriate attitudes, skills, and habits. But suppose this is done, as we will discuss in later chapters on capabilities. Does not the question persist? Even when understanding is nurtured in the context of a complex set of capabilities, does it not have to be transformed into conviction before it is translated into consistent moral action? The question can be asked in a different way. Is not conviction an aspect of the kind of understanding that engenders action? Further, would not any conviction such as "I must be truthful" only make sense if it were part of a whole system of knowledge and practice within which the moral nature of a given action would be assessed?

The extended reality proposed by Nagel seems to be relevant again. In nurturing the belief that "I must be truthful"—not as the habit of a well-trained child but as a strong conviction that can resist rampant forces of corruption in the world—we can ask if it is not necessary to see truthfulness as an element of a reality that goes beyond the physical, and if we do not need to introduce the concept of a soul as an element of that reality to which truthfulness is somehow attached as a property. Nagel himself sets his limits categorically. He sees no reason for the assumption that a soul exists. He recognizes that the assumption has other implications—for example, the possibility of life after death. What is interesting is that the language Nagel uses in this regard is one of belief; he does not attempt to prove or disprove the existence of the soul. He simply explains that he does not believe in such a continuation of individual life and, while lamenting death, accepts it as an end to his consciousness. A Bahá'í-inspired educational framework would necessarily disagree with Nagel on this point. It would assume the existence of a soul, although it would not pretend that there is an objective way to understand its essence. In this sense it would venture further into the exploration of the non-physical than Nagel seems willing to do. It would call a certain dimension of the extended reality spiritual and try to understand some of the attributes associated with it. But it would be wary of speculations about the nature of spiritual reality. It would agree with Nagel that all of reality is not available to some transcendental perspective we can reach. In fact, it would claim that most of it is beyond our reach. Yet it would not be willing to abandon religion's claim that we can gain insight into the forces and powers associated with the spiritual dimension of reality. It would argue that the exploration of this dimension through religion facilitates the transformation that understanding gained through ethical reasoning must undergo to become the kind of conviction that is conducive to moral action.

In the context of science education, Howard Gardner's illustration of the results of research on the extent to which students of leading American universities mastered what they studied demonstrates how ephemeral understanding of scientific facts is if it is not translated into a proper set of convictions. He states:

In a typical example, college students were asked to indicate the forces acting on a coin that has been tossed straight up in the air and has reached the midway point of its upward trajectory. The correct answer is that once the coin is airborne, only gravitational pull toward the earth is present. Yet 70 percent of college students who had completed a course in mechanics gave the same naïve answer as untrained students: they cited two forces, a downward one representing gravity and an upward one from the "original upward force of the hand."[51]

We could explain away this, and similar results of the research, by asserting that the students had not understood things well. But whatever our definition of "understanding well" may be, we would have to accept that what was operating in the minds of the students was a set of beliefs acquired since childhood, beliefs that scientific knowledge had not been able to replace. In the case of the above example, the belief in question is that "an object cannot move unless an active force has somehow been transmitted to it from an original impelling source (in this instance, the hand or arm of the coin tosser) and that such a force must gradually be spent."[52]

Gardner attributes this predicament of American education to the failure of educators to realize that *"in nearly every student there is a five year-old 'unschooled' mind struggling to get out and express itself."*[53] Valid as this statement may be, the challenge of education cannot be to empty the mind of the student from "belief" in order to fill it with "scientific knowledge." The constant process of formulation, modification, and sometimes destruction and reconstruction of scientific conviction cannot be ignored. Every text of modern science teaches the atomic theory of matter, for example, as one of the grand scientific theories of physics. Teaching the theory clearly involves nurturing the understanding of such concepts as particles, atoms and molecules, chemical bonds, and so on. But there is a point at which the understanding of the statement that "matter is made of particles" becomes a conviction; a profound conviction that wins over naïve beliefs which seem to contradict it.[54] This is particularly so because the conviction that matter is made of atoms is not equivalent to the acceptance that, say, such and such a beach is made of innumerable particles of sand. The former does not arise from direct observation but is the result of the ownership of a scientific theory by a person who has internalized its claims.

The arguments presented in the above paragraphs are by no means conclusive, but they prepare the ground for examining possible complementarity of convictions pertaining to science and religion. What is at stake here is the adoption of a realist position. The debate between realists and anti-realists in science—uncannily similar to the one between the religious believer and the unbeliever—brings to focus other convictions that underlie belief in the existence of constituent elements of atoms, say, the electron. According to Okasha "anti-realists advocate an attitude of complete agnosticism towards claims about the unobservable part of reality."[55] But Grover Maxwell, for example, argues that seeing through different instruments such as glasses, binoculars, low- and high-power microscopes represents a continuum. While the concept of the observable varies in each case, the sophistication of the device used cannot be the criteria by which one can draw a line between observation and theory. In the case of the electron, although an instrument is not yet devised that allows "seeing" it, "indirect ways of observing" are sufficient to convince us of its existence. In cultivating the conviction in the all-pervading existence of atoms and molecules, then, an educational process would have to, among other things, help shape the mindset of a realist in the student. A similar mindset helps the formulation of convictions about spiritual entities, for instance, spiritual qualities such as truthfulness and justice, when we accept the existence of an extended reality with a spiritual dimension. It seems reasonable, therefore, to state that education in the process of moral empowerment would have to cultivate scientific and religious convictions alongside each other. For, if the habits of a realist are not acquired through rigorous scientific thinking, how will one make sure that the search for understanding spiritual reality does not degenerate into the play of a fanciful and superstitious imagination? How does the premise of the existence of a soul, which is to be explored soberly, not end up in the belief that Napoleon's spirit resides in a tree? The Bahá'í teachings are unequivocal in this respect: Religion without science degenerates into superstition. Conversely, if realism about spiritual qualities is not cultivated, how would one ensure that scientific conviction about the nature of matter is not channeled to the detriment of humanity, to create weapons of destruction for example? Furthermore, what motivates humanity to resist the force of crude materialism—a force which both gives rise to, and is continually reinforced by, ideologies of rampant consumerism?"

Complementarity of Languages

Complementarity also needs to be examined in the context of the languages that characterize various "forms of knowledge." It is possible to think of a number of concepts usually associated with science itself as attributes of its language. In one of its texts, FUNDAEC examines the language of science, not so much as what it is, but in terms of what it seeks, exploring such statements as "the language of science seeks to eliminate ambiguities," "the language of science seeks objectivity," and "the language of science seeks rationality." In this exploration, scientific language ceases to be viewed as a series of exact definitions, precise observation statements, sound hypotheses and unquestionable conclusions reached through flawless logical reasoning. Such a rigid language would not permit the operation of faculties like intuition and imagination in scientific inquiry. Scientists do find it necessary to speak a language in which words and concepts mean the same to everyone in a given community. Yet, they are not intolerant of ambiguity. They seek to overcome it through a process of progressive clarification of ideas, allowing a notion, vague and intuitive in the beginning, to gradually evolve into a relatively well-defined concept. The process involves sorting out implications and identifying subtle meanings. It demands the ability to see possible contradictions further down the road, and depends on "the capacity of the mind to take creative steps, not chaotic ones but calculated leaps that more often than not allow one to land on surer ground."[56]

This process of progressive clarification coded into the scientific language enables scientific communities to clarify ambiguities and reach agreement in relation to certain concepts.[57] The most common concepts in science have evolved over decades and centuries to mean the same things to all scientists. For a long time, for example, words such as *force, energy,* and *power* were used by scientists in a variety of ways. As the field of physics advanced, each concept became better and better defined and, today, phrases like solar energy, kinetic energy, gravitational force, or electrical power, have unique meanings understood by all physicists.

The objectivity sought by scientific language is achieved progressively through an iterative process. This process is in accord with Nagel's view regarding objectivity as a method of understanding. Objectivity as the way to detach ourselves from how things appear to us in order to make statements about reality is valid if we are willing to include in a later stage our perceptions as part of a larger reality. Scientific language has to allow for this iterative process. The rationality that scientific language seeks cannot be defined too narrowly either. Not only does it have to include statements that employ such tools of reasoning as deduction, induction, falsification, analysis, inference, contextualization, and justification, but it also has to leave room for conclusions that result from the workings of intuition, intelligent guess, and leaps of faith.

The above three characteristics can also be attributed to the language of philosophy which science has to use, at least if it is to reflect on itself. In a sense, it employs the languages of mathematics and philosophy to achieve two different objectives. The former enables it to become increasingly more precise, the latter ensures that it does not lose its awareness of context. The language of science, in all its complexity, is not of course limited to the description of elements and properties of the physical universe; it extends its function by exploring social phenomena and the workings of the mind, as well as examining, with the help of philosophy, its own metaphysical foundations. However, it achieves what it seeks to a lesser degree, or at least with more difficulty, as it moves to aspects of reality less accessible to experiment. Take the question of objectivity. No one has difficulty accepting as an objective statement the sentence "the colour of things is a property arising from the way they interact with light." But in the realm of the social, the statement "the poor are lazy" only has the appearance of objectivity. It can easily be the expression of personal judgment, for example, of someone engaged in exploiting the poor, by paying them low wages, charging them exorbitant prices for the necessities of life, and blocking ways in which they could change their conditions. Such a person would be reluctant to make the subjective statement "I like to amass riches at the expense of the poor" or "I will simply squeeze every ounce of energy out of these people." He would be apt to pronounce instead, the apparently objective statement "the poor are lazy; they don't try hard and therefore they stay poor."[58] There is a thin line between a language that seeks objectivity and one that tries to justify one's subjective stance.

Clearly the need for the application of scientific language to the social and the metaphysical cannot, and should not, be denied. What has to be explored is whether the application of this language, though necessary, can be sufficient on its own, or whether it should be complemented by other languages. Concepts such as "the power of love," "the power of unity," or "the power of humble service" are good examples to consider, for they are all relevant to the question of moral empowerment as discussed in chapter 2. Today, these concepts have entirely different meanings for different groups, the very existence of such powers having little relevance to much of the prevalent discourse on power. Can the same clarification process, one may ask, that enabled scientists to reach agreement on the concept of physical power in terms of the expenditure of energy per unit of time, be used so that statements about these other kinds of power become increasingly clear, objective and rational, and incorporated in a language that can then be employed in an educational process aspiring to be scientific? While this is a process worth undertaking, it would not by itself prove adequate, for, the language of science does not exhaust meaning.

That languages other than the one associated with science are needed to convey meaning is, of course, a rather trivial statement. The languages of the arts and of poetry are clearly indispensable, and an educational process seeking moral empowerment has to employ them. "Where science does not reach, art, literature, and narrative often help us comprehend the reality in which we live."[59] To illustrate this point for its students, FUNDAEC presents them with two statements about the daffodil. The first is: "A daffodil is a species of narcissus with a large bell-shaped corona growing from the perianth, cultivated for its ornamental yellow flowers." The second is a poem by William Wordsworth, in which he describes a field of daffodils he saw as he "wandered lonely as a cloud that floats on high o'er vales and hills." To this "crowd" he refers as "a host, of golden daffodils"; "fluttering and dancing in the breeze"; "a jocund company" that would often "flash upon that inward eye which is the bliss of solitude;" and his "heart with pleasure" fills.

The first statement, students are reminded, is only the beginning of a series that would lead to a scientific description of the plant. Such a description would give insights into many aspects of the plant's existence, its evolution, the functions of its various parts and their relationships, its interactions with the environment and its uses; it could even include the fact that the daffodil has been the subject of a poem by Wordsworth. But can this set of statements ever express the kind of meaning that the poem conveys? And conversely, is the language of poetry an appropriate tool for describing a set of increasingly more complex scientific models of the plant? In reflecting on the characteristics of the two languages, students are asked to avoid simple claims that, for example, the language of poetry is subjective, or that it thrives on ambiguity. Why, they are asked, is not the heart of the poet dancing with the daffodils as much a part of reality as the flower itself?

> After all, once Wordsworth calls our attention to it, we too see the images he had in mind and our heart too is moved by the imagery. Could it not be said that there is inter-subjective agreement on the dance of the daffodils? Yet the agreement is not of the same kind as the one we can reach on a scientific description of the plant. What are the differences? And as to ambiguity . . . it would not be fair to call the language of the poem ambiguous either; it certainly conveys meaning with admirable clarity.[60]

The distinction FUNDAEC identifies in the above seems to be present in the way the designative theory of language and the expressivist view of it are explained in linguistic philosophy. The designative theory treats words as representatives of things and objects and sentences as "unambiguous and incontrovertible statements about the world itself." The task of linguistic philosophy in this case is to test the logical validity of propositions both on their own and in relation to other propositions. The expressivist view, on the other hand, focuses on the "power of language to express, specifically the power to express what it is to be human."[61] In the arts, for example, the expression of emotions has a central role. As R. G. Collingwood puts it, expressing emotions is a prerequisite of being conscious of them: "Until a man has expressed his emotion, he does not yet know what emotion it is. The act of expressing it is therefore an exploration of his emotions."[62] By coming at language from the side of expression, it seems as if Collingwood is attacking a certain view of language: the view that "language consists of a set of signs which have, or ought to have, clear and precise meanings and whose combinations are, or ought to be, subject to invariant rules—a double 'ought' which at the limit would sanction the abandonment of natural languages altogether as 'ill designed for their purposes,' and their replacement by a 'scientifically planned philosophical language.'"[63]

However, according to Dunne, Collingwood did not envisage the expressivist language of arts in conflict with this orthodox view of language as long as the limitations it contains (of grammar, logic, and so on) were realized in relation to "language in actual use, or as an activity."[64] Collingwood's treatment of language and his refusal to make it an instrument, even for expression, but rather an activity in which we are caught up that is already expressive, is helpful in thinking about various "languages" students need to be taught. The question being posed here is this: Is it sufficient for an educational process identifying itself with moral empowerment to initiate students in the languages of science and the arts and humanities viewed as activities, or is there need for initiation in the language of religion as well?

In a Bahá'í-inspired educational framework, the answer to this question would, of course, be positive. This is how one can begin to scrutinize the position: If religion is to be in harmony with science and not superstition respectably dressed, its language cannot be characterized by irrationality, arbitrary opinions, complete subjectivity and impenetrable ambiguity. It too would have to lend itself to intersubjective agreement, be able to express a rationality that, although broad, does not contradict the one sought by science, and be a medium through which progressive clarity about core spiritual and moral concepts and precepts can be achieved. It is not difficult to point to numerous passages in religious literature that fulfill these conditions. But religion does not allow itself to be confined by these boundaries and, for example, employs metaphor[65] as well as poetic imagery to convey meaning beyond that which is possible for the language of science. Its value, however, is not simply in its freedom to move from one form of expression to another. The structure of its language, which allows for this freedom, is such that it can express commandments, exhortations, prohibitions, instructions, and admonitions; these together with its more descriptive components give insights into the nature and purpose of human existence and elicit response to moral imperatives. When it is not misused to create fear, it is a language that accommodates both authority and love so as to nurture understanding in a unique way. This is particularly relevant to education, which needs to tap the roots of motivation and arouse the noblest of sentiments. It is not clear whether a combination of science, philosophy, the arts, and the humanities can accomplish this task without the language of religion.

In the specific context of ethics, Graham Haydon asks the following:

Religious belief can help to make sense of morality by enabling moral demands to be experienced within a wider framework of meaning, so that, while these demands can still be seen as in- dependently valid, they are not isolated from other aspects of a person's life. It seems to be true of us as human beings that we can act in a certain way, not just because doing so serves some self-interested desires, or even because it serves non-self-interested desires related to particular others, . . . but because it makes sense as part of a life that in turn is understood as part of something larger. Religion can provide a set of concepts and beliefs in which the 'something larger' can be expressed. It is worth asking whether there is some wider framework of meaning within which morality can be located that might be available to the non-believer.[66]

He then goes on to refer to the question of language: "Here it is interest- ing that some modern religious thinking has allowed traditional beliefs about God or the transcendent to be questioned, while retaining the traditional language; so that the language can still provide a framework of meaning even though it is not interpreted in the traditional way."[67]

In this regard, it is important to make a distinction between language of religion in general—which, akin to Collingwood's language as activity, is already expressive in the practice of a community—and language of revelation in sacred scripture, the source in which meaning of varying levels of depth is found. The latter language continually creates and reshapes the former. As we have already argued in this chapter, an expanded rationality creates the condition for the finitude of the human mind to relate to God's infinity. Language is essential to discovering this correspondence. According to Dunne, Gadamer gives a formulation and an answer to the problem of the correspondence between "intellect" and "being" in a world that can no longer rely either on the Greek metaphysical idea of an Infinite Mind, nor on the knowledge of salvation:

Hence we must ask: are there finite possibilities of doing justice to this correspondence? Is there a grounding of this correspondence that does not venture to affirm the infinity of the divine mind and yet is able to do justice to the infinite correspondence of the soul and being? I contend that there is. There is a way that attests to this correspondence, one toward which philosophy is ever more clearly directed—the way of language.[68]

"All human speaking," Gadamer further comments, "is finite in such a way that there is laid up within it an infinity of meaning to be explicated and laid out."[69] A Bahá'í-inspired educational program, of course, affirms the existence of the infinite Divine. And it does not attempt to confine it to a relative finitude of "being," as certain philosophers have done. Yet, a process of moral empowerment has to pay considerable attention to the language that provides the larger framework of meaning proposed by Haydon. A question that needs to be explored in this regard is the relevance of "hermeneutics." For, as Paul Ricoeur has said, it is "by *interpreting* that we can *hear* again . . . it is in hermeneutics that the symbol's gift of meaning and the endeavour to understand by deciphering are knotted together."[70] He points out how the present age offers two simultaneous possibilities for language:

> The same epoch holds in reserve both the possibility of emptying language by radically formalizing it and the possibility of filling it anew by reminding itself of the fullest meanings, the most pregnant ones, the ones which are most bound by the presence of the sacred to man.[71]

An examination of hermeneutics that surveys its evolution and addresses both the profound treatments of it by philosophers such as Gadamer and Ricoeur and the corresponding criticisms is beyond the scope of this inquiry. However, as a way to demonstrate possible lines of explorations we may briefly mention three features of Gadamer's hermeneutics as cited by Dan Stiver from his examination of *Truth and Method.*

First, Gadamer has argued that "there is an experience of truth in a work of art that is not purely subjective or a matter of taste."[72] He has shifted the emphasis away from the "aesthetic consumer"—the aesthetic feelings associated with works of art—to the "nature of the artistic product itself, and what the artefact is able to disclose or open up." In this context, he has drawn on Martin Heidegger's work for whom art, like truth, is a disclosure—"an opening up onto the world." Van Gogh's painting, "Shoes of the Peasant," for example, is not a mere drawing of a pair of worn out shoes; it discloses fundamental truths about the life and the world of the peasants.[73] Heidegger writes:

> From the dark opening of the worn inside of the shoes the toilsome tread of the worker stares forth. In the stiffly rugged heaviness of the shoes there is the accumulated tenacity of her slow

trudge through the far-spreading and ever-uniform furrows of the field swept by a raw wind. On the leather lie the dampness and richness of the soil. Under the soles stretches the loneliness of the field-path as evening falls. In the shoes vibrates the silent call of the earth, its quiet gift of the ripening grain and its unexplained self-refusal in the fallow desolation of the wintry field.[74]

A first line of inquiry, then, can focus on exploring how this feature of hermeneutics—expressed in the above in the context of works of art—can be employed to enhance our understanding of sacred texts and their application to the improvement of individual and social life. Religious truth is frequently relegated to the realm of the subjective. Divine Revelation is the channel through which God speaks to each individual human being and to humanity as a whole. However, in-dividual interpretation is oftentimes given undue significance in dis-covering the truth of sacred scriptures. Yet, truth is not the property of the individual alone, even spiritual truth. Collective inquiry and a spirit of cooperation both in reading the Word, and in attempts to apply it to the betterment of life on earth build shared understanding. This shared understanding is vital to the conduct of a community which—in collaboration with other communities and institutions—is concerned with personal and collective transformation. In order to ob-tain greater and greater measures of truth, then, language of religion cannot be approached merely from the perspective of the subjective. The truth expressed by it combines in a unique way the objective and the subjective. Consider as an example the worldwide Bahá'í commu-nity's reflections over the years in the context of its collective action as well as personal introspection on the statement: "The betterment of the world can be accomplished through pure and goodly deeds, through commendable and seemly conduct."[75]

Second, Gadamer has explained that prejudices or "preunderstand-ings" should not always be seen as obstacles to truth. While they can become prejudices in the negative sense, they are sometimes necessary

193

steps to understanding. We have "a historically shaped consciousness," and our prejudices constitute the historical reality of our beings. In this sense we belong to history, but are not necessarily trapped by it. Gadamer employs the term "fusion of horizons" to describe the process through which we overcome the alienation we experience as modern beings in relation to the past. Through acculturation and the use of language we acquire a "horizon," a perspective on the world. Gadamer remarks that the "concept of 'horizon' suggests itself because it expresses the superior breadth of vision that the person who is trying to understand must have."[76] Understanding anything from the ancient past, according to Gadamer, is the fusion of horizons; it is not "a matter of being fully conscious of the present horizon, then being fully conscious of the past horizon through some strict 'scientific' methodology, and then taking from it what one will."[77] In particular, when we encounter ancient texts we do not absorb the horizons of the ancients into our modern one, but we fuse with them. "That means that we are challenged, criticized, and changed by them."[78] Furthermore, understanding a text's meaning and its application are inseparable from each other. "Gadamer argues that some notion of what a text means when it is applied in the present is at least implicitly involved in interpreting what the text meant in the past. . . . He acknowledges that we can and must distinguish between a text's original meaning and how it may be applied in the present, but such sharp division is already a secondary and derivative process. Application has played a prior role as part of the current horizon that enables us to grasp and understand the past horizon."[79] Understanding the meaning of a text from the past can rightly be viewed as a "constructive activity." It evokes the image of a "dynamic conversation":

> . . . the language in which something comes to speak is not a possession at the disposal of one or the other of the interlocutors. Every conversation presupposes a common language, or better,

creates a common language. Something is placed in the center, as the Greeks say, which the partners in dialogue both share, and concerning which they can exchange ideas with one another. Hence reaching an understanding on the subject matter of a conversation necessarily means that a common language must first be worked out in the conversation. This is not an external matter of simply adjusting our tools; nor is it even right to say that the partners adapt themselves to one another but, rather, in a successful conversation they both come under the influence of the truth of the object and are thus bound to one another in a new community. To reach an understanding in a dialogue is not merely a matter of putting oneself forward and successfully asserting one's own point of view, but being transformed into a communion in which we do not remain what we were.[80]

There is much insight to be gained from this element of Gadamer's hermeneutics in relation to the language of religion already expressive in the practice of a community, language that is being continually re-shaped by the power of the sacred word. Gadamer mentions sensitivity to a text's otherness: "the important thing is to be aware of one's own bias, so that the text can present itself in all its otherness and thus assert its own truth against one's own fore-meanings."[81] This is one way we become aware of our own unexamined assumptions.

A second line of inquiry related to the first would have to explore a series of questions in the light of Bahá'í teachings. For example, how does a hermeneutically trained consciousness decipher the sacred in the language of revelation, the sacred that stretches across time "from all eternity to all eternity"? How do religious texts help one gain awareness of one's own prejudices and fore-meanings? What is the collective shape of these prejudices? Are they all historical? If not, what are some ahistorical assumptions that contribute to limited or distorted understanding? How does fusion of horizon take place across traditions that succeed one another in the context of progressive revelation of religious truth?

Third, Gadamer tries to overcome the dichotomy between authority and reason. The authority of a text or of a person, say, a teacher, is based on "an act of reason itself which, aware of its own limitations, trusts to the better insight of others . . . indeed, authority has to do not with obedience but rather with knowledge."[82] In a hermeneutical process, one does not accept "only what can be fully confirmed by reason . . . but what has a reasonable claim to insight and knowledge superior to one's own."[83] Postmodern attitudes toward authority as an antithesis of freedom are so ingrained in our times that they shut us out from seeking knowledge in sources endowed with a valid claim to authority. What is left then is a vacuum often filled with the voices of those who have greater access to power asserting their truth claims. As Williams has pointed out: "There are some very reductive criticisms of traditional academic authority that do seem to leave us in this position. If the canon of works or writers or philosophies to be studied, and the methods of interpreting them, and the historical narratives that explain those things, are all equally and simultaneously denounced as ideological impositions, we are indeed left with a space structured only by power. This is bad news from several points of view. One is that it leaves the critics themselves with no authority, since they need to tell a tale [in order] to justify *that* tale: this is the point that, for instance, the denunciation of history needs history. They also need a tale to explain why they are in a position to tell it."[84] Gadamer considers "a willingness to make a reasoned acknowledgement of authority" crucial for education. This willingness also has implications for religion. "It allows for a way to affirm the authority of Scripture, for example, without basing it upon blind faith or measuring it completely by the current deliverances of reason."[85] A third line of inquiry into hermeneutics with respect to religious language in light of Bahá'í teaching has to do with the exploration of the intricate relationship between authority, knowledge, and reason.

The purpose of this brief discussion of Gadamer's hermeneutics and his proposal for fusion of horizons, has been to demonstrate possible lines of inquiry into the nature of religious language. However, it remains to be seen how much such exploration would shed light on the notion of complementarity between the languages of science and religion. For according to Bernstein, Gadamer seems to speak of hermeneutical understanding "as an 'entirely different type of knowledge and truth' from that which is yielded by Method and science."[86] To argue, with the aid of hermeneutics, complementarity between science and religion in the dimension pertaining to language is only possible if one can stay free from Gadamer's apparent mistrust of science, and therefore, from the duality between knowledge generated through hermeneutics and the methods of science.

The discussion of these two last sections, on the complementarity in conviction and action and between the languages of science and religion, is intended to expand on the main theme of this chapter, namely, the centrality of knowledge from both science and religion, treated as complementary sources, to the process of moral empowerment. The aim of the arguments in this chapter has been to bolster the claim that the word "knowledge" is in fact applicable to the content of both systems. Faith, beliefs, and convictions are present, although somewhat differently in each system. Science and religion both seek truth, and the fact that reason can only approach it in measurable steps—faith being capable of much larger leaps—does not alter this truth-seeking nature of either of the two systems. The knowledge accumulating in both is fallible, but so is all human knowledge. In its generation, application, and diffusion, the various faculties of the human soul as well as experience enter. Each system has its own ways to test knowledge and reach some level of certainty that allows it to go forward in its practice. It seems imperative for an educational process that seeks moral empowerment of its students to see both systems as sources of knowledge and to draw on their contents and methods.

CHAPTER 7

INTEGRATION

This is the third of the chapters in which the nature of objects of understanding is being examined, first in the most general context, then in relation to science and religion as sources of knowledge, and now in an exploration of the way knowledge needs to be integrated in the content of an educational program seeking moral empowerment. We began our discussion in the last chapter with a brief reference to Hirst's conception of forms of knowledge. In suggesting complementarity between religion and science we argued that education should not deal exclusively with one part of reality—consisting of what is accessible to the physical senses and that which reason produces in response to it—but should also draw on the abundance of insights to be gained from religion, viewed as a system of knowledge and practice concerned with the spiritual dimension of an extended reality.

The dual purpose of pursuing personal development and contributing to the transformation of society—purpose which gives direction to the process of moral empowerment—demands deliberate and sustained action. The knowledge that students must make their own through education cannot be acquired in isolation from the imperative that they are to act on the reality of their own lives and of society. Reality, then, must be studied in a way that results in the understanding of concrete problems faced by individuals, groups, and communities, as well as the development of capacity to work on them. Students need to identify the causes of the problems they have to address and learn to deal with the forces that operate in society, struggling against the negative forces of apathy and inaction and aligning themselves with positive constructive forces. How and in what form does knowledge come to play in this complex process, not merely focused on cultivating the privileged few but in the education of the majority of the peoples of the world? In trying to answer this question one faces an immediate challenge: There is no one-to-one correspondence between the many sets of profound and interwoven social, cultural, political, and economic problems that societies face and the content of the disciplines that enter educational programs. The knowledge and skills acquired in careers and professions may include elements critical of the present order, but more often than not, prepare the student to work in a "normal" mode and not for the change in paradigm—to borrow Kuhn's terminology—that the transformation of society entails.

There are, of course, certain approaches to the generation, application, and diffusion of knowledge that try to meet this challenge. One is the establishment of interdisciplinary groups. Governments and organizations of civil society have often brought together groups of "experts" from various disciplines deemed pertinent to the study of a given set of problems in order to devise strategies for action. Education itself is also willing to put together knowledge from different fields to create new programs that can deal with emerging realities, for example, by trying to incorporate relevant content from the social sciences into technical fields. Disciplines themselves have not been static, they have grown, divided, and have given rise to new fields, say, biophysics or biochemistry.

However, in those areas of endeavor concerned with goals such as overcoming poverty or doing away with oppression, these approaches have not proven entirely adequate. In trying to address the problems of marginalized populations, interdisciplinary groups have often found it difficult to overcome the distance that separates not only the knowledge of experts in different fields but also the ideological positions that seem to characterize them. Emerging new fields often focus narrowly on certain problems, usually those that affect the industrialized world rather than the majority of humanity. Indeed, nowhere within the global network of universities—a network built according to the conception of a university in the industrialized nations, and engaged in the generation and diffusion of knowledge according to that conception—have appeared educational programs that, going beyond a vision of "modernization," would empower the peoples of the world to contribute to a fundamental transformation of their societies. Faced with this situation, many endeavors have sought answers in non-formal education, consciousness-raising, and the delivery of specific training packages. These efforts have certainly had a positive impact on society, for example, by enabling millions of people to participate in struggles against injustice. But the polarization created between such approaches and formal schooling—coupled with a romantic and exaggerated emphasis on "what people already know"—takes energy away from the development of programs that seek the empowerment of young people who do wish to attend school and whose families see in education the only hope for improving their condition.

The concept of integration enters this inquiry in the context of a need for educational programs, structured and substantial in knowledge content, that empower students to act on their reality and transform it. This involves the proper choice of objects of understanding, as well as their integration into an organized whole in such a way that would enable the students to apply what they learn to complex sets of real problems they encounter as they progressively try to contribute to the transformation of society. That education in some form has to take on such a challenge is by no means a given. Many programs are content with incorporating ethical propositions into a curriculum that consists of traditional subject matters or is organized around objectives and outcomes, which are precisely expressed but increasingly procedural and empty—activity for the sake of activity. Over the years a number of efforts to move away from curricula based on subject matters have also flourished here and there. Some of these have been formulated on the basis of hastily defined notions of "fragmentation," "compartmentalization of knowledge," and "collection of unrelated experiences," on the one hand, and "wholeness," "synthesis," and "unity" on the other. The results include units of instruction that, for example, try to teach physics, chemistry, and biology around a theme or help students sort information and develop a few skills and attitudes through the discussion of some social issue. But at this level, integration and fragmentation tend to become a pair of labels implying good or bad for whatever it is that is either being promoted or attacked, be it curriculum, method, or any other aspect of a specific educational approach. If integration is to mean more than this, the concept needs to be scrutinized at more depth. We will be able to do this here only to a limited extent, by first presenting some of Paul Hirst's explanation of the problematic assumptions underlying criticisms raised against traditional subject-based curricula which often have given rise to a call for integration. In light of his arguments, we will look at a few criteria for the organization of knowledge in curricula, showing in the process that replacing "subject matter" with "social practice," which is what Hirst himself later advocated, is not an entirely satisfactory solution. Apart from the organization of knowledge, integration needs to be dealt with in the context of the values knowledge embraces, and at a fundamental level, it has to overcome the dichotomy between thought and action. This chapter is intended to prepare the way for the analysis of the notion of capability in the next.

Distinct and Interrelated: A Defense of Forms of Knowledge

In the formulation of his original position, Hirst views "integration" as a term used to attack "subject-structured" curricula. He notes that existing school "subjects" "have boundaries that are the products of a number of historical factors, primarily the growth of knowledge and the changing social demands placed on schools. But within this historical framework certain logical factors have played a significant, if limited, part, so that the structure of subjects is not entirely a contingent matter."[1]

The structure of a subject matter is the result of the interplay of logical factors and sociohistorical forces. The knowledge of the physical world, for example, is different from the knowledge of the mind, and the difference lies in the nature of concepts, logical structures of propositions, and the truth criteria involved in each. Based on these three features, Hirst identifies "forms of knowledge," to which reference was made in the last chapter, as autonomous entities distinct from other organizations of knowledge including the most longstanding university "subjects" and "disciplines." He asserts that by attacking the logical structure of existing knowledge, the critics of traditional curriculum are in effect attacking the wrong thing: the very nature of what most educators still want to teach.[2]

A given form of knowledge, albeit not immune to change, is irreducible to other forms. Hirst points out that some advances in knowledge have indeed broken down divisions between traditional subjects, but have not in fact bridged the *logical distinctions* between different forms of knowledge. "A new science which bridges areas of physics and chemistry is not breaking down any logical distinctions between two forms of knowledge, for physics and chemistry belong to the same form. Many new organizations for research and teaching are, however, developing new concepts that are significant in more than one distinct form of knowledge. These bring to the fore the inter-relations between the forms of knowledge. . . . It is, however, not in general the case that even such domains are examples of new, emerging, fundamental forms of knowledge."[3] Thus, although different forms of knowledge cannot be unified under the same kind of concepts, they are nevertheless interrelated. The concepts and truth criteria in one form of knowledge may well presuppose the concepts and truth criteria in another. For example, "many moral and religious concepts manifestly presuppose concepts we have for distinguishing features of the observable physical world. But religious or moral concepts do not thereby become reducible to physical concepts."[4] The interrelations between concepts, truth criteria, and the logical structures of different forms do not in themselves constitute "an integration of different forms of knowledge," rationalizing "an inter-form or topic structure," just as the "differentiating characteristics" of forms of knowledge do not justify "a curriculum of isolated 'subjects.'" What is needed is, "a detailed map of the logical relations between objectives and then the best curriculum structure for attaining these, whatever that is."[5]

This short reference to Hirst's analysis illustrates the dangers inherent in dealing with the question of integration as a mere reaction to the inadequacies of curricula based on subject matters. A closer look at the nature of some of the objections made to such curricula, and Hirst's answers to them, will clarify the issues at hand further.

The first objection, which Hirst refutes, is expressed as exclusive focus on abstract knowledge. He argues that the assumption of a division between common-sense and theoretical knowledge underlying this objection is based on the mistaken notion that the former is not differentiated into logically distinct forms. It is true that the two types of knowledge represent different levels of abstraction, but there is a logical continuity from one to the other. In any form of knowledge, the same conceptual structure and truth criteria can be found across its entire spectrum, from the level of common-sense to the highly academic, albeit in varying degrees of complexity. That a subject structured curriculum is too theoretical for children, then, does not by itself justify a claim for integration.[6]

The next criticism, which Hirst contests, relates to the lack of attention a traditional subject-based curriculum gives to the student's practical and moral concerns. Since the freer ways of organizing knowledge are just as prone to this weakness, the criticism, he points out, misses the cause of the problem. In some cases, application of knowledge could be addressed under subject matters by extending the theoretical to the practical. In other cases, where input from different areas is required, a more complex approach would have to be adopted. Certain interrelations between forms of knowledge rather than their distinctions, for example, become particularly significant when it comes to issues of a moral and practical nature. But such interconnections in themselves do not indicate the need for a "new non-subject type of curriculum unit." Moral education, for example, could be treated either as a subject that presupposes the knowledge of other forms or in the context of teaching the knowledge of other forms to which are attached relevant moral issues. It is immaterial whether the units that deal with moral and practical issues are called subjects or not. What is crucial is that curriculum units "come to recognise both the differences and the relations that are necessary features of knowledge."[7]

The third objection to subject-based curriculum, the flawed nature of which Hirst tries to expose, rests on a psychological premise. It is claimed that "the mind or consciousness of a person either is, or ought to be, a unity which we distort by the compartmentalization of the curriculum." But the picture of the mind this conception evokes is, according to Hirst, faulty. The "structure of an individual's consciousness is certainly the structure of the concepts, knowledge, judgments that he has acquired and it has that unity which these elements possess."[8] Education cannot aim at "unity of consciousness" outside these logically organized elements. Concepts, truth criteria, and logical structures are the very elements of consciousness students need to acquire, and educational objectives should be organized around them.

Yet another criticism, also based on a psychological premise, is expressed in terms of the curtailment of the freedom of mind introduced by the boundaries of subject areas. To condition the mind "to classify situations in pre-determined ways, to entertain limited considerations about them," it is said, will make the mind incapable not only of "wider unrestricted thought" but also of "other forms of response and feeling." Hirst rejects this assumption and argues that any level of coherent thought beyond the merely superficial involves "the sustained, persistent use of limited ranges of concepts." Education should develop the ability of the mind to move between diverse forms of knowledge. At the same time, it should train the mind to sustain thought within a given category. Freedom of thought exists "within a rule-governed structure of concepts. Outside such structures freedom is, in general, only freedom to be irrational."[9]

There are lessons from this outline of Hirst's rebuttal of the assumptions of certain proposals for integration that we will carry forward in our exploration. The main one, particularly relevant in light of much contemporary practice, is that whatever the divisions of knowledge are called—forms, disciplines, subjects—there is a certain logic internal to them that cannot be ignored. To simply make weak connections between pieces of knowledge brought together from various disciplines because they are relevant to a problem or to a topic does not create the kind of structure that integration should seek.

Moral empowerment as discussed up to now sets a broad aim for integration. But much has to be said before objectives for curriculum-units are established in programs that adhere to this conception of educational aim. We will do this in the next two chapters on capabilities and on pedagogical choices, keeping in mind Hirst's analysis of the issues surrounding the question of integration. Of particular value, in this respect, is his insistence that the objectives of any unit of study should be grounded firmly in the logical structure of knowledge. He actually agrees that when there are unclassifiable objectives that fall outside the distinct forms of knowledge, they "offer a basis for curriculum units which will demand some form of genuine integration and thus run counter to the construction of sharp subject divisions." However, "qualities of mind" like enquiry, imagination, and critical thinking are not constants across the different forms of knowledge and cannot, therefore, be the basis for curriculum integration. There is not a common unit of "imagination" that could apply equally to "imaginative writing" and "imaginative scientific investigation." Where such general qualities exist, Hirst asks: "must they not be first developed within some specific area of knowledge and then be generalized to apply to other areas?"[10] He also remarks:

> . . . the concepts on which our knowledge is built form distinctive networks of relationships. If we transgress the rules of the relationships which the concepts meaningfully permit, we necessarily produce nonsense. If we talk about magnetic fields being angry, actions being coloured, beauty having weight, or stones being right or wrong we have simply produced conceptual confusion.[11]

Criteria for Curricular Integration

This brief examination of Hirst's early treatment of forms of knowledge, his criticism of the reasoning behind superficial conceptions of integration, and the caution with which the theme has to be approached opens the way for an exploration of certain basic characteristics of the process through which the content of curricula may be elaborated in the general context of moral empowerment. A discussion of a number of these characteristics follows:

STRUCTURE

There is a wide spectrum of educational approaches, ranging from radical constructivism at one extreme to firm attachment to the boundaries and structures of disciplines at the other. Although Hirst's insightful analysis is a warning against schemes of integration that ignore the structure of knowledge, there are a number of difficulties with the concept of structure as applied to knowledge. Some of these have been presented by D. C. Phillips and are relevant here. Phillips notes that Hirst's proposal for the anatomy of forms of knowledge falls short of successfully demonstrating the distinction each form supposedly enjoys: There are overlaps between the forms with respect to their distinguishing criteria and there is more than one logical structure within some of the forms. Psychology as a branch of the human sciences, for example, embraces both Freudianism and behaviorism with dissimilar central concepts, logical relations, tests against experience, techniques, and skills.[12]

In seeking to ensure that the content of a curriculum does not ignore the structure of knowledge, we need to be reminded that the word "structure" has different meanings in different contexts. As Phillips explains, it loosely means arrangement of parts, elements, or constituents. In this sense, as "most things have parts or constituents, most things have a structure."[13] But "structure" carries with it normative connotations as well, which implies that some theory in each instance has to back up the usage of the term. Yet, too often, the underlying theory is not made explicit. Disparate domains become confused or conflated when various types of structure are not kept separate. The result is that "one type of structure is thought of, or discussed, in terms only appropriate to another; modes of measurement that are appropriate for one type of structure are misused in the forlorn attempt to measure other types of structure," The example below by Phillips is telling:

Consider the "Alice Through the Looking-Glass" situation that arises in the following case: a teacher is presenting a piece of science curriculum to a student, and the whole transaction is being studied by a cognitive psychologist who is preparing a paper for a conference presentation. The lesson has a structure; the science discipline being taught has a structure . . . ; the physical universe has a structure that the science discipline in some sense is reflecting; the teacher has a cognitive structure (pertaining to what he or she wants the pupil to learn); the pupil has a cognitive structure (pertinent to mastering the discipline); the researcher has a cognitive structure (pertinent to studying this complex situation); and the researcher might use his or her own cognitive structure to construct a mental model which postulates a structure that hypothetically is what is present in the mind of the learner. If all goes well, even the researcher's conference paper will have a structure (and maybe even some content).[14]

In the above situation difficulties arises when these structures get conflated; when the successful acquisition of science by the student becomes "isomorphic" with the structure of the science that was learnt, or the mental model that the cognitive scientist constructs is considered isomorphic with what is located in the student's head. Phillips points out that "to say that there is isomorphism between the conceptual structure of the discipline of physics and the structure of the real physical world, or between the cognitive structures of a learner and the structure of physics, is to postulate isomorphisms between entities that occupy different 'universes of discourse.'"[15] In research methodology, for example, a method appropriate for structures in one universe of discourse cannot, without some reasonable justification, be adopted in another. The research methodology that would shed light on the cognitive structure of the student cannot be conflated with that which would assist in discovering how well he or she has learned the concepts of a discipline.

Thus . . . to ask a pupil some questions about the relationships between concepts in a discipline is, indeed, to do just that—it is to seek to find how well the pupil understands the discipline. It is not a good way to discover the pupil's cognitive structure. If a pupil was to say that "energy in physics is the same as force," this would show that the pupil did not understand part of the discipline of physics—he or she has incorrectly linked the two concepts (incorrectly, that is, in terms of the rules of the discipline of physics). And presumably, too, there is something going on in the head of the pupil that caused him or her to make that statement, but whatever the *cognitive-psychological* story is, it is not identical with, and is not fully describable in terms of, the *discipline of physics* story.[16]

While Phillips examines all these difficulties, he is not willing to do away with the concept of structure as applied to the content of education. He even seems to hope for some kind of classification of structural models in which relations between "ontological elements"—among the physical or cognitive or psychological or conceptual elements or building blocks—and relations between "functional units"—among functioning elements or processes—are given different treatment.

We, too, while sharing Phillips' caution, recognize the need to be aware of structure in developing curricula in the context of moral empowerment. As Phillips mentions, there is a "heuristic" value to the concept of structure. That is to say, the concept can at first play a suggestive or guiding role in the organization, say, of a given experience. As reflection and investigation advances, it becomes possible to replace the notion of structure with something more specific and more accurate. Hypotheses could then be formed about types of organization, "so that eventually the useful but potentially misleading heuristic notion could be dropped."[17] He further asks:

. . . human experience . . . does seem to be orderly; it is not all "booming, buzzing confusion." But what is the nature of this order? Will cognitive psychology resolve the mystery? What role is played by social forces of the sort that interested Vygotsky? And what role—if any—do the traditional disciplines play in helping me to order my experience? Are these disciplines themselves organized in some way?[18]

These, as well as the role structured social practices play in bringing order to experience, are important issues that have not yet been resolved. As far as the development of curricula is concerned, however, the mere heuristic value of the concept of structure points to promising directions. One can begin, for example, by examining structures within disciplines but then step over their boundaries to the degree needed and possible in order to organize the curriculum according to specific aims. In this way, it would be possible to retain the rigor of the educational program—not trivializing the treatment of subject areas such as mathematics, science, and language—while allowing sufficient fluidity that would open space to deal with relevant theoretical and practical concerns, drawing on knowledge from various fields and practices. This dynamic interplay between an established form of knowledge at a given stage of its development and successful efforts to bend it, not only avoids the ossification of an existing organization of knowledge, but also safeguards against the kind of superficiality of which hasty attempts at integration are rightly accused.

RELEVANCE

The process of integration being examined here needs to take into account the dangerous tendency to make education an exclusive enterprise. This implies that moral empowerment as a discourse cannot become too attached to the instrumentalism of the industrial world, thus ignoring the role its protagonists, constituting the majority of the peoples of the planet, would have to play in humanity's transition to its age of maturity. A criticism of the liberal arts education offered by Richard Pring speaks to this concern. Pring draws on Michael Oakeshott's metaphor of a "conversation" to make his point: We all inhabit "a world of ideas," ideas that make sense of who we are and of our experiences. What is significant is that we all participate in this world of ideas; we form our individual perceptions from sources that are publicly accessible. We learn, say, about democratic values through separate experiences, but there is enough in common between them "to enable a 'conversation' to take place about those democratic values—and the conversation itself becomes a part of [each individual's] self-enacted history."[19] Education as a transaction between generations of human beings in which newcomers are initiated into the world they are to inhabit, perpetuates this ongoing conversation. In Oakeshott's words, "we may recognize liberal learning as, above all else, an education in imagination, an initiation into the art of this conversation in which we recognize the voices; to distinguish their different modes of utterance, to acquire the intellectual and moral habits appropriate to this conversational relationship and thus to make our 'début dans la vie humaine.'"[20] Pring, citing the failure of liberal education to include the voices of the majority in "the conversation of mankind," asks:

What sort of conversation is it which, dealing with issues that affect us all, excludes so many people? Ought not the topics of conversation to be extended to those which the majority find an interest in? And should not questions about the relevance of education to their future lives (the central concern of most young people) be regarded as legitimate within that conversation? The liberal ideal excludes so many and, unexamined, will continue to do so, for 'relevance' is seen as an irrelevant consideration in an activity which is engaged in for its own sake and for no external ends.[21]

Important as Pring's observations are, the requirement of relevance has pitfalls of its own, particularly when the notion that knowledge is "socially constructed" is overemphasized. An example presented by Michael Young is instructive in this respect. In post-apartheid South Africa it was natural for policy makers to wish to make a break with the past and "hand power to create a new curriculum to teachers, students and more broadly to the 'democratic forces.'" In the process, however, the social construction of knowledge "became a slogan for opposing the idea that the role of the curriculum is to enable learners to develop their thinking through engagement with specialist bodies of knowledge that are not available to them in their everyday lives."[22] The resulting "outcome-based" curriculum intended to express broad educational goals of a political movement, but it ended up "largely free of content" as it refused to offer to Black South Africans the expertise and specialist knowledge from which they had been excluded under apartheid. Young's example illustrates the dangers of emphasis on narrowly defined notions of "relevance" in the development of educational content. It points to the requirement that the integration of knowledge be carried out within an "inclusive" discourse on education, but one in which the disciplines of knowledge are respected.

THE ROLE OF THE COGNITIVE

Whatever degree of attention to forms of knowledge the framework being sought in this inquiry may recommend, it is important that the role of the cognitive be not exaggerated. In his initial approach, Hirst seems to go too far in making the concern for cognitive development the cardinal feature of curriculum design, hoping that "other objectives can be catered for adequately only by elaborating on a curriculum structure that copes with the cognitive."[23] Later, in criticizing his own position, he makes explicit the philosophical doctrines that influenced the thinking and practice in education during the years he was formulating his early views.

Hirst admits that his original proposal for a liberal education presupposed a certain conception of the human being, whose diverse capacities were divided into three main categories: the cognitive, the affective, and the conative. The latter two involved emotions, actions, and dispositions, and were dependent for their intelligible operation upon "the concepts, beliefs and knowledge achieved by the cognitive capacities." It was through developing these cognitive capacities that justifiable bodies of rational beliefs, rational actions, and rational emotions could be acquired. Connected to this conception of a 'rational person was the notion of the ideal form of life to which all should aspire. In this ideal form of life, there could be "no more ultimately justifiable pursuits than the intrinsically worthwhile pursuit of reason in all its forms," and "the successful ordering of all other human concerns in terms made possible by the achievements of reason into a coherent and consistent whole."[24] This conception of a good life was consistent with the ideals of democracy to which freedom of choice was central.

Hirst highlights two main assumptions of this worldview: First, "the development of reason is seen as a fundamentally social construction." Objective judgments are reached through shared conceptual schemes by drawing on cognitive capacities and knowledge formed through the creation of public languages. Second, "society is itself seen as simply a collection of freely associating individuals." Survival and achievement of goals necessitate the organization of human society into families, groups, and communities. Bonds are formed primarily through each individual's pursuit of the good life according to rational principles. "It is the good will of each member that holds communities and groups together." It is not difficult to see how this particular view of the rational, autonomous life would provide a framework for the formation of educational aims. Within this framework, the practice of education would be conceived in terms of "rational determination of the ends to be pursued," "determination of the best means possible," and "the implementation of the conclusions reached."[25]

Educational aims were defined broadly in terms of the development of knowledge and understanding, the pursuit of which is worthwhile both intrinsically and as a way of ordering progress in all aspects of personal and social life. To achieve these aims, forms of knowledge were "logically mapped and the diversity of the cognitive objectives involved was explored for their logical interrelations." A notion of liberal education was postulated in terms of "initiation into the forms of knowledge as characterised by their distinctive internal, logical features." These forms of knowledge were seen as the core of a wider education—a domain considered secondary, containing useful knowledge and skills as well as "personal and social education to promote the development of character necessary to the conduct of rational living both individually and in social contexts." The development of character was considered to be "a matter of moral education in the light of rationally justified principles both universal and local." Here the education of emotions and dispositions would "combine to provide an appropriate network of virtues for the exercise of rational choice and the practical living of the good life."[26]

According to Hirst, this rationalist approach to education was criticized for its "philosophical underpinnings" and its "internal contradictions" even as it was being developed. The value of the kind of "disengaged knowledge" that, according to this approach, reason would generate—isolated from both the external environment and from all human attributes including reason itself—was being seriously questioned. Parallel to it, the "utilitarian" approach was gaining stature and power, bringing into focus the practical dimension of the good life. Reason, knowledge, and understanding were no longer seen as capable of "determining from a detached point of view the ends that constitute the good life for individuals or society"; they became instead the instruments that help us "discern, develop, and order coherently those basically given elements of wants and satisfactions from which the good life is to be composed."[27] Capacities such as reason and will, it was said, should be appropriately directed in order to harness the dominating power wants and satisfactions have over our lives. This instrumentalist view denies reason any direct role in motivation. Society is just "a collection of atomic individuals associating together for their personal satisfactions," and social relations are nothing more than "contingent arrangements that promote personal satisfactions." Individualism is now particularly strong as "all judgments of what is good, and the motivation to attain that, rest ultimately in personal subjective states." In line with these presuppositions, education is "rationalistically planned," now according to a different rationality: the goals it serves "are ultimately generated individually by rational choice in relation to personal wants and contextual constraints."[28]

Having identified the shortcomings of the cognitive and utilitarian approaches, Hirst argues for an education based on "social practice." Yet, the alternative conception of reason he proposes in this context does not seem to represent a fundamental shift, but a convergence of the two previous conceptions. He recommends that we should first recognize the intrinsic value of reason, acknowledging that the satisfaction derived from pursuing and achieving true beliefs and justifiable actions is as motivating as that of fulfilling our other wants and desires. We should then realize the practical nature of reason and the extent to which it is directed by our interests. Reason discriminates between activities that lead to states of satisfaction and dissatisfaction and "these activities themselves become objects of satisfaction." The practical nature of such activities involves know-how, skills, and judgments which are often tacit. "Individual objects, situations or events are conceptually distinguished because of their practical significance for our wants and desires. Propositional knowledge and belief are thus developments within the context of practice and are . . . in the form of practical principles. The primary propositions that reason delivers are generalisations concerning successful and unsuccessful practice rather than disinterested truths."[29] Education in his modified proposal is to equip the individual to pursue the "good life," one that allows each person to seek satisfaction of pursuing and achieving true beliefs and justifiable actions for its own sake alongside the satisfaction of practical needs and desires.

The rationality underlying Hirst's proposal, autonomous and at the same time directed by interests and desires, we can argue, is the rationality of the well-educated, well-meaning proponents of modernization to whom we referred, quoting Mahbub ul Haq, in the previous chapter. We have already expressed misgivings about the rationality of the "modern man" and concluded that he is a poor candidate for the "subject of understanding" being sought in this inquiry. In trying to define the role of the cognitive in what we would accept as a reasonable conception of integration, it is important to ask if an educational process shaped by a convergence of the two rationalities as advocated by Hirst, could lead students, particularly the youth of the villages and the marginalized neighborhoods of the burgeoning cities of the world—a significant pool of human resources that has to be seriously taken into account—to participate in a process of transformation, which, while global in outlook, is set in motion in the context of local community? The answer may well be positive if the task before humanity today is the mere reform of the present world. But will the qualities of mind acquired through such an education be up to the tasks that need attention in the transition of humanity from childhood to adulthood, the inevitability of which is one of the fundamental elements of the educational framework being explored here? Would such education prepare the kind of "revolutionary" envisioned by Marc Belth in the following excerpt to work for the construction of a new order which humanity's transition to adulthood demands?

> . . . man is continuously shaping his experience into a whole which can be recalled readily and used in confronting and explaining new events. In this constant shaping, he borrows from everywhere. . . . The ordinary human being, growing up in his own culture, inherits all of the models available to him, and has no alternative but to use them. . . . When he becomes a radical, a revolutionary, he is in fact coming to reject some or all of the models which he has inherited.[30]

To determine the proper role for the cognitive in curricula in such a way that students do acquire the qualities of mind called for by the knowledge system that defines the modern world, but at the same time attain the freedom to reject obsolete "inherited models" is not an easy task. In this inquiry, we have tried not to isolate the role of the cognitive in nurturing understanding or to reduce rationality to the satisfaction of wants and desires, no matter how legitimate they may be in specific contexts. It is for these reasons that we examined in chapter 4 the nurturing of understanding and the fostering of spiritual qualities as an inseparable whole. Our attempt to refute narrow definitions of rationality in the context of the complementarity of science and religion in the previous chapter was to some extent due to the same concern.

SOCIAL PRACTICE

Attention to social practices, using them if necessary as contexts within which specific educational content may be elaborated, is another valid criterion for integration. Once again, Hirst's views on the subject are helpful. Later in his career, he advocated that the shortcomings of a discipline-based curriculum can be addressed by the priority given to the "consideration of current practice, the rules and principles it actually embodies and the knowledge, beliefs and principles that the practitioners employ in both characterising that practice and deciding what ought to be done."[31] We have already mentioned that this shift from a view of education centered on forms of knowledge to one primarily concerned with social practices occurred as he identified flaws in the conception of reason in both the "rationalist" and the "utilitarian" positions. Yet how, we may ask, does he try to transcend the "radical individualism" with which, he believes, the two positions are "infected"? And what are his conceptions of the individual and of society in the context of social practices?

Hirst states that persons "are necessarily social constructions," and society is a "network of socially constructed individuals who within that network have the capacities for choice for the formation of their own patterns of life and the modification of their social networks."[32] Thus, the good life for the individual is only possible within the networks of existing social relations and traditions. Initiation into practices is vital to the good life of the individual. In a way similar to MacIntyre's, Hirst defines practices as "patterns of activity engaged in individually or collectively which have been socially developed," as "complex interrelated packages of such elements as actions, knowledge, judgements, criteria of success, values, skills, dispositions, virtues, feelings . . ."[33] Education will have to select practices according to emerging capacities of individuals and their social and physical contexts. Hirst suggests that such practices fall into at least three domains: first "those very varied basic practices necessary for any individual to be rationally viable in their given everyday physical, personal and social contexts," second "practices from that much wider range of optional practices available for the construction of each individual rational life," and third those practices that are "second order" to the first two categories, constituting "critical reflection" on them.[34]

We have already discussed in chapter 4 in the context of virtues the kinds of difficulty an educational program would face were it to anchor moral development solely in the "internal goods" and "standards of excellence" found in practices. Hirst's proposal for a practice-centered educational approach presents additional challenges. His categorization of practices with which education should be concerned is too broad, and the defining characteristic of each rather vague; as a result it is difficult to see how it would lead to the actual choice of relevant practices and ultimately to "structured" educational content. But even assuming that such a task can be carried out, how useful is the hierarchy he establishes as an organizing principle of curricular design? A fundamental question to be asked in the context of moral empowerment is whether the aim of education is merely to initiate individuals into certain practices as they are, or is it also to enable them to reshape existing practices? If the latter is the case, then one must decide the extent to which the student should develop the capacity to reflect critically on the nature of the practice into which he or she is being initiated. Hirst, of course, recognizes the role education has to play in reshaping a given practice, but assigns this function, which involves identifying presuppositions within a given practice through "abstracted theoretical study," to that part of education which deals with "initiation into the practices of critical reflection on the fundamental substantive practices."[35] Further he envisions a small minority of people participating in such theoretical practice and claims that "it is in general impossible for worthwhile education to engage directly in these theoretical pursuits." He places this social responsibility on "theoretical specialists" who should "engage in wide public dialogue about the significance of their work for non-theoretical pursuits, thus providing a context of public critical reflection on social practices on which educators can draw."[36]

That specialized theoretical pursuits involving critical reflection on social practices are desirable is a statement with which it would be difficult to disagree. But that such reflection should be mostly the concern of a relatively small number of individuals in a hierarchical arrangement is a conclusion based on an unnecessary sharp division between the theoretical and the practical, between know-that and know-how. One important criterion for the kind of integration we seek here is the ability to transcend this dichotomy as much as possible. This requires that theoretical knowledge needed for reflection on the nature of a practice into which one is being initiated be incorporated into it from the beginning, albeit progressively. This does not necessarily invalidate Hirst's scheme of categorization, but does suggest that better ways of thinking about the role of practices in the design of curricula may be available.

The sharp division between know-that and know-how—between propositional and practical knowledge—present in Hirst's original position appears again when social practices rather than forms of knowledge take center stage. In both proposals, insisting on such a dichotomy hides from view essential elements of the desired framework for curricular design. Paddy Walsh, for example, in agreeing with Hirst's own criticism of his original position, questions the one-way dependence of every kind of development on propositional knowledge and points out that the theory of forms of knowledge ignores "the likelihood that the affective, the moral, and the practical are properly interdependent with the intellectual." As a result, among other things, the effect of the environment, the importance of practice, the role of values, "the engagement of the heart to the propositional in contemplative-appreciative knowledge," and "the common belief that moral insight is as much a fruit as it is a condition of good will and right action" are not addressed. Walsh states that such a theoretical stance could legitimize the "distortion of many subjects that has resulted from isolating their propositional from their deliberative, technical and contemplative elements." He also points to a next level of difficulty: overlooking the possibility that "the relationship of propositions to value and action within forms of knowledge is just as integral to their logic or 'grammar,' and just as distinctive in each form and as significant a variable across forms, as those features of propositions,"[37] on which the theory of forms of knowledge stands.

As to the consequences of overemphasizing the value of practical knowledge, it seems sufficient to remind ourselves that even in the moral, religious, and aesthetic domains—areas where initiation into the corresponding practices is an imperative—education accomplishes relatively little if a good grasp of theoretical and propositional knowledge is not achieved. The statement "a kindly tongue is the lodestone of the hearts of men. It is the bread of the spirit, it clotheth the words with meaning, it is the fountain of the light of wisdom and understanding . . ."[38] is an example of the kind of propositional knowledge that abounds in religious texts. Understanding it contributes as much to the development of a kindly tongue on the part of a religious practitioner as does the practice of speaking kind words in the community in which she or he is a member. The relationship between theory and practice in releasing human potential is not one in which the theoretical consideration of moral principles and religious teachings is either secondary to their practical application or takes precedence over them. On the contrary, the relationship is sustained by a multidimensional web of connections that education cannot disregard.

Rather than choosing either forms of knowledge or practices as the axis of a scheme of curricular integration, we may argue, it is necessary to pay attention to the dynamic interplay between theoretical and practical knowledge. The mind seems not to move in only one direction. There is the dialectic of "concrete" and "abstract" which has to be respected. Instead of seeing the "concrete" only as something palpable through our senses and as a necessary requirement of abstraction ("a conceptual or mentally constructed process"), one can also see it as the "systemic interconnectedness" of things rooted in phenomena and therefore as the outcome of thinking.[39]

Pring's analysis of the interrelationship between theory and practice clarifies the issue further. He states that "practical activities are themselves permeated by understandings that can be more or less intelligently held. . . . There is an embryonic theory contained within intelligent practice." Once the theoretical understandings within practices are made explicit and systematically formulated they can be examined. It is also true that "the way into theory is often best reached through this intelligent reflection upon a practice that might otherwise have been pursued mechanically." Pring offers the example of attempts in theology to theorize about the intimations of immortality: "Theory, and the propositional knowledge which constitutes the theoretical position, are a provisional formulation of a set of ideas through which we make sense of reality, including the practical reality of worship, of work, or of moral struggle."[40]

The duality between theory and practice, Pring points out, is at the heart of the rift that separates liberal and vocational education. To close this gap, the need for reflection is often stressed, reflection that can logically lead us "to the explicit formulation of the implicit theoretical position." In this context the "intelligent 'doing' (intelligent because it demonstrates insight, adaptability to circumstances, openness to criticism) is . . . to be seen as both vocationally significant (not just bookworms or articulate talkers, but 'doers') and academically respectable (not just 'doers', but systematic thinkers about 'doing')."[41]

While Pring acknowledges that "the logical connection between thinking and doing and between theory and practice are too often neglected in education, to the detriment of the intelligent practice essential to moral and working life," he voices caution against the kind of "reflective exercise through which 'action' becomes an intelligent activity and practice becomes theoretically sound." Reflection cannot simply consist of rendering explicit the ideas and beliefs within a practice; it involves situating them "in the objective world of critical enquiry developed through the various intellectual disciplines." It is not enough, for example, "to make explicit the quaint ideas of healthy living implicit in one's daily eating habits" without subjecting them "to some form of science-based criticism. And yet to have that critical perspective requires some mastery of basic and relevant concepts in science."[42]

Moreover, Pring mentions that this emphasis on the need for reflection expressed by many of the "vocationally oriented curriculum developments" is to encourage "independent 'doing' and 'making.'" The motto being that "it is the process rather than the product which counts." He feels, however, that another false dichotomy is introduced here. This dichotomy arises from the inability to see that the "process" itself "embodies ideas (bad as well as good) and beliefs (false as well as true) which can be rectified only through engagement with that critical conversation which is the product of other people's enquiries." He reminds us that the "academic disciplines are the resources upon which the teacher must draw in helping the 'doer' to be more intelligent in the doing."[43]

In the context of the kind of curricula being explored here, overcoming the dichotomy between theoretical and practical would help guard against the kind of educational content that too easily relegates the majority of humanity, the very people who are to participate in the processes of change and reconstruction, to the acquisition of a few manual or technical skills. By focusing on the interplay of practical and theoretical knowledge, it will be possible to have the freedom to choose among different available options for integration according to the specific aim of a given set of educational activities. At times, initiation into social practice could be the starting point, but in such a way that the corresponding theoretical knowledge can be incorporated from the beginning so as to enhance the understanding of the students. On other occasions, it would be the logic and truth criteria of a discipline or form of knowledge which would set the process in motion, while drawing on relevant practices in order to ground theory in experience. These two paths, each in its own way, would bring together *doing* and *knowing*, but doing and knowing cannot be integrated in isolation from our state of *being*. It is in this respect that neither social practice nor forms of knowledge would on their own suffice to fulfill the aims of integration. Truths about the extended reality mentioned earlier also need to be incorporated into curricular content. The oneness of humankind and the interconnectedness of existence in all its dimensions are truths corresponding to the core of our being; their source is not merely social practice or forms of knowledge. Spiritual qualities introduced in chapter 4—as distinct from virtues rooted in social practices—are other examples of such truths, which are not bound to a practice or a form of knowledge, although both provide grounds for aspiring toward such truths. As David Cooper, drawing on Plato's conception, points out, ". . . truth is not, in the first instance, a property of sentences, beliefs, or other purported representations of reality. Rather, it is a property of reality itself. . . . Knowing truths is acquaintance with the true. It results from a 'turning away' from less true objects, 'the world of change,' towards the 'brightest of all realities.'" He further explains: "An aspect of this 'turning around' which needs stressing is that as a person comes 'in contact with the truth,' he becomes *more* like the true world. He comes to partake in its 'immortality,' so that his 'divine quality' . . . appear(s) quite clearly."[44]

Historically opposing tendencies have fragmented our conception of truth. Yearning for truth in its transcendent Platonic form has been sharply separated from seeking fulfillment in every day social practices or in the study of sciences and the kind of knowledge that pertains to this world. Often an ascetic life has been advocated as a requirement for attaining truth beyond the merely human. However, in the sense that we use the concept here—as intimately connected with our state of "being" both individually and collectively, truth shapes social practices and academic disciplines in such a way as to advance the real good of humanity.

Values of Knowledge

Selection of objects of understanding and their organization into some structured but fluid whole requires the examination of values associated with knowledge. This may immediately suggest the often-cited contradiction between knowledge as an end in itself and knowledge as a means to other ends. But we need not be confined to the longstanding debate on the merits of one or the other. M. A. B. Degenhardt, for example, mentions that some knowledge "is valuable neither as a means to an end, nor as an end in itself, but because it helps us to determine our ends."[45] Once we overcome the duality, we are free to reflect on the values that knowledge itself embraces. Walsh offers a rich perspective in this regard. He orders four types of values—the possessive, the experiential, the ethical, and the ecstatic—in a line of argument that "brings us up sharp against the idea of persons, objects, and aspects of the world having value in themselves as a condition of their being values for us, and of love of the world as a rational condition of our other prizings."[46] He compares the possessive values to those of wealth, status, and power, in that all three can be possessed in different amounts and varying degrees of security, and cites unqualified vocationalism and encyclopaedism—"distinguished from measured concerns, situated within a larger value context, for the vocational and for the breadth and the retention of knowledge"[47]—as manifestations of a rampant possessive instinct in education which he criticizes in a decisive way.

Walsh attacks vocationalism on the ground that it promotes a narrowly instrumental view of education: Education is the means to establishing a working life and the working life is an instrument to securing money, status, and power. This view of education is characterized by a "narrowness of attitude" that leads to the "narrowing of curriculum," for it would be inconsistent to "value other aspects of work, like comradeship, service or intrinsic satisfaction, without valuing them in other contexts as well and then allowing those contexts their broadening influence on curriculum." "This kind of vocationalism," according to Walsh, "is the natural educational expression of vulgar materialism, for which possession is the overriding value and passion."[48]

Walsh considers encyclopaedism "a subtler manifestation of the possessive instinct, and a kind of mental materialism." It is this possessiveness that characterizes, for example, the crammer for an examination or the person who glorifies in the store of information in his head. However, the irony is that, even in the case of the latter, "he does not make knowledge really 'his own.' In some sense he kills it in his attempts to possess it. 'Knowledge' for him has no connection with action, intimacy, or contemplation, does not yield life experience or wisdom . . ."[49]

The experiential values of knowledge emphasize "richness of experience." Walsh suggests that these should rest on "host values" of truth, respect and justice, as well as an acknowledgement of the independent value of objects of experience. He warns against the perils of the kind of value placed, for example by John Dewey, on experience, rejecting in a sense the proposition that "the objects of experience can possess values in themselves."[50] Denial of such intrinsic value and the insistence that 'objects' are the mere constructions and reconstructions of 'subjects' are the basic flaws of Dewey's pragmatic theory of an education "of, by and for experience." By retaining the "wedge between experience and the world-in-itself in the notion of knowledge as fundamentally a construction," one destroys the wonder of the paradox that is knowledge: "an 'assimilation' of the world that yet of itself leaves the world as it is."[51]

The ethical values of knowledge are associated with the regulative rationality held up by open-ended formulations and injunctions conjuring such notions as respect, care, authenticity, and justice. These rational values are to be "added to possessive and experiential values as their ethically necessary corrective."[52] But even a virtue like respect for persons—defined as that virtue by which we treat people as ends rather than means—loses its ethical value if it does not "underline its basis in a positive acknowledgement of the independent value of other persons, the paradigm of which is a loving relationship." No amount of generalization and abstraction will lift "respect" from the level of a mere injunction if it is not shown as a "subsidiary to love." A lover's primary response is to the value inherent in the world. For the religious believer "the praise of God, just because He is God" is the "primary religious response—more fundamental than his search for salvation through relationship with God." The scientist, the artist, and the historian find respectively that the order of the universe is marvelous, that beauty is to be contemplated because it is there, and that people are everywhere in history and they are in themselves worthy of our interest. "And education can be conceived as, in large part, the loving initiation into these, and other such, mysteries."[53]

In Walsh's argument, "security of possession" as a value is subordinated to "richness of experience," which in turn "becomes a pursuit of one's tail unless, first, it allows itself to be constrained and limited by the demands of truth, respect and justice, and, second, it transcends both itself and a negative conception of its ethical limits, in an acknowledgement of the world that is properly called love."[54] Conversely, "only from the perspective of love of the world can the values of the ethical life, of the rich or the full life, and of possessions be balanced and integrated." It seems clear that the contemplation of this love can yield many an insight into the values of knowledge which should be taken into account in elaborating curricula. But we can take this conclusion a little further.

Love of the world in its broadest sense—and love of any particular object of understanding—has to be accompanied by consciousness of the interconnectedness of all things and, in particular, of the oneness of humankind. Love is always in danger of being individualistic. Love of the world helps the "subject of understanding" transcend the possessive values of knowledge, but only if she is fully aware that knowledge gained is not to be used as an instrument of power. The self-absorbed lover can easily forget that generous sharing of knowledge and insight is a requisite of understanding. Likewise, focus on the value inherent in the object of inquiry helps save education from the fetish of "radical constructivism," but one must be wary as well of the individualism that may become attached to independent discovery and mastery of intricacies of objects of understanding. Empty and generalized ethical injunctions are transformed through love of the world, but it is a love that is continually deepened by a sense of belonging to the whole. The consciousness of the oneness of humankind breaks the individualistic limits of the values of knowledge and imbues love of the world—and hence love of an object of understanding—with a sense of the collective. What is at stake is not a search for knowledge on which we embark individually; it is a journey we traverse together with others. To the extent that we act on the reciprocity that the consciousness of the one-ness of humankind awakens in us, we are empowered individually and collectively to transform ourselves and the world.

The transformative power of knowledge is another value that is in-tertwined with the love of the world. In ordinary friendship, the wish to transform the object of one's love is to be frowned upon; friends are not our projects, we are to love them for who they are. But in the case of the world, transformation is a requirement that existence itself demands from us. The transformative power of the physical sciences cannot be extracted and isolated from them; technology is not merely a product of science but intrinsic to it. Inherent in scientific knowledge of the universe is the human ability to transform the physical environ-ment. Placing love for the universe at the heart of one's determination to acquire knowledge of it and at the same time striving to rearrange its elements, according to the demands of an advancing civilization, poses no contradiction.

The transformative power of knowledge is, of course, a value of great significance to the process of moral empowerment defined in terms of a twofold purpose of personal and societal transformation. At the level of the individual, self-knowledge—not a mere awareness of one's thoughts, feelings and intentions, but a realistic growing un-derstanding of one's abilities and potential—has to accompany the development of character. Such knowledge is acquired against the background perception of human nature and the purpose of one's ex-istence. In the context of a Bahá'í-inspired framework, human nature would be seen as that complex fusion of its material dimension, the product of physical evolution shaped by the struggle for survival, and its spiritual dimension, characterized by such qualities as love, mercy, generosity, and justice. That the material nature is necessary and that, operating in its proper space, it helps the realization of human po-tential would not be denied. However, insights into one's own nature would be sought with the conviction that the human being is noble in

essence, and to attain true nobility, one has to strengthen one's spiritual nature, recognizing that which leads to "loftiness or lowliness, glory
or abasement, wealth or poverty."[55] In the absence of such recognition
it becomes impossible to set oneself commendable goals and choose
worthy means to achieve them. Further, this self-knowledge is not possible without an understanding of the nature of the relationships that
can be cultivated with other human beings. As D. W. Hamlyn puts it,
"a case can be made for the thesis that no proper understanding of the
concept of a person can be had in independence of an understanding
of the concept of a human relationship."[56] The knowledge that em-
powers us to transform the relationships of dominance and control to
those of solidarity and cooperation impels us to transform our own
character, and the insights that aid the individual to have a generous
personality are gained as he or she strives to forge bonds of love and
fellowship with others.

Thought and Action

We have approached the question of integration first in the context
of knowledge itself and then in relation to values of knowledge. It is
important to note, however, that integration cannot be achieved if, at
a fundamental level, the dichotomy between "thought" and "action"
is not transcended. The powers of thought operate in the world by
means of action, and action is endowed with meaning through the
exercise of human intellect and moral capacities. The last chapter of
this book is about the continuity of thought, language, and action.
A brief examination of the nature of the problem, however, seems
warranted here.

In this section we will draw on a debate between John McDowell
and Hubert Dreyfus in order to highlight some of the issues surrounding the relationship between thought and action, on the basis of which
we can reach certain conclusions. In chapter 5 we examined briefly
some of McDowell's arguments in *Mind and World*. It is necessary to

say a few words about Dreyfus' ideas as expressed in the first chapter of *Mind over Machine* before we look at the debate between the two philosophers. The purpose of the entire book is to present a challenge to artificial intelligence by demonstrating the unique way in which human beings acquire various kinds of skills. The locus of the argument of the first chapter is on know-how and the stages of learning that take an individual to the level of an "expert." It is stated that in acquiring skills learners do not suddenly leap from "rule-guided 'knowing that' to experience-based know-how."[57] Five stages are identified in a "skill acquisition model" through which an individual typically moves: novice, advanced, competent, proficient, and expert.

The first stage of learning, that belonging to a novice, consists of recognizing various "objective facts and features relevant to the skill," and acquiring "rules for determining actions based on those facts and features." Facts and features of the situation considered relevant are extracted and objectively defined for the novice learner without reference to the overall context within which they occur. These elements are called "context-free elements," and the corresponding rules to be applied regardless of what else is happening "context-free rules."[58] Below are a few examples from different skill areas:

> The beginning automobile driver learning to operate a stick-shift car is told at what speed (a context-free feature) to shift gears and, at any given speed, at what distance (another such feature) to follow a car preceding him. These rules ignore context. They do not refer to traffic density or anticipated stops. Similarly, the beginning chess player is given a formula for assigning point values to pieces independent of their position and the rule "always exchange your pieces for the opponent's if the total value of pieces captured exceeds that of pieces lost." The beginner is generally not taught that in certain situations the rule should be violated. The novice nurse is taught how to read blood pressure, measure

bodily outputs, and compute fluid retention, and is given rules for determining what to do when those measurements reach certain values . . .[59]

In the examples above, being able to follow each set of rules determines how well a novice performs. But in order to proceed to the level of an advanced beginner, the learner should be able to do more than just follow predetermined rules. An advanced beginner has gained enough experience in real situations to recognize certain elements which are not the "context free features" to which the "context free rules" apply. These new elements are called "situational." "Rules for behavior" at this stage of skill acquisition include both the new situational and the context-free elements:

The advanced beginner automobile driver uses situational engine sounds as well as context-free speed in his gear-shifting rules. He also learns to distinguish between the behavior of the distracted or drunken driver and that of the impatient but alert one. With experience, the chess beginner learns to recognize and avoid over-extended positions. Similarly, after much experience he can spot such situational aspects of positions as weakened king's side or a strong pawn structure despite the lack of precise and universally valid definitional rules. The student nurse learns from experience how to distinguish the breathing sounds that indicate pulmonary edema from those suggesting pneumonia. . . . In all those cases, experience seems immeasurably more important than any form of verbal description.[60]

For advanced beginners experience continues to grow until the number of recognizable situational and context-free elements becomes unmanageably huge. To cope, people will have to learn to "adopt a hierarchical procedure of decision-making." They need to come up with an organizing plan in order to examine "only the small set of factors that are most important." The ability to do so is the characteristic feature of "competence." At this stage, a competent individual who has a goal in mind sees the situation as a set of facts, the importance of which depends on the presence of other facts. "He has learned that when a situation has a particular constellation of those elements a certain conclusion should be drawn, decision made, or expectation investigated."[61]

> A competent driver . . . is no longer merely following rules designed to enable him to operate his vehicle safely and courteously but drives with a goal in mind. If he wishes to get from point A to point B very quickly, he chooses his route with attention to distance and traffic, ignores scenic beauty, and as he drives selects his maneuvers with little concern for passenger comfort or courtesy. He follows other cars more closely than normally, enters traffic more daringly, and even violates the law. A competent chess player may decide, after studying his position and weighing alternatives, that he can attack his opponent's king. He would then ignore certain weaknesses in his own position and the personal losses created by his attack, while removal of pieces defending the enemy king becomes his overriding objective.[62]

> The competent nurse will no longer automatically go from patient to patient in a prescribed order but will assess the urgency of their needs and plan work accordingly. With each patient, such a nurse will develop a plan of treatment, deciding that if certain signs are present a certain number of days after surgery, say, the time has come to talk with a patient about his wound and its care outside the hospital. When discussing the matter, various medical aspects of the patient's condition will be ignored, and psychological aspects will become important.[63]

In the next two levels, performance surpasses "the slow, detached reasoning of the problem-solving process" and is characterized by "a rapid, fluid, involved kind of behavior."[64] In performing a task, the proficient person will be deeply involved in it. Recent events will lead him to some specific perspective that will bring to the fore certain salient features of the situation while others recede to the background.

> As events modify the salient features, plans, expectations, and even the relative salience of features will gradually change. No detached choice or deliberation occurs. It just happens, apparently because the proficient performer has experienced similar situations in the past and so associates with present situations plans that worked in the past and anticipates outcomes that previously occurred.[65]

A proficient performer relies on the ability called "holistic discrimination and association," the ability "to intuitively respond to patterns without decomposing them into component features." At this level "while intuitively organizing and understanding his task" the person "will still find himself thinking analytically about what to do." Intuition, "the understanding that effortlessly occurs due to discriminations resulting from previous experiences" are still, however, followed by "detached decision-making."[66]

> On the basis of prior experience, the proficient driver, approaching a curve on a rainy day, may intuitively realize that he is driving too fast. He then consciously decides whether to apply the brakes, remove his foot from the accelerator, or merely reduce pressure. The proficient chess player can recognize a very large repertoire of types of positions. Grasping almost immediately, and without conscious effort, the sense of a position, he sets about calculating a move that best achieves his intuitive plan. . . . The proficient

nurse will *notice* one day, without any conscious decision-making, that the patient is psychologically ready to deal with his surgery and impending release. However, during the conversation, words will be carefully and consciously chosen.[67]

At the highest level, an expert is "deeply involved in coping with his environment." He transcends all earlier skills which to differing degrees involve detached and deliberate thinking. An expert's skill becomes "so much a part of him that he need be no more aware of it than he is of his own body." "The expert driver becomes one with his car, and he experiences himself simply as driving, rather than as driving a car, just as, at other times, he certainly experiences himself as walking and not, as a small child might, as consciously and deliberately propelling his body forward." "Chess grandmasters, engrossed in a game, can lose entirely the awareness that they are manipulating pieces on a board and see themselves rather as involved participants in a world of opportunities, threats, strengths, weaknesses, hopes, and fears. When playing rapidly, they sidestep dangers in the same automatic way that a teenager, himself an expert, might avoid missiles in a familiar video game . . ."[68] "Expert nurses will sometimes sense that a patient lies in danger of an imminent relapse and urge remedial action upon a doctor. They cannot always provide convincing, rational explanations of their intuition, but very frequently they turn out to be correct."[69]

Having briefly described the skill acquisition model presented in *Mind over Machine,* let us look at the debate between Dreyfus and McDowell, which focuses on the nature of our perception and its relation to the world as it pertains to action. McDowell's position is that our perceptual experience and agency are permeated with rationality. Dreyfus, on the other hand, in line with the above, asserts that at higher levels of performance we are absorbed in mindless embodied coping. Embodied cognition as opposed to the information processing of the computer model of the mind emphasizes the features of the body's coping with the world beyond the brain itself. Dreyfus claims that there is a "ground-floor level" of coping that is "preconceptual, preobjective/presubjective, prelinguistic,"[70] and he accuses McDowell of focusing exclusively on "the conceptual upper floors of the edifice of knowledge," ignoring "the embodied coping going on on the ground floor."[71]

Dreyfus expresses the view that monitoring what we are doing "leads to performance which is at best competent. When we are following the advice of a coach, for example, our behavior regresses to mere competence. It is only after much practice, and after abandoning monitoring and letting ourselves be drawn back into full involvement in our activity, that we can regain our expertise. The resulting expert coping returns to being direct and unreflective," which he takes to be "the same as being nonconceptual and nonminded."[72] In this sense, "the enemy of expertise is thought."[73]

In chapter 5, we referred to McDowell's treatment of "openness to the world," an openness that accounts for the possibility of thought. Dreyfus contends that from a phenomenological perspective "what we are directly open to is not rational or even conceptual; it is not part of the world at all as McDowell understands 'world.'"[74] According to such an understanding, he points out, the rational world is made up of "facts about what affords what"—a fact such as an opening in a wall "affords" us passage through it. He argues that "instead of the affordance-facts that on McDowell's view we are directly open to, it is the affordance's *solicitations*—such as the attraction of an apple when I'm hungry—to which I am directly open." It follows that the world is "the totality of interconnected solicitations that attract or repulse us. Thus, the solicitations and the world they make up are inseparable from our ability to be directly solicited."[75]

McDowell supports the project that seeks insights into the "phenomenology of our embodied coping." But he maintains that such insights should not be construed as a "corrective to the thought that our orientation towards the world is permeated with conceptual rationality, but as a supplementation . . ."[76] He rejects the assumption that reason operates only in those cases "in which one acts some content fully specifiable in detachment from the situation."[77] He does not believe in the conception of rationality as situation-independent.

He further denies that his view of openness to the world is openness to a world of facts, requiring in a sense "separation from anything with practical significance." He considers a "subject to whom the world is disclosed an agent"; for an agent trying to get to the other side of a wall, "the fact that a hole in the wall is of a certain size will be a solicitation." Therefore, according to McDowell, Dreyfus' insistence on a distinction between affordances and solicitations, the former drawing on rational capacity, and the latter on motor skill intentionality, seems pointless. This is an attitude that keeps the "contemplative" state in opposition to a state in which one is "practically engaged."[78]

For McDowell, "the fact that perception discloses the world to us is intelligible only in a context that includes the embodied coping competence." However, responsiveness to affordances, although similar in some of its features to how nonrational animals perform, is not the mere coping with an environment; it is an openness to the world that "transforms the character of the disclosing that perception does for us." Further familiarity with affordances, such as the size of a hole in the wall, "comes to be a background to what there is." In a distinctly human way of being, then, affordances "are no longer merely input to a human animal's natural motivational tendencies; now they are data for her rationality, not only her practical rationality but her theoretical rationality as well."[79]

We do not need to get into the technical details of the different ways in which McDowell and Dreyfus use such terms as "affordances" and "solicitations." No doubt, we gain valuable insights from Dreyfus' account, and his argument against naïve versions of artificial intelligence. However, as far as the debate between the two philosophers is concerned, we must side with McDowell despite the difficult language in which he expresses his thoughts. To create such a definitive model of learning, as Dreyfus does, admittedly based on a large set of cases with certain predetermined similarities, is not warranted. Even in the specific case, say a nurse, the model applies to some aspect of her practice, and not the totality of her "being, doing, and knowing" as an agent. Dreyfus' view suggests an inherent contradiction between situational embodied coping that makes us reach the summit of an expert and the disembodied intellect used in decontextualized thinking. He claims that the latter, which involves the capacity to monitor what we are doing, can only take us to the level of "competence." As human beings, we have the freedom to step back from our actions and reflect on them, but we also have the freedom to get involved in non-conceptual bodily-coping, without which we will not attain to expert performance. Dreyfus in his argument against McDowell creates a dichotomy between "thought" and "action," presumably deep in our psyche: There is the world of "propositional structures" and the world of "solicitations to act." Dreyfus sees openness to the world, as a state of "being" in which, at a given time, there is contact with one part of the world and not the other. We must "distinguish motor intentionality, and the interrelated solicitations our coping body is intertwined with, from conceptual intentionality and the world of propositional structures it opens onto."[80]

Dreyfus' position could easily give credence to the popular view that certain higher levels of thought are entirely removed from context, and that engagement with the world at lower stages of performance is purely rote. What is puzzling is that in trying to move away from the reductive reconstruction of the mind in cognitive psychology's computer model, he consolidates another reductive position. He extends his skill acquisition model to every action. How useful would it be for us, for example, to use the analogy of an expert basketball player when we are concerned with the protagonist of moral empowerment engaged in thought and action directed toward his or her twofold moral purpose?

That the powers of the mind are operative in everything we do, even in actions seemingly requiring less reflective thought, is only one aspect of the relationship between thought and action. The other more significant aspect, at least for the purposes of this inquiry, is the *pervasiveness* of context in all we undertake, especially those activities that demand high levels of abstraction. The perceptible is never a single, independent sense datum; the perceiving agent could not perceive it without an understanding, albeit tacit, of the wider context surrounding it, context which is "taken for granted, but for the most part not focused on."[81] But context cannot be understood by the students only in physical or even social terms, although this would be highly desirable; it should expand to include the extended reality examined in chapter 5. Otherwise, there is always the danger in education of reducing context-bound understanding of complex concepts and the corresponding actions to a number of predetermined algorithms. Is the context, one can ask, in which a driver masters the skills of driving really no different from the context in which a nurse is to acquire the knowledge, the insights, the attributes, and spiritual qualities that tending to the healing of people requires? To take the example even further, what constitutes context for the empowerment of the disenfranchised peoples of the world? Why should the learner, say FUNDAEC's Promoters of Community Well-Being, be free at any stage of the learning process from such context? Is that not precisely what needs to be avoided?

FUNDAEC seems to have been well aware of the significance of context in the development of understanding. For example, in a series of lectures on the subject of Bahá'í-inspired curricula the following ideas are presented:

There are at least two extremely powerful tools that the human mind uses to achieve understanding. One is analysis, breaking things into smaller parts and then examining the relations and interactions of these parts. The other is placing things in larger and larger contexts in order to gain insights into causes and reasons for their existence and behavior. Now suppose that you want to understand the internal workings of a clock—just that, not its social function or the physical laws that govern it. It is obvious that your approach has to be one of analysis. You take the clock apart, examine each part, figure out its function and then put the clock back together again. But suppose you want to understand why someone behaves in a certain way. Undoubtedly you could use some of the methods of analysis to break up that behavior into its component parts—its rational component, its emotional component, and so on. But could you possibly arrive at a satisfactory understanding of a person's behavioral patterns without examining, for example, his or her background, culture, and family situation, each of which serves as a context within which the individual's behavior can be understood?

This is one example of how different methods are needed to facilitate the comprehension of different categories of objects of understanding. Now suppose you wish to understand a certain theory of social progress. In the case of the clock your study was almost entirely objective. You did not need to "go inside yourself" and examine your own feelings and convictions. In fact to have done so would have confused you and hampered your understanding. Whether you like things that monotonously tick away forever, or whether you are fed up with the pressures of a society that puts too much emphasis on time, has nothing to do with your attempt to understand the workings of a clock. But to understand a social theory, a process which, in spite of what many claim, inherently involves valuation, you need to look inside yourself and examine your own world view, your views of social reality, and your basic attitudes towards life and its purpose. In fact, only if you do this carefully, will you be fair and objective. Otherwise, you will end up hiding behind pretentious veils of false objectivity.

I hope these examples of distinct approaches to investigating reality clearly demonstrate that teaching/learning approaches and methods must be suited to the category of the object of understanding being addressed by a given educational activity. I have already mentioned that this is self-evident but, for some reason, it is often neglected by educators. One of the results of this neglect is that over the past decades an increasing number of educational systems throughout the world have dedicated themselves to shaping minds and characters that are slaves to the analytical method. The basic approach of these often very sharp-minded individuals to intellectual inquiry is to zero in on more and more minute parts of reality, to the point that they seem incapable of seeing things in larger and larger contexts. In general, they tend to be almost totally ahistorical and demonstrate little capacity to see the moral and ethical implications of their actions. They are capable of denying to themselves the most noble human sentiments in the name of the "bottom line" and expediency. The havoc these apparently polished and educated minds, with alarmingly narrow ranges of understanding, have brought to both our physical and social environments is only gradually being recognized. The harm they will continue to inflict on society in the future is difficult to estimate as their grip on numerous fields of human endeavor becomes increasingly strong.[82]

One lesson of a text dedicated to the development of capabilities related to the power of expression illustrates how FUNDAEC has tried to nurture the understanding of the significance of context in its students. In this lesson, the students are asked to reflect on the acts of service they undertake in the community by describing these acts in wider and wider contexts. A case is provided in which a promoter of community well-being has held conversations in the community on the subject of sanitation. The first description they are asked to consider is one emphasizing the circumstantial aspects of the action:

241

On Monday afternoon I visited the community of La Dominga. I spoke with eight adults and twelve youth, spending approximately twenty minutes with each of them. We spoke about the importance of environmental sanitation and the possibility of organizing a study group on this subject. That evening at 7:00 p.m., we had a meeting at the Community Center and after a pleasant discussion, in which all those present actively participated, we decided to hold a study class every Monday and Wednesday at 7:30 p.m. beginning next week.[83]

The students are then reminded that the information in the above description simply answers a certain kind of questions: When did the conversation take place? Where? With how many people did the promoter speak? For how long? What did she or he speak about with each person? When and where did the meeting take place? When will the study class be held? When will it begin? This type of information, they are told, is useful for a variety of purposes, for example, for gathering statistical data or administering a community educational program in a region. However, it is possible to describe the same action in a wider context, placing the event in the context of the promoter's own education. In this context, elements considered before take on added meaning, and new, maybe more important meanings, appear:

It is my personal conviction that one of the most significant activities in my life, which allows me to work with the greatest personal satisfaction, is that of contributing to the education of a community. It is very disturbing to observe the precarious sanitary conditions in which many children are raised. I think that by teaching courses on sanitation I can effectively contribute to the welfare of my fellow human beings. Therefore, I have decided to organize a study and action group on environmental sanitation in a nearby village. On Monday afternoon I visited the commu-

242

nity of La Dominga. I spoke with eight adults and twelve youth, spending approximately twenty minutes with each of them. We spoke about the importance of environmental sanitation and the possibility of organizing a study group on this subject. That evening at 7:00 p.m., we had a meeting at the Community Center and after a pleasant discussion, in which all those present actively participated, we decided to hold a study class every Monday and Wednesday at 7:30 p.m. beginning next week. After the meeting, I went back home and thought about the challenge of facilitating community education. Assuming this responsibility will require that I continue to develop certain attributes such as constancy, integrity, and patience. I must pursue my own education more vigorously than before.[84]

After an exercise in which the students are asked to compare the nature of the two conversations, a third one is presented:

Some of the most serious health problems afflicting our communities result from poor sanitary conditions. The high rate of disease, especially among children, requires vigilant action by community organizations and by individuals who are familiar with health problems and are motivated by a spirit of service. For this reason, one of the objectives of a rural educational program must be to help the students and the communities it serves learn about environmental sanitation. This is one of the subjects I like most in my studies at FUNDAEC. It is my personal conviction that one of the most significant activities in my life, which allows me to work with the greatest personal satisfaction, is that of contributing to the education of a community. It is very disturbing to observe the precarious sanitary conditions in which many children are raised. I think that by teaching courses on sanitation I can effectively contribute to the welfare of my fellow human beings. Therefore,

I have decided to organize a study and action group on environmental sanitation in a nearby village. On Monday afternoon I visited the community of La Dominga. I spoke with eight adults and twelve youth, spending approximately twenty minutes with each of them. We spoke about the importance of environmental sanitation and the possibility of organizing a study group on this subject. That evening at 7:00 p.m., we had a meeting at the Community Center and after a pleasant discussion, in which all those present actively participated, we decided to hold a study class every Monday and Wednesday at 7:30 p.m. beginning next week. After the meeting, I went back home and thought about the challenge of facilitating community education. Assuming this responsibility will require that I continue to develop certain attributes such as constancy, integrity, and patience. I must pursue my own education more vigorously than before. Also, I am more convinced than ever of the great human potential and vast resources of rural communities, for many of those who attended the meeting seemed to be people willing to learn not only for themselves, but also for the betterment of society. I also believe that the meeting had a very positive effect, generating more unity in the community. We all agreed that achieving success in our endeavour to better our lives and those of our children will require resolution, concerted effort, and sacrifice.[85]

After another exercise comparing the nature of this description with the previous ones, the students are asked each to choose an act of service in which they have recently participated, write descriptions of it in ever widening contexts, and then divide into small groups to discuss what they have written. Thus, upon completing the lesson, the students have not only examined the context of certain descriptions, but have also thought about the significance of "community service" for their actions and their studies at FUNDAEC. And, as the lesson itself reminds them, their understanding of the word "context" has deepened a great deal.

The many and varied ways in which an individual's powers of the mind come into play differ according to circumstances, but it is the understanding of the wider context surrounding it that furnishes each action with meaning. A grasp of the intimate connection between thought and action in the context of an extended reality, itself not broken into a world of "inanimate causal interactions" and an "animate," "enchanted" world of reason, as elaborated in chapter 5, is fundamental to any genuine effort at integration in education.

CHAPTER 8

CAPABILITIES

Our examination of the philosophical framework of an educational process concerned with moral empowerment up to now has been mostly focused on three interrelated themes: the subject, the object, and the process of understanding. In our search for the "subject of understanding," we abandoned a number of candidates proposed, explicitly or implicitly, by various trends in education some of the presuppositions and arguments of which were analyzed. While the exploration so far has brought to light several inadequacies of the candidates we have considered, not enough has been said about the characteristics of the subject of understanding envisioned—the participant in the process of moral empowerment and its principal protagonist. It seems apparent that if this protagonist is not to be merely characterized by a set of virtues, competencies, and skills, we need a way of thinking that would not confine us to these categories, and a language sufficiently expansive that would enable us to describe the progress of the subject of understanding on the path of moral empowerment, a path on which individual growth and contribution to social transformation are inseparably linked. It is argued in this chapter that the concept of capability—the notion that the moral empowerment of an individual may be described in terms of a wide range of capabilities he or she acquires progressively—is central to this way of thinking.

The exploration in this inquiry of the characteristics of the subject of understanding, as mentioned before, takes for granted the validity of the claim that humanity as a whole is entering its age of maturity and that during this transition the great majority of the human race will need to develop capacities that the required transformation demands from them. In fact, the convulsions of the present-day society are in part, according to this outlook, effects of the forces that destroy barriers to such realization of potential and, while undeniably causing a great deal of suffering, finally serve to open possibilities for the gradual construction of a global civilization of unprecedented material and spiritual achievements. But this vision, no matter how fundamental at the level of conviction, is too general and has to be brought to bear on the immediate concerns of Bahá'í-inspired educational endeavors, key elements of the framework of which we are examining here. The arena of action where the educational process unfolds is, to a large extent, the community in which the student is immersed and many of the educational goals are related to the social, economic, cultural, and spiritual development of the community. We have already included, in our examination of science and religion as two complementary sources of knowledge, a brief discussion of "development" with its emphasis on modernization. As we now turn once again to the theme of the "subject of understanding," we need to seek a more appropriate conception of development as the immediate context within which many Bahá'í-inspired educational programs would be elaborated. The starting point for the analysis of the concept of capability, then, will be a discussion of its place in the discourse on development.

As already mentioned in chapter 1, Bahá'í-inspired efforts adhere to the idea that man's inner life is organic with the environment, and that lasting change can only occur as a result of the mutual transformative interaction of the two. However, it is difficult to translate the conviction that in a process of transformation the human heart cannot be segregated from the environment outside it into activity conducive to the social and economic development of a people. One condition is clearly necessary at the level of thought: An educational program concerned with releasing the potentialities of individuals to contribute to the betterment of their communities needs to be embedded in an appropriate paradigm that would govern the development of the society in which these communities function. Above all, the subject of understanding imbued with the desired twofold moral purpose is to be a protagonist of the development of his or her people, not according to all theories of development, but those for which the empowerment of the people themselves is a central concern.

Much has been said about the failure of development, particularly the global programs that began in the mid-twentieth century. At least at the level of theory, the idea is sometimes expressed that the very notions of "developed" and "underdeveloped" suggest that nations and people are judged by standards, which, claiming objectivity, are formulated by outsiders. The distorted and self-contradictory perception of reality at the heart of such divisions has been vehemently criticized for the way it has shaped the practice of development. Gustavo Esteva, for example, states that underdevelopment began on January 20, 1949 when President Truman in his inaugural speech announced a bold new program to make the benefits of the scientific advances and industrial progress of his nation available for the improvement and growth of the underdeveloped areas. He remarks:

On that day, two billion people became underdeveloped . . . from that time on, they ceased being what they were, in all their diversity, and were transmogrified into an inverted mirror of others' reality: a mirror that belittles them and sends them off to the end of the queue, a mirror that defines their identity, which is really that of a heterogeneous and diverse majority, simply in the terms of a homogenizing and narrow minority.[1]

Social and economic development approaches that divide reality in this way and define the identity of the inhabitants of so many regions of the world as underdeveloped people reduced to "individual units with input requirement," to "points below or above the poverty line" and to "mathematical aggregates revealing the rate of growth of a country" are incompatible with the kind of education being discussed in this inquiry. If we had to question the suitability of candidates for the subject of understanding suggested by certain educational theories because of the incomplete picture of the human being they painted, how much more will we have to stay away from the type of characterization in which individuals are depicted as immersed in the throes of underdevelopment—a state of malaise from which mainstream development efforts are supposedly trying to save them. In fact, the subject of understanding we are seeking has no resemblance to the social character that, fabricated to benefit from development's global programs, engraves in the mind images of need and dependency which serve to justify the enterprise and perpetuate it.

Development as Freedom

A notable departure from theories that fail to see the majority of the inhabitants of the planet as potential protagonists of development is Amartya Sen's conception of *development as freedom*. For Sen, development is principally the process through which people's real and substantive freedoms are expanded. By adopting this definition, he distances himself from views that identify development with "growth of national products," with "rise in personal income," with "industrialization," with "technological advance," and "social modernization." These, he points out, are means—not the only ones—through which freedoms are expanded, but they are often mistaken for goals. There are other factors that contribute to development, for example, social and economic arrangements that make available education and healthcare, as well as political and civil rights. Sen contends that viewing "development in terms of expanding substantive freedoms directs attention to the ends that make development important, rather than merely to some of the means that, inter alia, play a prominent part in the process."[2] He draws on Aristotle's statement that "wealth is evidently not the good we are seeking; for it is merely useful and for the sake of something else,"[3] in order to argue that ends and means should be distinguished if we are to achieve a comprehensive grasp of the nature of development which cannot be reduced to economic growth.

Placing the concept of freedom at the heart of development thinking moves it in a direction that allows greater focus on the protagonists of the process. It makes it possible to incorporate into the theory such factors as the "liberty to participate in political affairs" and the "opportunity to receive basic education or healthcare," not only as contributors to economic growth but more fundamentally as "constitutive components" of development. Freedoms are counted among the primary ends of development as well as its principal means. A conception of development as a process through which freedoms are expanded does not neglect poverty, but demands its removal, along with conditions like tyranny, as sources of "unfreedom." It represents a shift from the more traditional approaches that adopt variables such as utility, primary goods, procedural liberty, and real income as informational base for evaluation. Moreover, expansion of freedoms fosters individual initiative and social effectiveness. It enhances the "ability of people to help themselves and also to influence the world."[4]

These features, among others to be discussed below, suggest that Sen's theory of development may serve as a suitable background to the exploration of the characteristics of the subject of understanding in the process of moral empowerment. Yet, to draw upon certain insights from Sen's theory does not imply adherence to it. There are also causes for uneasiness. Pursuit of individual freedom, even when it is in accord with the highest social ideals, can easily turn into the promotion of individualism. To be fair, Sen avoids the individualistic slant that one would expect from an approach to development with the notion of individual freedom at its core by situating his discourse in the context of the lives of distinct groups, particularly marginalized majorities suffering from a host of deprivations in so many nations. In doing so, he provides a picture of the empirical connections that link freedoms of different kinds. Social opportunities and participation in political processes, for example, promote economic security, just as provision of economic opportunities to take part in trade and production contributes not only to the generation of personal wealth, but also to the enhancement of public life. His treatment of "development as freedom" acknowledges, in addition to the centrality of people's ability to choose and act, the indispensable role social arrangements and social structures play in providing opportunities for people's participation in the development process.[5]

Notwithstanding the depth of Sen's analysis, an approach that would use freedom as a super-value, an umbrella under which all other values exist without any tension, faces certain problems. Nussbaum mentions some of the difficulties: "Some freedoms limit others." For example, the "freedom of rich people to make large donations to political campaigns limits the equal worth of the right to vote. . . . The freedom of the landowners to keep their land limits projects of land reform that might be argued to be central to many freedoms for the poor." Not all freedoms are "desirable social goals" and they cannot be given equal status. Some freedoms "lie at the heart of a view of political justice, and others do not. Among the ones that do not lie at the core, some are simply less important, but others may be positively bad."[6] Sen, of course, would respond that only certain freedoms such as the liberty to participate in political affairs, to achieve basic nutrition, or to receive basic education and healthcare fall in the category of "substantive" freedoms. But such an argument would only illustrate how, as stated by Gasper and Staveren, Sen "can bring values other than those related to the independent self under his language of freedom. . . ." As they explain, when "our agenda is not only evaluation, but also explanation and prescription . . . a more differentiated language becomes essential."[7]

"Development as freedom" has clearly proven to be a valuable approach to the evaluation of development strategies and goals, as demonstrated by the prominence "human development" has received over the years. However, in considering the development process itself, and within it the question of education, "explanations and prescriptions" do become necessary and a number of values, either implied by "freedom" or not addressed by it at all, have to be brought into focus. This seems possible if the analysis of development goes beyond the exploration of enlightened social policies and their relevance to progress in the material realm. Of particular importance, at least as indicated by the premises of this inquiry, is the explicit treatment of an extended reality which, as elaborated in chapter 5, would not only embrace the material and social dimensions of civilization in the construction of which the protagonist of development will have to participate, but would also pay sufficient attention to the spiritual dimension of human existence. Once such a step is contemplated, we can argue, development strategy would need to seek coherence between the material and the spiritual. And it would not be possible to respond to this demand adequately if religion were seen as nothing more than a set of beliefs one should have the freedom to choose, and less so if it were treated as a mere instrument for the achievement of material progress. Yet even a sophisticated theory such as Sen's could ultimately assign only an instrumental role to religion in the development process.

Dennis Goulet describes how religious beliefs are often viewed as means that could accelerate or slow down the achievement of development goals set by those outside a given value system.

Even development agents who are sensitive to local values usually derive their goals from outside these values: from development models or the common assumptions of their respective scientific disciplines. Thus, a demographer will strive to "harness" local values to his objective of promoting contraception or achieving zero population growth. Similarly, the agronomist will search for a traditional practice upon which to "graft" his recommendation to use chemical pesticides. Similarly, the community organizer will "mobilize" a population for political ends around traditionally cherished symbols.[8]

In development strategy, science too is often viewed from an instrumental perspective. It is ever present in name, but mostly in the shadow of technology—an unfortunate condition contributing much to the ascendance of technique over substance. The consequences of an instrumental view of science are detectable, of course, not only in development thought but in many fields of human endeavor. In his book "*Scientific Knowledge and Its Social Problem,*" Jerome R. Ravetz offers penetrating insights into the problems such a view is bringing to scientific inquiry itself. Although his concern is with the natural sciences, the perils he mentions exist in the area of human and social sciences as well. "The activity of modern natural science has transformed our knowledge and control of the world about us," he states, "but in the process it has also transformed itself; and it has created problems which natural science alone cannot solve." A particular concern in this respect is the way the "production" of scientific knowledge increasingly assumes the attributes of industrial production. But as a "product of a socially organized activity, scientific knowledge is very different from soap." The profound difference has to be understood, but according to Ravetz, neither the academic science of the past, nor the industrialized system of production of today have the tools or the attitudes that would lead to such understanding. "The illusion that there is a natural science standing pure and separate from all involvement with society is disappearing rapidly; but it tends to be replaced by the vulgar reduction of science to a branch of commercial or military industry. Unless science itself is to be debased and corrupted, and its results used in a headlong rush to social and ecological catastrophe, there must be a renewed understanding of the very special sort of work, so delicate and so powerful, of scientific inquiry."[9]

A common feature of development thinking that is slowly taking shape in Bahá'í communities around the world is the conviction that in seeking coherence between the spiritual and the material, the flow of scientific and spiritual knowledge needs to be the main concern of development strategy. Like Sen's, this kind of thinking does not deny the significance of economic activity but suggests that it should be given its proper place in the context of the production and distribution of means. By focusing on the flow of knowledge, this conception of development, the elements of which are barely taking shape in grassroots efforts of the Bahá'í communities worldwide, brings to the fore the role of science and religion as complementary sources of knowledge in the development process, and regards the participation of a people in the generation and application of knowledge as vital to their progress. This emphasis on knowledge opens ways to examining the subject of understanding beyond that which the concept of development as freedom seems able to do. The assumption is that as a population becomes empowered to participate in the generation, application, and diffusion of knowledge, it will be able to create the conditions in which it can exercise the substantive freedoms called for by Sen. But the process would achieve more. It would make explicit within the population the values now hidden under the umbrella of freedom, and would shed much needed light on the concept of freedom itself.

As Bernard Williams has explained, various conceptions or understandings of freedom "involve a complex historical deposit."[10] Take, for example, Sen's substantial freedom to participate in political affairs. So much of today's discussion on this kind of freedom has its roots in the political thought of liberal democracy. Such a framework is tied to conceptions of power which can be analyzed and evaluated through intricate arguments of political science, some of which were included in the cursory treatment of the subject in chapter 2. But development thinking that would accept the complementarity of science and religion, as discussed in chapter 6, would also use the language of religion to gain insights into the nature of both power and freedom. In the language of religion, one can find explanations of the kind of freedom that inspires human beings to transcend various forms of bondage resulting in inaction or harmful action in the world. We may, for example, explain the consequences of greed on the physical environment from a scientific perspective, but it is the language of religion that helps us see it as inner bondage, curtailing our freedom. The language of religion confirms the incompleteness of the objective view of reality, no matter how far we advance in that view. With its aid, we do not only seek external freedom: "the absence of obstacles to doing what we want," as Nagel puts it. We seek the ability to detach ourselves from "the motives and reasons and values" that influence our choices and "submit to them only if they are acceptable."[11] Consider the insights into freedom one can get from the following passages:

O My Servant! Purge thy heart from malice and, innocent of envy, enter the divine court of holiness.[12]

O Son of Spirit! Burst thy cage asunder, and even as the phoenix of love soar in the firmament of holiness. Renounce thyself and, filled with the spirit of mercy, abide in the realm of celestial sanctity.[13]

O Children of Desire! Put away the garment of vainglory, and divest yourselves of the attire of haughtiness.[14]

O children of understanding! If the eyelid, however delicate, can deprive man's outer eye from beholding the world and all that is therein, consider then what would be wrought if the veil of covetousness were to descend upon his inner eye. Say: O people! The darkness of greed and envy becloudeth the radiance of the soul even as the clouds obstruct the light of the sun. Should anyone hearken unto this utterance with a discerning ear, he will unfurl the wings of detachment and soar effortlessly in the atmosphere of true understanding.[15]

O My Servant! Thou art even as a finely tempered sword concealed in the darkness of its sheath and its value hidden from the artificer's knowledge. Wherefore come forth from the sheath of self and desire that thy worth may be made resplendent and manifest unto all the world.[16]

Agency

Sen's "freedom-centered" conception of development represents at the same time an "agent-oriented" approach. He makes a distinction between his use of the term "agency" and how it is employed in, say, the economics literature, where it is attached to an individual who is acting on someone else's behalf and whose achievements are to be assessed in light of someone else's goals. Rather, the agent is "someone who acts and brings about change, and whose achievements can be judged in terms of her own values and objectives, whether or not we assess them in terms of some external criteria as well."[17] Sen claims that when processes that advance substantive freedoms also provide social opportunities, individuals will be able to shape their own futures; they will no longer be seen as constituents of an "inert population," objects of "fine-tuned 'targeting'"[18] of policy makers, and "passive recipients of the benefits of cunning development programs."[19] By the same token, the removal of "unfreedom" in its various forms is essential as these wipe away people's choices and do not allow them to exercise "their reasoned agency."[20] For example, viewing the rights of women in a larger context by including their role as free agents alongside other entitlements related to their well-being has helped transform the conception of women from "passive recipients of welfare-enhancing help" to "active agents of change: the dynamic promoters of social transformations that can alter the lives of *both* women and men."[21]

Like freedom, the concept of agency helps define development in a way that could admit the notion of education as a process of moral empowerment. It brings into development thinking a conception of the human being as an active rather than a passive entity, as someone able to draw on his or her physical, mental, and moral resources to effect change, rather than a patient who, bereft of such resources, is waiting to be saved by others. Yet, here too, one has to be aware of the dangers of an individualistic interpretation of social existence. In formulating a conception of education for development, it is necessary to extend the notion of agency to the collective life of humanity. Communities and the institutions of society together with the individual constitute the three protagonists of the development process. The empowerment of the individual must occur simultaneously with that of the other two. In a world where the individual continuously clamors for more and more freedom and institutions seek ever-growing control, directly or through propaganda and manipulation, the combination of agency and freedom as concepts central to the social and economic development of peoples needs to be adopted with care.

Capability

A third concept closely connected to freedom and agency is "capability." Sen laments that the "technocratic sound" of the word does not contribute to the sense in which the expression was picked by him in order to "explore a particular approach to well-being and advantage in terms of a person's ability to do valuable acts or reach valuable states of being." For him, the capability represents "the alternative combinations of things a person is able to do or be—the various 'functionings' he or she can achieve."[22] Functionings in this context correspond to "parts of the state of a person—in particular the various things that he or she manages to do or be in leading a life."[23] They embrace such elemental states as being adequately nourished, being in good health, having mobility, as well as more complex ones, say, being happy, achieving self-respect or being socially integrated.[24] Here is how Sen defines the concept of capability: "In the space of functionings any point, representing an n-tuple of functionings, reflects a combination of the person's doings and beings, relevant to the exercise [of evaluation]. The capability is a *set* of such functioning n-tuples, representing the various alternative combinations of beings and doings any one (combination) of which the person can choose."[25]

According to Sen "the freedom to lead different types of life is reflected in the person's capability set";[26] a person deprived of a capability set is not free to lead the type of life she values. His treatment of poverty, not synonymous with low income but as "capability deprivation," demonstrates the power of his approach to the evaluation of development strategy. Income is only an instrument in generating capabilities, and in formulating policy one should be aware that "the instrumental relation between low income and low capability is *variable* between different communities and even between different families and different individuals." Variations such as age, gender, social role, and physical location should be taken into consideration in efforts aimed at poverty reduction. Age, disability, or illness not only reduce the ability to earn an income, they also make it harder to convert income into capability. Thus real poverty in terms of capability deprivation may be significantly "more intense than what appears in the income space."[27] Further, the income approach to poverty pays little attention to the distribution of income within the family. For example, if the family income is used predominantly on boys, then the extent of deprivation of girls will not be adequately taken into account. Such deprivations are better assessed by looking at "capability deprivation (in terms of greater mortality, morbidity, undernourishment, medical neglect, and so on)."[28] Finally, "*relative* deprivation in terms of *incomes* can yield *ab-*

solute deprivation in terms of *capabilities*." A relatively poor person in a rich country may earn a "high" income in terms of "world standards," but be deprived in terms of capabilities, including participation in the social life of the community.[29]

As Sen explains, the capability perspective in poverty analysis enhances the understanding of the nature and causes of poverty by "shifting primary attention away from *means* to *ends* that people have reason to pursue." Emphasis is now on the freedoms that enable a person to pursue the desired ends. And deprivation is "seen at a more fundamental level—one closer to the informational demands of social justice."[30]

Sen employs the concept of capability to explore the workings of development policy in impressive depth.[31] He speaks of "two different distinctions." The first is between "the promotion of the person's *well-being*" and "the pursuit of the person's overall *agency goals*," and the second between "*achievement*" and "*freedom to achieve*."[32] These two distinctions produce "a fourfold classification of points of evaluative interest in assessing human advantage":[33] well-being achievement, agency achievement, well-being freedom, agency freedom—each requiring different evaluative exercises for policy.

The "well-being achievement" is viewed in terms of "well-ness" of an individual's state of being and assessed by the different functionings—"the constituent elements of the person's being seen from the perspective of her own personal welfare." This does not imply that a person's well-being cannot be "other-regarding." However, one's concern for others would operate through some feature of one's own being. "Doing good may make a person contented or fulfilled, and these are functioning achievements of importance." Functionings, then, are seen as "central to the *nature* of well-being, even though the *sources* of well-being could easily be external to the person."[34] The claim here is that "the functionings make up a person's being, and the evaluation of a person's well-being has to take the form of an assessment of these constituent elements."[35]

When the purpose shifts from assessing well-ness to appraising the success in achieving individual goals, then the exercise is one of evaluating "agency achievement," rather than "well-being achievement." For the evaluation of the former, the category of functionings presents a rather restrictive space, since a person's agency goals may well include objectives that go beyond his or her own personal well-being. Apart from this distinction in the *space* of evaluation between well-being achievement and agency achievement, there are also differences when it comes to weighing their shared elements—functionings that are pertinent both to one's well-being and to one's other objectives.

Sen's analysis of the two latter points of evaluative interest—"well-being freedom" and "agency freedom"—sheds light on some of the reasons impelling him to go beyond mere achieved functionings and to introduce the concept of capability sets. "Achieved functionings" in isolation from freedom to choose states of doing and being do not prove adequate for all evaluation purposes. One has to assess both "well-being achievement" and "well-being freedom." That Sen includes freedom to achieve one's well-being and agency goals in his capability set points to the value he places on the exercise of choice. Freedom is crucial to both one's well-being achievement and one's agency achievement. "Acting freely and being able to choose" is directly conducive to well-being because "choosing is seen as a part of living" and "'doing x' is distinguished from 'choosing to do x and doing it.'"[36] To illustrate his point, Sen asks us to assume that two persons have identical actual functionings, which include the state of being in hunger. One is a rich individual who has decided to fast and another a poor starving person who cannot exercise such a choice. The functionings of the former are of a different quality; they are refined because they incorporate the exercise of choice. Sen contends that "the well-being a person actually enjoys is often more closely related to such *refined* functioning achievements." This view supports the idea "that good life is inter alia also a life of freedom."[37] He admits that freedom of choice is an ambiguous concept and states that his view of it is different from that of a standard consumer theory in which "the contribution of a set of feasible choices is judged exclusively by the value of the best element available."[38] "It is odd," he states, "to conclude that the freedom of a person is no less when she has to choose between three alternatives which she sees as 'bad,' 'awful,' and 'gruesome' than when she has the choice between three alternatives which she assesses as 'good,' 'excellent,' and 'superb.'"[39] The sophistication Sen introduces by incorporating choice in his "refined" capability set still leaves too many issues unresolved. It is one thing to assert that the development process has to eliminate the condition under which so many people do not even get to exercise their freedom of choice to pursue worthwhile goals, it is quite another to make "choosing states of beings and doings" so central an element of capabilities. Especially when it comes to education, which has to concern itself with the development of capabilities, a host of crucial questions have to be asked. Take Sen's own example of an individual who is enjoying his lunch by the bank of a river and decides to jump into the river to save a drowning person. This person has chosen not to continue having his lunch without anxiety, which would have presumably enhanced his well-being. But why is freedom of choice so central to his capabilities in this case? Should we not ask what motivated him to exercise his agency freedom in this way? The fact that he had freedom to choose does not explain why we tend to admire his action. Is not emphasis on "choice" itself rather than on "choosing between right and wrong" one of the characteristic features of emotivism that has given rise to the emotivist self according to MacIntyre? How would Sen propose to protect society from the ills of emotivism?

In Nussbaum's treatment of capabilities—somewhat different from Sen's—the question of choice also receives particular attention. Nussbaum employs Aristotle's conception of political distribution, the aim of which is not the simple allotment of commodities, but the enabling of people to function in certain ways. Sen adopts the concept of capabilities in order to define the space within which quality of life is assessed; Nussbaum uses it "as a foundation for basic political principles that should underwrite constitutional guarantees."[40] She formulates a list of "central human functional capabilities," stressing that any such list cannot be but "a proposal put forward in a Socratic fashion, to be tested against the most secure of our intuitions as we attempt to arrive at a type of reflective equilibrium[41] for political purposes."[42] The list covers capabilities having to do with life: bodily health; bodily integrity; senses, imagination, and thought; emotions; practical reason; affiliation; other species; play; and control over one's environment, political and material. The composition of the list is, according to Nussbaum, of "*separate components*" all of which have "central importance" and are "distinct in quality."[43] Although the items on the list are interrelated in many ways, the increase in one item does not make up for the deficiency in another below a certain basic level.

Nussbaum identifies the capabilities of practical reason and affiliation as paramount since "they both organize and suffuse all the others, making their pursuit truly human."[44] Her emphasis on practical reason—the ability to form a conception of the good and to engage in critical reflection about the planning of one's life—is particularly significant as it relates to "choice." Practical reason is the activity that is common to all functionings in a truly human sense. She points out that from an Aristotelian perspective there is "something less than fully human about a life devoted to pleasure alone, the life that many humans claim to want. It seems to leave out something that we think a human life should have. This something is hinted at in the work of 'choosing,' . . . namely the exercise of choice and practical reason."[45]

Nussbaum extends her conception of capability to the field of education, particularly education aimed at human development. She states:

> . . . an education for human development . . . has a twofold purpose. First, it must promote the human development of students. Second, it must promote in students an understanding of the goals of human development for all—as goals inherent in the

very idea of decent, minimally just society—and it must do this in such a way that when they are empowered to make political choices, they will foster these capabilities for all, not only for themselves.[46]

As to how education can accomplish this aim, she elaborates on the significance of three key abilities: the ability for critical thought, the ability to "see oneself as a member of a heterogeneous nation—and world—and to understand something of the history and character of diverse groups that inhabit it" and the ability to feel sympathy. The type of education to nurture these abilities is one in which through "carefully crafted instruction in arts and humanities" students are brought into contact with "issues of gender, race, ethnicity, and cross-cultural experience and understanding," and one in which critical thinking "informs the entire spirit of a school's pedagogy." She mentions that these abilities are being developed well in the liberal arts colleges and universities in the United States, while they are poorly treated in earlier stages of education, in the years K–12.[47]

Important as Nussbaum's arguments are, they deal with discrete ideas not easily translatable into curricular objectives and content. Moreover, they should be treated with caution. Attributes like "critical thinking" and "sympathy," and outcomes such as "choice" and "freedom" have their place in education. But, as mentioned in the discussion of Hirst's conception of integration in the previous chapter, focusing on them—along with qualities of the mind like creativity and imagination—as key goals determining educational content and methods is not as fruitful as it may seem at first.

Building Capacity

Having discussed the concept of capability in the context of development as freedom, we can now turn to the task we set for ourselves in the beginning of this chapter: to examine the claim that the moral empowerment of the individual may be described in terms of the progressive acquisition by the student of a wide-range of interrelated capabilities. To analyze this claim, however, we will describe these capabilities in a language that is not identical to the one used by Sen and Nussbaum.

What is being argued in this chapter is that it is possible to formulate an approach to moral empowerment that employs the concept of capability to make appropriate pedagogical choices. To advance toward such a formulation, however, the notion of capability has to be recast in terms that are of more immediate use in education. Here, we must turn once again to FUNDAEC's experience. Unfortunately, a straightforward account of how the organization developed the concept of capability is not easy to come by; it has not presented a systematic philosophical treatment of the concept, but has utilized it in the development of curricula and strategies. What we will do is to draw on some twenty-five units[48] constituting the content of a two-year program to prepare "Promoters of Community Well-Being" and relevant statements in documents elaborated by the organization in order to analyze the notion of capability and its relation to moral empowerment. The next chapter will be dedicated to the examination of certain pedagogical implications of the concept of capability as advanced here.

We have already mentioned in chapter 2 that FUNDAEC has used the concept of capability as "developed capacity to think and act in a particular sphere of activity and according to an explicit purpose." Capabilities in this particular sense refer to "complex spheres of thought and action." A capability is not something a student either has or does not have; it is developed progressively as one acquires a set of interrelated skills and abilities, assimilates the necessary information, advances in the understanding of relevant concepts, and acquires certain attitudes, habits, and spiritual qualities. The conclusion easily reached after one attempts to define the concept with more precision is that the exercise is counterproductive. FUNDAEC insisted from the outset that it would use the concept mostly as a heuristic device, a way of thinking about educational objectives and content, a strategy to organize elements of a curriculum according to a specified overall aim. Reflection on the way an ongoing discussion of capabilities has assisted FUNDAEC to tackle the challenges of integration in determining curricular content and methods leads to the realization that to be useful in making pedagogical choices, a given capability would not need to have a definable or measurable existence as might a skill, an attitude, or the knowledge of something. The attributes that would contribute to it—the skills, the assimilated information, the understanding of concepts, the attitudes, habits, and spiritual qualities—would not be its components; they would somehow interact and take on a comprehensive meaning in the context of action in the community. A capability would not be reducible to a list of such attributes.

Language, of course, allows the word capability to be used in a wide variety of ways. To be capable of doing something may refer to a simple skill or to a most complex set of functionings, one of the n-tuples proposed by Sen. One could be considered capable of identifying types of nutrients in foods being bought in the market, or could be called capable of critical thinking. In formulating objectives corresponding to a given educational aim, only capabilities in a certain range of "sizes" and certain levels of specificity would be useful. For example, "typing" is too small in size and would be relegated to the realm of skills; "critical thinking" is too broad and the capabilities that assist in its gradual realization would each be formulated in relation to a specific objective. Again, no formula would exist for determining the range; "rules of thumb" would emerge through action and reflection in the elaboration of educational content.

We have already discussed that the overall vision of a civilization manifesting the powers of humanity in its stage of maturity gives rise to certain immediate concerns of education bearing on the development of the community in its various aspects—social, economic, cultural, and spiritual. In the life of the individual student these concerns can be organized around the concept of "service to the community." As mentioned in chapter 4, the image being used widely in Bahá'í communities worldwide is that of walking a path of service. Walking this path implies study, action, and reflection on action. As one advances on the path of service, one acquires progressively the set of capabilities that "seeking personal growth" and "contributing to the transformation of society" necessitate.

Various kinds of capabilities are always present in a given set. A first category consists of capabilities that have to do with the moral dimension of the path of service. In any program of the kind being explored here, the students would have to become increasingly capable, for example, of building unity of thought and action while pursuing a common aim, of managing personal and community affairs with rectitude of conduct, of participating effectively in processes of community consultation, and of accompanying others in their acts of service without imposing one's own will. These and other similar capabilities are essential requirements of walking a path of service associated with moral empowerment. They also seem to be of the "right size" to be included among the objectives of an educational program, knowing that the objective would never be the definitive acquisition of a given capability, but advancing in it. The objectives of each unit would be expressed in terms of contributing in some measure to the understanding of the concepts, the assimilation of the information, the development of the skills, the habits, the attitudes, and the spiritual qualities that together make advancing in some set of capabilities possible.

A few words about one example, building unity of thought and action while pursuing a common aim, may be helpful here. To assist the students advance in this capability, the educational process would have to ensure that they give sufficient thought to such fundamental concepts as unity, diversity, unity in diversity, unity versus uniformity, unity of vision and purpose, unity of thought, and unity in action—

sometimes in theoretical discussions but often in practice in the context of the actual work for which they are being prepared. Skills, abilities, and habits would include those of listening carefully to others, of identifying elements of agreement in a given situation upon which unity can be built without trivializing differences, and of avoiding false dichotomies. A necessary attitude would be detachment, and one to be avoided at all costs a posture of superiority. General discussions as well as personal and collective reflection on the effectiveness of specific acts of service would contribute to the acquisition of the appropriate attitudes, but these would be fragile unless they are established on the firm foundation of spiritual qualities such as love, humility, and selflessness, pertaining to a state of being; to these the program would have to pay ample attention. Finally, the development of the capability would also imply a profound knowledge of the community including its history based on a great deal of accurate information accumulated systematically in the context of various acts of service.

A second category of capabilities to be addressed consists of those having direct bearing on the acts of service that give practical expression to the aims of a given program. To move from an aim, no matter how well stated, to the identification of the needed capabilities calls for a definite procedure. In the case of the "Promoter of Community Well-Being" program—community meaning a village or the neighborhood of a city in a micro-region with clearly definable social and economic challenges—FUNDAEC proceeded in the following way. It considered the chains of activity that people carry out in the micro-region and conceptually organized them into what it called "processes of community life." Examples of the wide range of such processes are production in small farms, preservation and improvement of the physical environment, socialization of small children, formal education of children and youth, individual and community healthcare, secondary production such as the processing of food, the buying and selling of primary and manufactured goods, artistic expression and cultural

enrichment. In every micro-region, FUNDAEC observed, the processes of community life are being affected by the forces of integration
and disintegration characterizing the age of humanity's transition
from childhood to maturity. In so many communities the destructive
forces, generated globally or locally, are the strongest, disempowering
the population and maintaining or deepening material poverty. FUN-
DAEC embarked on setting in motion, initially in one micro-region, a
"learning process" alongside each of the processes of community life
consisting of research and action close to the grassroots in which the
population itself would increasingly participate. The purpose of these
learning processes was to apply and generate knowledge, thereby creating forces that would empower the population to take ownership of
its own social and economic development. The moral empowerment
of the promoters of community well-being, the students of FUNDAEC,
would involve acquiring capabilities that would enable them to engage
in these learning processes, to promote them through acts of service,
and to help individuals and groups in the micro-region to participate
in them.

A brief look at the problem of environment helps illustrate this
approach. If a community is moving toward prosperity, people within
it should be engaged in chains of activity that not only maintain but,
in the long run, also improve the quality of the physical environment.
In most communities of the world forces, both from outside and from
within, are reversing the direction of this process leading to progressive
environmental deterioration. A promoter of community well-being
should be able to promote the kind of learning within the population
that leads to effective environmental action. One necessary capability,
FUNDAEC decided, would be that of raising the consciousness of a community about environmental issues, and another closely related to it,
the capability of making a diagnosis of the state of an ecosystem and
participating in the search for possible solutions to its problems. Again
these capabilities are of a "size" so as to become objectives of units of

curriculum that impart sufficient knowledge of the environment, nurture a deep enough understanding of the relevant scientific and moral concepts, and cultivate desirable skills, habits, attitudes, and spiritual qualities. As already mentioned, the objective of such units would not be the definitive acquisition of these capabilities; all that a student can do is to advance in them, and the units could only contribute to this advancement. The capabilities themselves need not be confined to the sphere of action at the level of the local community. The knowledge, the skills, the attitudes, the habits, and spiritual qualities required of the promoter capable of raising the consciousness of the local community about environmental issues, for example, represent the beginnings of what would be needed if life were to take him or her to become an executive of a sophisticated agency concerned with environmental policy at the national level.

A short mention of a few other capabilities directly concerned with acts of service in the "Promoter of Community Well-Being" program may shed further light on the nature of the approach undertaken. To participate in and promote effectively the learning process on production of food on small farms would require that the promoter be capable of both designing and cultivating certain plots suitable for the ecological, social, and cultural conditions of the micro-region, and of using these plots as educational tools for the propagation of appropriate agricultural practices. Through extensive research, FUNDAEC developed over some two decades a methodology for the cultivation of what it called "diversified high efficiency plots," applying the latest advances in the science of agriculture and animal husbandry, but with due regard for the rationality of small farmers and not in the manner of large commercial enterprises. Based on the results of its research, it elaborated units of text focused on the development of the above two capabilities. In relation to the process of the education of children and youth, to take another example, one aspect of the learning process set in motion by FUNDAEC had to do with preschool education. Relevant capabilities in this respect range from those needed by preschool teachers and administrators all the way to those required of individuals engaged in educational research and the development of curricula. In the education of promoters of community well-being, it was decided, two capabilities would have to be addressed. The first would include concepts, information, skills, and qualities that would enable them to carry out informal educational activities with small groups of children, and the other the attributes that would enable them to converse with parents on issues related to the education of young children. Two units under the title *Nurturing Young Minds* focus on the development of these two capabilities. Similar lines of reasoning led to the identification of other capabilities related, for example, to primary healthcare, to the strengthening of the local economy, and to theatre and other performing arts—the latter both as powerful tools for raising social consciousness and as elements of the learning process related to the enrichment of culture.

A significant characteristic of FUNDAEC's approach, and one that can be deduced from our discussion so far to be an essential element of the framework being explored in this inquiry, is that the development of capabilities in the two categories described above does not take the student far enough on the path of moral empowerment. There are a large number of capabilities associated with the intellectual heritage of humankind—say, with the forms of knowledge described by Hirst—some of which would have to be carefully selected and addressed according to the specific aims of a given program. Without these capabilities, it would be difficult to achieve a proper balance between *knowing* and *doing*, and between information, skills, and attitudes, on the one hand, and understanding and spiritual qualities, on the other. A few examples may be necessary to illustrate this point.

In the case of the promoters of community well-being, an intimate knowledge of the micro-region requires classification of a wide variety of things, from flora and fauna of the region to the occupations of its inhabitants. Classifying things is a capability built on certain basic mathematical concepts and logic, the understanding of which creates a foundation for its development. A unit dedicated to the enhancement of this capability, using the language of mathematics, mostly of set theory, containing an extensive treatment of taxonomy and guiding students in the collection and classification of data about the various physical and social features of the micro-region is among the first to be studied. The promoter would need other capabilities, also belonging to the realm of mathematics, that would, for example, enable him or her to make numerical statements of various degrees of precision about the world—capabilities that begin developing when a child learns to count, and reach extraordinary levels of complexity in the application of mathematical equations to the workings of the universe. Another example is the capability of applying arithmetic, including operations with fractions, to the analysis of data. One of the units that contributes to this capability treats systematically the subject of fractions as any good text of arithmetic would do, but now in relation to a rather extensive survey of the state of health in the community.

The promoter of community well-being is not to be a mere technician applying formulae to a process of transformation which calls for much more than technique. Thus the need for a set of capabilities associated with science, say, those of making organized observations of phenomena, of seeking patterns in data gathered about a phenomenon, of designing experiments to test a hypothesis and even of creating models within a theoretical structure. We will refer to these capabilities in the next chapter in the discussion of pedagogical choices. Here it suffices to mention that they are not merely treated instrumentally but in units that teach science at the appropriate level of rigor, fostering a scientific culture in the community the promoter is to serve. Another area in which the students have to develop a number of capabilities is language. The question of language, of course, arises in a number of ways in relation to the broad aim of moral empowerment; we have touched on the subject in chapter 6 in the context of the complementarity of science and religion, and will come back to it in the last chapter. Capabilities to be nurtured in any program that focuses on the twofold moral purpose explored in this inquiry have to do with describing the world around oneself—precisely when needed and in metaphors if required—with formulating ideas and expressing them clearly, with reading the literature of relevant fields at a good level of comprehension, and with depicting events and processes in their historical contexts.

Having described the nature of capabilities in the three broad categories—those related to the moral dimension of the path of service, those that have a direct bearing on the acts of service which give practical expression to the aims of a given program, and ones associated with the intellectual heritage of humankind—we can turn to the examination of certain pedagogical issues in the next chapter. Before bringing the present argument to a close, however, one point needs to be emphasized: The universe of concepts, information, skills, habits, attitudes, and spiritual qualities is not being divided here into sets each corresponding to a capability. Capability, as mentioned in the beginning of this chapter, is used heuristically to allow for a way of thinking about the attributes of the subject of understanding—the protagonist of moral empowerment—and their interrelations as one tries to formulate objectives and elaborate a curriculum for a program of specified aims. There is no call for a taxonomy of desired attributes. A given attribute clearly contributes to more than one capability; thus there is overlap among capabilities. Relationships, however, are not simple. The treatment of an attribute, say, understanding a certain concept or possessing a certain spiritual quality, varies as one focuses on different capabilities in the same curriculum. For example, the quality of honesty has to be addressed in the context of the capability of managing personal and community affairs with rectitude of conduct, together with related concepts, skills, and attitudes as well as the knowledge of issues involved in specific instances when the capability is to be exercised. Fostering the same quality needs to be treated together with other sets of attributes in the context of unity building, and yet others in relation to engagement in scientific inquiry. In the totality of these contexts, honesty as a spiritual quality is endowed with far more meaning than when it is addressed in the context of a single capability. In an appropriate pedagogy, then, the conception of capability serves to integrate theoretical and practical knowledge. This is of particular importance when we recognize that the way the concept is being used here does not confine it to functionings—the refined forms of which, according to Sen, are the freedoms to choose doings and beings that are of value to a person—but places it in a much wider space of learning in which *knowing, being,* and *doing* are brought together to contribute to a dual process of individual and social transformation.

CHAPTER 9

Pedogogical Choices

The previous chapter was dedicated to a general discussion of the concept of capability, first in the context of development following the ideas set forth by Sen and Nussbaum, and then, defined in a different manner, as a strategy to analyze and organize educational programs concerned with moral empowerment. Throughout this inquiry, we have sought insights from relevant literature so as to make explicit elements of a conceptual framework for such programs, and have said little about the teaching-learning experience per se. It seems necessary at this point to enter the hazy area that separates philosophy and pedagogy[1] in order to clarify the nature of some of the challenges we have already identified, particularly in dealing with the question of integration.

Even when it is taken for granted that the concept of capability provides a valuable mode of thinking about the organization of the teaching-learning experience and the formulation of objectives, there is no guarantee that its use will lead to a curriculum conducive to moral empowerment. For one thing, as it stands, the notion is vague and can easily transmute into other concepts, for example, competencies or life skills. Numerous pedagogical choices have to be made if the proper experience is to be created. A full discussion of such choices is beyond the scope of this book; what we can do is to select a few pedagogical issues of significance for our inquiry, hoping that by so doing we will be able to make explicit some features of the desired teaching-learning experience. But first a few words about the way one may envision progress in pedagogy to occur, at least in the space created by the expanding network of Bahá'í-inspired organizations. The approach that is gradually finding acceptance by these organizations calls for groups of educators working at the grassroots to identify educational needs, consult on them, develop a coherent set of ideas, and create a series of teaching-learning experiences in which these ideas are put into practice. Each group is to see itself engaged in a systematic process that involves action—carrying out educational activities and evaluating them—reflection on action, consultation and analysis of advances in educational theory, not as a linear sequence but often in parallel, leading to repeated modification of ideas, methods, and materials. In this way, through a series of approximations, curricular elements emerge to be shared with others in the network engaged in a similar process. The development of these elements, it is accepted, does not need to await the emergence of a comprehensive theory of education for moral empowerment; the process itself contributes significantly to theoretical advance as long as action is carried out within an evolving conceptual framework, the knowledge being generated from various experiences is systematized and shared, and theory, no matter how well established, is considered a source of insight and not a statement about reality as it is.

The attitude toward theory being promoted by this approach has its roots in the belief that a search for a pedagogy seeking moral empowerment will only be successful if those involved in the practice of education set aside a number of deeply-rooted dichotomies. Dewey expresses the challenge succinctly:

> Mankind likes to think in terms of extreme opposites. It is given to formulating its beliefs in terms of *Either-Ors*, between which it recognizes no intermediate possibilities. When forced to recognize that the extremes cannot be acted upon, it is still inclined to hold that they are all right in theory but that when it comes to practical matters circumstances compel us to compromise.[2]

276

In the field of education, this habit of thought seems to exert undue influence on theory, and even when not explicitly stated, certain dichotomies are able to engender endless debate on a host of other opposites. "Development from within" against "formation from without" is one such dichotomy as is its parallel "progressive education" vs. "traditional education" mentioned by Dewey. The concept of capability as elaborated and used by FUNDAEC has the potential to harmonize different elements related to the subject, object, and process of understanding—elements which educational debate has often held in opposition to each other. By bringing together, for example, the acquisition of skills, the assimilation of information, and the understanding of profound concepts in the formulation of each objective it helps one get away from such categorical statements as "schools must not aim at imparting knowledge but focus on offering tools for in-depth understanding and thought" or "schools should reduce the amount of material students are required to learn and teach them how to think." In an approach where theories are to be treated as sources of insight and not positions to be defended at all cost, it seems more useful to consider sets of related ideas with all the tension that naturally exists among them and see how a pedagogy is built out of their interactions. In this chapter we will only discuss two such sets of ideas.

Banking Education and Problem Posing

A first set of ideas to be sorted out in the search for a pedagogy centered on the development of capabilities is related to a dichotomy which is often expressed in terms of banking vs. problem-posing education or rote learning vs. critical thinking. In our analysis of the notion of power in relation to the aims of an educational program concerned with moral empowerment, we referred to the work of Paulo Freire and his exploration of the kind of education that would cultivate critical consciousness. In that context, he masterfully criticized certain approaches to education and examined the characteristics of an alter-

277

native, which served to revolutionize thinking about adult literacy. But the two notions—banking education and problem-posing—took on their own lives, and gradually became, as such extreme contrasts tend to do, synonymous with good and bad education. To make valid pedagogical choices that would allow the concept of capability to show its potential, any kind of debate that pitches process against content in education needs to be set aside.

Freire's account of banking education does not simply refer to its substance and method, but more significantly to the interactions between the teacher and the students. He seems to suggest that the role assumed by the teacher determines the nature of banking education. The teacher in this case is a narrator whose task is to "fill" the minds of students with the contents of his narration. Such contents, whether concerned with social, moral, or physical dimensions of reality become "detached from reality, disconnected from the totality that engendered them and could give them significance." Students receive, file, and store what teachers deposit in them and are themselves in the end "filed away through the lack of creativity, transformation, and knowledge . . ."[3]

Freire argues that inquiry and praxis are what makes us human and that knowledge "emerges only through invention and re-invention, through the restless, impatient, continuing, hopeful inquiry human beings pursue in the world, with the world, and with each other." The process of inquiry cannot begin when knowledge is considered a gift bestowed by the so-called knowledgeable upon the so-called ignorant. In such a relationship, the teacher "presents himself to his students as their necessary opposite; by considering their ignorance absolute, he justifies his own existence. The students, alienated like the slave in the Hegelian dialectic, accept their ignorance as justifying the teacher's existence—but, unlike the slave, they never discover that they educate the teacher." The contradiction is deeply ingrained in banking education and is reflected in the attitudes and practices that characterize oppressive societies. So, "the teacher teaches and the students are taught";

"the teacher knows everything and the students know nothing"; "the teacher thinks and the students are thought about"; "the teacher talks and the students listen—meekly"; "the teacher disciplines and the students are disciplined"; "the teacher chooses and enforces his choice, and the students comply"; "the teacher acts and the students have the illusion of acting through the action of the teacher"; "the teacher chooses the program content, and the students (who were not consulted) adapt to it"; "the teacher confuses the authority of knowledge with his or her own professional authority, which she and he sets in opposition to the freedom of the students"; "the teacher is the Subject of the learning process, while the pupils are mere objects."[4] In banking education, the teacher dulls students' critical abilities and stifles their creativity because he first grasps "a cognizable object while he prepares his lessons in his study or his laboratory," and then he expounds "to his students about that object." The students do not "practice any act of cognition, since the object towards which that act should be directed is the property of the teacher rather than a medium evoking the critical reflection of both teacher and students." The students merely memorize what the teacher narrates. Education, therefore, in the name of "preservation of culture and knowledge," creates "a system which achieves neither true knowledge nor true culture."[5]

Freire calls for an education that frees human beings of their state of passivity and enables them to be active participants in the transformation of oppressive structures. Such liberating education "consists in acts of cognition, not transferrals of information. It is a learning situation in which the cognizable object (far from being the end of the cognitive act) intermediates the cognitive actors—teacher on the one hand and students on the other." He sees problem-posing as the approach that would allow acts of cognition to take place and the teacher-student contradiction to be resolved. It is in problem-posing education that vertical patterns are broken and "dialogical relations—indispensable to the capacity of cognitive actors to cooperate in perceiving the same cognizable object," are fostered. The teacher is no longer the absolute authority, neither is he "merely the-one-who-teaches, but one who is himself taught in dialogue with the students, who in turn while being taught also teach."[6]

No doubt, Freire's criticism of the practice of education he encountered is insightful, and the banking analogy imaginative. It is difficult to find fault with his analysis of the inability of such education to liberate oppressed peoples of the world from structures that imprison them. The success of his work in adult literacy testifies to the theoretical and practical contribution he has made to the field of education. For Freire, a problem-posing educator is a cognitive collaborator and at no point assumes the role of a narrator. Objects that are to be problematized— cognizable objects as he calls them—are reflected upon in dialogue between the teacher and the students. The teacher "constantly re-forms his reflections in the reflection of the students" who are "critical co-investigators in dialogue with the teacher." The role of the teacher in this sense is "to create, together with the students, the conditions under which knowledge at the level of the doxa [opinion and magic] is superseded by true knowledge, at the level of the logos."[7] Attaining true knowledge occurs as one passes from the state of semi-intransitive to that of critical transitive consciousness,[8] a state in which the oppressed can no longer be manipulated by the internalized reality imposed on them by the oppressor. In the context of the political empowerment of certain sectors of society, this formulation of an educational process, with its accompanying techniques such as the use of generative words and selected pictures, works extremely well. Yet, freedom from oppression is but one step in a people's path of development. It is doubtful that a pedagogy so heavily dependent on problem-posing would ever be able to empower the students to deal with the complex reality they have to understand and transform. There is no evidence that a people thus liberated have been able to build a better society simply by the force of their new critical consciousness. Moreover, Freire and many others inspired by him have attempted to base even formal education in schools on the pedagogy of the oppressed. While it is easy to accept that in any kind of empowering education, problem-posing as a method will be employed judiciously when the occasion calls for it, giving it a central position in the overall conception of education—particularly one addressing the development of a wide range of society-building capabilities which is our concern here—seems unwarranted. Two points should be raised in this respect, one having to do with sources of knowledge and the other with consciousness.

In relation to educational activity that would act as both a "problem-situation" and "an antidote to the domesticating power of propaganda—from advertising commercials to ideological indoctrination," Freire gives the example of how the problem of cigarette advertising could be addressed by facilitating a discussion among a group of men who would "perceive the deceit in a cigarette advertisement featuring a beautiful, smiling woman in a bikini (i.e., the fact that she, her smile, her beauty, and her bikini have nothing at all to do with the cigarette)."[9] They develop the ability to recognize subtle associations of unrelated ideas as a strategy of propaganda in contrast to their own discussions as a method of liberating education. In this example, the state of transitive critical consciousness reached by these men enables them to take definite steps toward confronting the problem, to begin by not allowing themselves to be fooled by such propaganda, consciously resisting what advertising tries to do to them. This is clearly an illustrative example, but looking for solutions to most problems requires far more complex actions, which in turn require knowledge. Where should one look for the knowledge that enables "subjects" with a newly developed consciousness to participate in processes of transformation? In schools of thought akin to Freire's, emphasis is on the knowledge already possessed by the people. He advocates, for example, that "popular education" should turn to "epistemological research, antecedent to or concomitant with teaching practices, especially in peasant regions." The purpose, he recommends, is "to know how rural popular groups, indigenous or not, know—how they organize their *agronomic* knowledge or science, for example, or their medicine, to which end they have developed a broadly systematized taxonomy of plants, herbs, teas, spices, roots." He observes with great interest that "they integrate their meticulous taxonomy with miraculous promises—for example an herbal tea that heals both cancer and the pangs of unrequited love. . . ." He notes that "research in Brazilian universities has verified the actual medical usefulness of certain discoveries made by popular wisdom," and "to discuss with peasants this ongoing university-level verification of their knowledge is a political task of high pedagogical importance."[10]

To hold that respecting popular wisdom is a requisite of the education of adults in large numbers, and that, even in schools, a proper pedagogy would not neglect what the students know, and a good teacher would interact with them as possessors of valuable knowledge seems entirely valid. It represents a pedagogical choice that should definitely be made in the development of many a capability. But care has to be exercised not to give the impression, by the emotional content of the dialogue, that the knowledge of the medicinal effects of certain local herbs, for example, can replace the accumulating knowledge of humanity in the field of biology, chemistry, and medicine. When valuing what people know and helping them develop critical consciousness in the process of political empowerment gives way to an exaggerated romanticism about local knowledge and its transformative power, a kind of paternalism sets in that does not do justice to the oppressed.

Not all approaches to problem-posing, of course, have the tendency to underestimate the value of knowledge organized in specialized disciplines and fields. Ira Shor, for example, suggests that the problem-posing approach "views human beings, knowledge, and society as unfinished products in history, where various forces are still contending." According to him Freire's emphasis on "problem-posing as a democratic way for students to take part in the contention over knowledge and the shape of society" does not imply "that students have nothing to learn from biology or mathematics or engineering as they now exist." "As long as existing knowledge is not presented as facts and doctrines to be absorbed without question," he states, "as long as existing bodies of knowledge are critiqued and balanced from a multicultural perspective, and as long as students' own themes and idioms are valued along with standard usage, existing canons are part of critical education."[11] But even this statement does not go far enough to clarify the function of various sources of knowledge in education. Knowledge is not merely an instrument through which problems are posed. An individual who is learning to examine his or her physical and social reality at a less and less naïve level of consciousness would need, using Hirst's terminology, a grasp of concepts, logical structure, and truth criteria of relevant forms of knowledge to achieve "depth in the interpretation of problems" and guard against belief in "magical explanations"[12]—ends that were sought by Freire himself. But drawing on such knowledge requires "cooperation" with the source and not simply criticism. This requirement has been treated by M. J. Adler, for example, under the unfortunate term "docility." His two essays on the subject offer insights into how understanding is developed through a cooperative relationship between the student and knowledge, which does not imply subservience, passivity, and a propensity to be indoctrinated.[13]

Further, all the values the knowledge within disciplines and subject matters represent cannot be contained in a series of contentious questions the purpose of which is to help students think critically. The "contention" suggested by Shor is, of course, connected with other elements of the thought he expresses in the few lines quoted above. We need to question the relativism underlying the conception of a human being as an unfinished product who has a claim on knowledge by virtue of his or her own perspective. And, why should all existing forms of knowledge be balanced and criticized from a multicultural perspective? An acceptable pedagogy will surely help students analyze what they are being taught, and there is certainly a place for problem-posing and the cultivation of critical consciousness in education. But this does not justify enlarging the domain of the corresponding content and methods beyond reasonable limits to become *the* defining features of good education. When views about the human being and knowledge are not shaped by extreme relativism, the teacher's role is not limited to that of a facilitator of dialogue who poses questions; he or she can also be a narrator and expounder of meaning.

The second point to be raised in relation to the dichotomy in question has to do with the notion of consciousness. The atrocities that have occurred throughout human history were not perpetrated by individuals with a semi-intransitive consciousness, but often by those who understood the forces operating in society, knew well what they wanted, and strove to accomplish their aims. In seeking a pedagogy that would cultivate capabilities associated with the twofold moral purpose of individual and collective transformation, a transformation that would not simply make oppressors out of the oppressed, one has to take into account that consciousness can be distorted. Consciousness "shares in the bipolarity of all thought: it has an intrinsic responsibility to be truthful while at the same time it can succumb to falsehood."[14] The possibility of the corruption of consciousness is another reason not to overemphasize the value of consciousness-raising in education. In a certain sense, the way capabilities have been conceptualized here allows one to resist the temptation to generalize and express educational objectives mainly in terms of critical consciousness.

One more thought about the dichotomy introduced by Freire is worth mentioning. The very image of a banking education, useful as it is at the time of initial diagnosis, creates difficulties when it is gradually extended to capture the totality of each and every educational activity that intends to impart knowledge. It is true that "restless, impatient, continuing hopeful inquiry" generates knowledge. But knowledge is not just generated; it is also applied and diffused, which implies the transference of knowledge. Clearly in education, imparting knowledge should not be done according to banking procedures; a sophisticated pedagogy that trains the many complementary powers of the human heart and mind is needed. To cite an example, memory and comprehension are two such faculties. They complement and reinforce each other. Consequently, memorization is not the antithesis of cognition. Indeed, memorization with the purpose of reflecting on and sharing knowledge often entails cognition. In so many cultures the memorization and recital of poetry and meaningful passages has been the vehicle for collective deliberation on meaning. The plight of "modern" American education points to the dangers of categorically rejecting certain educational approaches, which are rich in content, as "rote learning" only to find out that elsewhere these same approaches are proving themselves superior, at least in areas such as the physical sciences and mathematics. Furthermore, the desired pedagogy would need to address the question of information and its relation to understanding. As stated in the previous chapter, the assimilation of relevant information does play an important role in the development of capabilities, but the educational approach would have to meet at least two challenges. First it would have to pay due attention to credible accounts of how information is assimilated, and second, it would have to subordinate the assimilation of information to the understanding of concepts. While it is not possible to think of concepts without information, care must be exercised not to reduce the former to the latter.

A brief reference to Bruner's computational and cultural accounts of the mind, already mentioned in chapter 3, may serve to illustrate the point we are trying to make here. Bruner advocates that the development of intellectual functioning "is shaped by a series of technological advances in the use of mind." Growth according to him "depends upon the mastery of techniques."[15] In the evolution of species, the selection process has favored the ability to use "technological implements," and it is this ability that provides the means for future growth of human beings. Brunner suggests that the implement systems seem to be of three general kinds: "*amplifiers of human motor capacities* ranging from the cutting tool through the lever and wheel to the wide variety of modern devices; *amplifiers of sensory capacities* that include primitive devices such as smoke signaling and modern ones such as magnification and radar sensing . . . ; and finally *amplifiers of human ratiocinative capacities* of infinite variety ranging from language systems to myth and theory and explanation. All of these forms of amplification are in major or minor degree conventionalized and transmitted by the culture."[16] The effectiveness of any such implement depends on the production of an appropriate internal skill that organizes our sensorimotor acts, objects in the environment, and our thoughts in a way that matches them to the requirements of the implement. Consequently, the development of the mind is to be measured in terms of those internal skills that are linked to techniques as amplifiers of human capacity. In the computational approach, the focus is on the mastery of the technique of establishing coding systems and of generating new information based on available data; the learner crosses the barrier from storing facts into thinking by creating generic codes. In culturalism, capacities are unlocked by techniques that "come from exposure to the specialized environment of a culture."[17] Storytelling, theatre, the forms of science and protoscience, even jurisprudence are all techniques for inflating the "forum-like" feature of culture, which education according to Bruner should imbibe.[18]

The manipulation and transformation of information to create more information, of course, cannot constitute the end of cognition. Nor can acquiring skills to negotiate meaning in a given culture meet the demands of moral empowerment. The second and more significant challenge not-ed above, that of understanding concepts, would need to be addressed. The mastery of the relevant techniques, in this respect, cannot replace the more demanding goal of advancing in understanding. The following example given by Bruner shows that, unfortunately, his approach, so focused on technique, does not take us far enough toward this goal:

> It would have been possible for Galileo to have published a handbook of the distances traversed per unit time by falling bodies. Schoolboys for centuries thereafter could easily have been tortured by the task of having to remember the Galilean tables. Such tables, cumbersome though they might have been, would have contained all the necessary information for dealing with freefalling bodies. Instead, Galileo had the inspiration to reorganize this welter of information into a highly simplified form. You recall the compact expression $S=1/2$: it not only summarizes all possible handbooks but organizes their knowledge in a way that makes manipulation possible.[19]

Presumably, Bruner himself would have not been happy with a pedagogy that presents this "formula" to the students and teaches them how to apply it to many situations of falling bodies, in tedious exercises, until they have mastered this coding of an infinite set of information. If the objective is the development of capabilities, in this case those associated with scientific inquiry, in parallel to acquiring the ability to work with information, students would need to "understand" such concepts as acceleration, distance, and time, and what it means to measure them, and be able to place the expression $S =1/2$ in the historical discourse of science, appreciating its significance in breaking away from the Aristotelian version of free fall—a version that is suggested by every student's initial intuition. And this kind of understanding cannot be achieved merely through problem-posing which itself has the tendency to yield to technique.

The Logical Order and the Psychological Method

The second set of ideas to be clarified in relation to our search for a pedagogy centered on the development of capabilities revolves around another dichotomy, not unrelated to the first. It is clear that in making pedagogical choices, one necessarily has to deal with accumulated human knowledge, as well as the attributes of the mind to be developed through education. Dewey points to some of the challenges that arise in the process by the tension between teaching according to the logical order of the subject matter and through the "psychological method." He argues that "the *intellectual* (as distinct from the *moral*) *end of education*" is "*the formation of careful, alert, and thorough habits of thinking.*"[20] This end cannot be achieved, however, if it is assumed that there is no relationship between an individual's psychological tendencies and his logical achievements. Ignoring this relationship leads to a perception of logical training as "something to be ingrafted upon the individual from without." Dewey points out that opposing schools of thought suffer from the consequences of this wrong assumption. In one way of thinking, "mottoes are freedom, self-expression, individuality, spontaneity, play, interest, natural unfolding, and so on," and *method* is conceived "to consist of various devices for stimulating and evoking, in their natural order of growth, the native potentialities of individuals."[21] In another, the focus is on, "*subject-matter*—upon matter already defined and classified," and its "mottoes are discipline, instruction, restraint, voluntary or conscious effort, the necessity of tasks, and so on."[22] Method in this latter case employs devices that would imprint the logic of subject matters on the mind of the student. Dewey argues that one should see "*the logical from the standpoint of subject-matter*" as representing "*the goal, the last term of training, not the point of departure.*"[23] When this is not done, the perfected form of knowledge acts as a stumbling block for the learner, whereas a method of teaching based on "problems selected from the material of ordinary acquaintance" allows the student to gain "independent power to deal with material within his range."[24] A good teacher would understand the "real problem of intellectual education" to be the "transformation of natural powers into expert, tested powers: the transformation of more or less casual curiosity and sporadic suggestion into attitudes of alert, cautious and thorough inquiry." The teacher will see that "the *psychological* and the *logical*, instead of being opposed to each other (or even independent of each other), are connected *as the earlier and the later stages in one continuous process of normal growth.*"[25]

In developing curricula that employ the concept of capability as a strategy one has to pay attention to Dewey's analysis of the logical and the psychological, but avoid a step that will finally lead to adopting the psychological as the basis of pedagogy, leaving the logical for later when the aim is to create experts. It is too easy to interpret Dewey's words to mean that the purpose of learning should be a personal or "psychological" organization of knowledge rather than a "logical" organization appropriate for research specialists. This ignores the very continuity that Dewey identifies between "earlier and later stages" of "normal growth." Finding an appropriate balance between the logical and the psychological is a challenge that must be met at every stage of the student's development. When the "psychological method" becomes a sign of "progressive education," the pendulum has swung too far toward the first of the two opposing schools of thought, which Dewey himself rejected. Hirst made an interesting observation early in the evolution of his own thought when he argued that if "our teaching methods are not to remain the hit and miss business they are at the moment, the careful, detailed analysis of the logical features of exactly what we wish to teach must be pursued far more thoroughly than it has been thus far."[26] Furthermore, the significance of truth criteria and tests of validity within disciplines of knowledge can easily be neglected if one sees the connection between the psychological and the logical only in terms of how they relate to the earlier and the later stages of normal growth. As Pring mentions, "the organisation of the learning (the acquisition of knowledge and understanding) might not follow the logical organisation of knowledge. For example, 'atom' may be a basic concept in science but it does not follow that science should begin with an introduction to the concept of the atom. The psychological process is not determined by the logical structure. The vocational and the practical interests of the learner can themselves be organising elements. For example, access to biology might be through moral concern over environmental pollution; access to physics might be through an industrial topic. But the criteria of valid fulfilment of those interests or of the correct grasp of the relevant biological or scientific points are themselves established, not by the vocational interests themselves, but by the tests of validity and correctness within the respective bodies of knowledge."[27]

Focusing on capabilities in the formulation of objectives and the organization of curricula facilitates the search for balance between the logical and the psychological. To begin, there is a shift from the "knowledge the student has to acquire" to the "attributes of the student." But the way these attributes are integrated into the concept of capability does not allow curricula to be developed in the context of personal experience alone. Capabilities are concerned with *doing* and *being*, and *being* is viewed not only as "functionings" but also in terms of the dynamics of advancing spiritual qualities together with *knowing*—the assimilation of information from relevant fields and the understanding of concepts that give structure to knowledge in those fields with the nuances mentioned in chapter 7 in the context of integration. A brief discussion of FUNDAEC's attempt to incorporate content from the natural sciences into its two-year "Promoter of Community Well-Being" program may prove useful here. Clearly our purpose here is not to argue the effectiveness of any of FUNDAEC's programs. That a number of evaluations have been performed and, in general, have shown positive results is a mere fact in the background. Repeated reference to FUNDAEC's educational efforts is, for us, a way of illustrating not necessarily accomplishments, although there are many, but attempts to address formidable challenges in developing curricula.

The "subject of understanding" in this example is the member of a group consisting of ten to fifteen students and one tutor that meets some 20 hours per week to study and to design, carry out, and discuss the results of action and research in the community. The students are youth trying to balance their lives between an education they highly value and whatever work is available in order to fulfill some of their obligations to their families. The tutor is not a teacher in the traditional sense, but neither is she a mere facilitator of discussion. She has received special training and is considered a collaborator of FUNDAEC in its effort to engage the population of the region in the generation, application, and diffusion of knowledge so as to take ownership of its own social and economic development. All the activities of the program are guided by units of written text, in the form of a dialogue between FUNDAEC as an institution of research and education and the group of students, the tutor being a member of both. The objectives of any set of activities are formulated in terms of contribution to the development of capabilities from the three categories mentioned in the previous chapter. A primary function of the tutor is to accompany the students as they "walk a path of service." But acts of service are not seen as the "practice component" or "practical application" of a theoretical study; on the contrary, it is the experience being created along the path of service that engenders the need to develop certain capabilities, to gain moral and practical insight, and to acquire knowledge.

Among the capabilities, the necessity of which arises naturally as experience advances, are those associated with participation in scientific inquiry. The capability of making accurate observations and organizing the corresponding statements and data in a way that lends itself to rigorous examination, for example, is one that students soon come to see as a requirement of their work as promoters of community well-being. Here, experience does not refer to haphazard occurrences in the students' lives, nor artificial situations created to facilitate learning by doing, but something that is being built systematically in the context of the transformation of the processes of collective life in the micro-region, a transformation that admittedly is not scientific in a strict sense but must involve the use of scientific knowledge and its methods. In this connection, then, a narrative of what scientists do in general becomes gradually woven into the dialogue with the students; the narrative, or certain aspects of it, gets repeated time and again and becomes more sophisticated with each repetition. In its rather simple initial formulation it is something like the following:

Scientists start with certain common observations that answer some of their questions and raise new ones. As questions become more complex, their observations need to become more sophisticated and this includes the development and use of instruments to make increasingly precise measurements. Observation and measurement are not carried out haphazardly; scientists select one or more systems in which they can observe some aspect of the process they are exploring. Thus observing, measuring, coming up with questions and partial answers are not things they do once but repeatedly and not always in the same sequence. Intermingled with these activities are the important tasks of elaboration and clarification of concepts; ideas may begin vague but over time have to be cast in a language that is as unambiguous as possible and as rational and objective as the human mind permits. Another aspect of scientific work is the identification of patterns in the data collected on some aspect of the process being studied. When patterns keep appearing consistently one may discover a law that governs the unfoldment of the process. But scientists are not satisfied with the identification of patterns. Their main task is to make models of reality. Models are sets of statements that explain observations related to a part of or an entire system or process. One can have models, for example, that explain what happens when water boils or when ice melts. But these models are always based on theories that are sets of profound statements about the nature of reality. In the example of a model explaining the boiling and freezing of water, the underlying theory is the atomic theory of matter.[28]

The pedagogical choices before FUNDAEC in relation to teaching science have had to do with the way students develop the capabilities that enable scientists to do what is briefly described in the above passage: which combination of information and concepts, skills and abilities, attitudes, habits, and spiritual qualities would have to be addressed and in what manner so that an educational activity can contribute to the development of one or more of these capabilities? The most immediate answer, of course, is that the challenge should be addressed in the very "development activity" in which the student is engaged in the community. To begin working in the area of health, for example, students are asked to carry out research on the knowledge the inhabitants of their micro-region already possess about how to maintain the health of their small children as well as the operation of health services available to them. Here, the development of the capabilities of a scientist is one of the themes explicitly treated in the corresponding text, which does not shy away from presenting the knowledge of biology relevant to the health issues being investigated. The same holds for actions related to agriculture and environment. But what is important for our exploration is that FUNDAEC has found this aspect of its pedagogy necessary but insufficient in relation to its goal of enabling promoters of community well-being to engage in scientific inquiry as an integral part of their work. It has felt that while acts of service related to the development of the community are valuable instances of learning about science in practice, they do not lend themselves to the kind of focused treatment of science that a systematic development of the desired capabilities requires. It has convinced itself that a step-by-step study of some areas of scientific knowledge respecting their "logical order"—to use Dewey's terminology—is necessary, albeit without ignoring the importance of the student's own experience.

When it comes to bringing the student's experience into the teaching of science, there are not that many choices readily available. As Michael Reiss puts it, most attempts leave the student with a "very narrow understanding of what science is and how it is carried out."[29] Children do not learn "to ask the sorts of questions that scientists actually ask or to ask the sorts of questions that the rest of us ask and to which science can make a contribution." Instead, pupils are restricted "to mind-blowingly dull questions about the bouncing of squash balls or the dissolving of sugar in what are misleadingly termed 'scientific investigations.'"[30] Such an approach persuades "most people that they aren't good at science."[31] FUNDAEC seems to have held similar views regarding the materials and methods associated with what has come to be known as "learning by discovery." It has observed that much of the experience artificially created for the student in the name of "scientific investigation" often leaves the student with the impression of science as a collection of imaginative, and almost magical, discoveries. It is worth noting here that even Bruner whose article, "The Act of Discovery,"[32] seems to have given the idea a boost became disillusioned with the direction "learning by discovery" took over the years. Early on he had argued:

> . . . emphasis upon discovery in learning has precisely the effect upon the learner of leading him to be a constructionist, to organize what he is encountering in a manner not only designed to discover regularity and relatedness, but also to avoid the kind of information drift that fails to keep account of the uses to which information might have to be put.[33]

In a follow-up essay he distanced himself from the excesses that had set in. "I am not sure any more what discovery is,"[34] he confided, and complained that "discovery was being treated by some educators as if it were valuable in and of itself, no matter what it was a discovery of or in whose service."[35] Here again the popularization of an idea had led to extremes, to unwarranted slogans, for example, learning by doing vs. book learning.

It seems that any attempt that tries to connect the logical order of the subject matter to the experience of the student would do well to reflect on Lev Vygotsky's insightful treatment of everyday and scientific concepts. His suggestion that the development of the child's spontaneous concepts may be seen to be proceeding upwards and the development of his scientific concepts downwards creates an image of the way the two are connected:

> The development of a spontaneous concept must have reached a certain level for the child to be able to absorb a related scientific concept. . . . In working its slow way upward, an everyday concept clears a path for the scientific concept and its downward development. It creates a series of structures necessary for the evolution of a concept's more primitive, elementary aspects, which give it body and vitality. Scientific concepts, in turn, supply structures for the upward development of the child's spontaneous concepts toward consciousness and deliberate use. Scientific concepts grow downward through spontaneous concepts; spontaneous concepts grow upward through scientific concepts.[36]

In the example being considered here, the students are not children but youth whose commitment to pursue their own moral and intellectual growth and to contribute to the transformation of their communities is being firmed up in an empowering educational process. They are becoming increasingly conscious of the need to develop capabilities among which those associated with scientific inquiry are of particular value for the work ahead of them. Their experience, apart from the usual occurrences of daily life, includes systematically guided activity that generates a wealth of concepts in need of "structures supplied by scientific concepts" in order to move toward "consciousness and deliberate use." This is an important justification for FUNDAEC's decision to dedicate a part of its curriculum to the treatment of a few areas of science according to their "logical order."

The approach FUNDAEC adopted in the particular case of its efforts to enhance the capabilities of promoters of community well-being is as follows: It chose the atomic theory as the set of statements that guide the students to move time and again through the series of steps suggested by the narrative on the nature of scientific inquiry, each time by examining one familiar process. The first process is the heating and cooling of matter which can be studied in some depth in light of the first and most general statement of the atomic theory, namely that matter is made of extremely small particles in constant motion. The corresponding conversation organized in written text takes the students through an inquiry into the nature of the process: everyday observations are remembered and organized; a substantial number of questions are generated; ordinary concepts such as heat, temperature, force, and pressure are clarified and are moved "upward" toward their scientific definitions; instruments for measuring these quantities are introduced as an aspect of the upward movement; measurements are made, data is collected and patterns are observed; the relationship between volume, temperature, and pressure in an ideal gas is "discovered" and discussed as an example of a law in science; a model of matter in its three phases—a solid as an organization of small particles bound together and oscillating around a point of equilibrium, a liquid as an aggregate of particles more loosely bound to each other and able to "slide" over each other, and a gas as the aggregate of particles moving in all directions and bouncing against each other—is presented and used to explain as many observations made about the process, and the patterns identified among them, as possible. Although at this early stage certain fundamental philosophical issues cannot be explicitly addressed, care is taken not to create notions of science in the mind of the student that later have to be erased. For example, the theory dependence of observation is clearly emphasized as is the finite range of validity of any set of theoretical statements. The study of the process ends with a discussion of the Aristotelian view of the universe in terms of the four elements of fire, air, water, and earth. It is shown how that theory also explains certain observations about the process of the heating and cooling of matter, yet the explanatory power of even the first statement of atomic theory is far greater.[37] In the study of three other processes, the growth of a plant, the transfer of energy, and photosynthesis, new statements are added to the atomic theory—the division of particles into atoms and molecules, the structure of atoms, the nature of chemical bonds, the transformation of energy from one form to another, the properties of photons and electrons—making it possible to create a number of theoretical models as sets of statements about the workings of such systems as the root of a plant, a cell or an electrical circuit.

In addressing the development of capabilities associated with scientific inquiry, directly in an exploration of science as a "form of knowledge," the experience of the student in the community is not neglected. The approach is similar to the way these capabilities are treated in the texts concerned with areas of "service" such as health and agriculture. There, science is brought in as needed; here, constant reference is made to systematic action in the community showing the significance of scientific concepts, information, skills, and attitudes being acquired. This is, of course, not the place to discuss and compare approaches to science education. But this brief account of one part of FUNDAEC's curriculum in a specific program demonstrates the way an approach based on capabilities lends itself to the resolution of a set of dichotomies revolving around the contrast between the "psychological method" and the "logical order" of subject matters.

Capabilities as Contexts

In general, one could argue that any effective pedagogy should deal with the kind of difficulties to which the two sets of dichotomies mentioned above as well as a host of others—child-centered vs. subject-centered, process oriented vs. outcome based, moral vs. intellectual development, skills vs. cognition, just to mention a few—give rise. That so many of the popular pedagogies fall on one or another side of rigidly defined opposing camps indicates that finding the necessary balance is not as easy as it may appear. We are not suggesting in this chapter that using the concept of capability by itself meets this formidable challenge. What is being stated is that the approach fosters the kind of thinking that pays simultaneous attention, say, to the student and the subject matter, to the acquisition of skills and cognitive development, to the process and the outcome, to the intellectual and the moral. But achieving this desired balance requires that capabilities not be taken apart and analyzed in terms of their "components." The understanding of a set of concepts, the assimilation of relevant information, the acquisition of some skills, and the development of certain spiritual qualities, attitudes, and habits all contribute to the enhancement of several interrelated capabilities, but at the same time, the capabilities give meaning to these attributes, serving as the context within which they are acquired. A given curricular element, of course, will necessarily focus on a few attributes—as little as one or two skills and a small set of related concepts—but in the context of the much larger constellation of attributes that contribute to the desired capabilities. Adopting such an approach in the elaboration of curricula involves the acceptance of a certain claim that the many attributes to be developed in the mind and the heart of the individual do lend themselves to fluid arrangements that somehow correspond to definite states of *being* and *doing* to which capabilities refer. But, there seems to be a notion underlying this claim indicating that capabilities may not be mere arbitrary constructs. The correspondence with actual states of being and doing, however, is not a simple one. For one thing, these states are moving in constant development. Those involved in the elaboration of curricula would have to be aware of the inadequacy of any description, fixed in time, of a capability in terms of a given set of attributes that contribute to it. While focusing on one such set may be sufficient to help the student advance in a capability at a certain point, once a new state of *being, doing,* and *knowing* is envisioned, further movement may require additional attributes to enter into the description of the capability.

CHAPTER 10

CONTINUITY OF THOUGHT, LANGUAGE, AND ACTION

The last two chapters were dedicated to an exploration of the promises and challenges of an approach that would use a particular formulation of the concept of capability to organize the teaching-learning experience in educational processes aimed at the moral empowerment of the student. To illustrate the approach, certain features of a specific Bahá'í-inspired program for the education of promoters of community well-being with notable achievements in certain areas of the world were presented. In that connection, three categories of capabilities to be progressively acquired by the promoters were mentioned, those directly concerned with the moral dimension of empowerment, those pertaining to the realm of action as the promoters systematically generate a growing body of experience through acts of service, and those related to humanity's accumulating knowledge in its various forms. Most of the discussion, however, was limited to the latter two categories; the only statement of consequence about the first was the claim that the development of the corresponding attributes—the understanding of concepts, the assimilation of information, the skills, attitudes, habits, and spiritual qualities—would have to be addressed in educational activities concerned with capabilities in the other two categories as well and, not necessarily, in a separate part of the curriculum dedicated to moral education. We should now go further and explore a few major considerations that must inform the cultivation of attributes directly related to the moral dimension of empowerment.

To begin, we may argue that, in an educational process aimed at moral empowerment, the development of moral capabilities have a direct bearing on what was referred to in chapter 2 as essential relationships—among individuals, between the individual and the institutions of society, and among the many elements of the community, underlying all of which is humanity's relationship with nature and more fundamentally with the Divine. These relationships define the individual, the community, and the institutions of society as protagonists of the immense transformation which entering the age of maturity demands. As mentioned before, the morality called for here is not a passive one, focused on functioning in the world as it is today. Desirable as it is, for example, to work constructively in unity with others and avoid being a cause of conflict and dissension, it is the capability of building unity of thought and action while pursuing a common aim that needs to be addressed by the empowering educational process. Honesty and truthfulness are qualities to be enhanced by any attempt at moral education, but those capable of managing personal and community affairs with rectitude of conduct are in need of attributes that help them, for example, to champion justice and be effective participants in struggles against corruption. To seek happiness without harming others is a valuable moral goal, but to be capable of bringing joy to others while accompanying them in an act of service seems to be a challenge that presents itself at a more active level of morality. These and myriad other capabilities of the same kind seem to be directed among other things toward the creation of environments[1] within which the essential relationships characterizing a mature human race are to take shape and manifest themselves. What are some of the ideas essential to any educational program hoping to enhance such capabilities?

It seems that foremost among the challenges of a curriculum concerned with the development of moral capabilities is that of language.

Clearly, students engaged in an empowering educational process need to develop a language that will allow them to progressively articulate their thoughts and experience with clarity. The language becomes refined and acquires depth as students are able to express more and more accurately and completely a range of moral concepts and their interrelationships. This refinement needs to take place in the ongoing reflection of a group of students on its experience in pursuing a two-fold moral purpose. However, this is not a theoretical exercise aimed at extracting general principles from particular instances of action. Profound collective reflection on action needs to be expressed in words that invest action with meaning and transform activity in the minds of the students from routine or dull performance of duty to that which is intrinsically linked to their aspirations and goals.

The phrase "growing into our language," which Dunne uses in his analysis of Gadamer's work, is relevant in this respect. Growing into our language is a process which introduces "differentiation and order into our world."[2] Gadamer states: "Experience is not wordless to begin with, subsequently becoming an object of reflection by being named, by being subsumed under the universality of the word. Rather, experience of itself seeks and finds words that express it."[3] Dunne points out that "this seeking and finding is, in fact, the primary process of concept formation which keeps pace with the growing complexity of the way in which we experience the world."[4] In the example of the promoters of community well-being, the students' arena of action is the community in a micro-region, with its physical, social, and ethical environment. As the students each advance in the relevant capabilities at their own pace, they "grow into a language" that increasingly corresponds to the complexity of the world they experience and the conditions of which they endeavor to transform. The development of the power of expression in this sense is rooted in the experience that is being generated in the community. On a personal level, it reflects the continuity between thought, language, and action. On a collective level, it lends impetus to the gradual elaboration of a shared framework which increasingly draws together the goals and aspirations of a growing number of people within a specific population.[5]

We have already touched on the question of language in the context of science and religion as two complementary sources of knowledge. In that discussion, we argued that, in addition to the language of science, an educational process concerned with moral empowerment needs to employ the language of religion, which, with the rational, the normative, and poetic forms of expression at its command, would speak to the heart and the mind in ways that are not easily accessible to science. At the time, we did not address the question of the arts in the kind of process being discussed here. The arts, of course, enter into education in their own right as essential aspects of humanity's cultural heritage. Depending on the nature of a given program, the development of certain artistic capabilities, contributing to the enhancement of such faculties of the human mind and heart as creativity and imagination, would constitute an important part of the totality of the objectives of the program. In exploring in this final chapter the continuity of thought, language, and action, it should at least be mentioned that, beyond their own intrinsic value, the various forms of art expand human ability to express experience, and need to be taken into account in the exploration of the language into which students "grow" as they advance in a given set of capabilities. One reason is that feelings and emotions have an important role to play in moral choices and acts. The language of science, or philosophy, is clearly not the most effective instrument for the expression of emotions, although it can help to analyze and understand them. The language of religion certainly deals with the affective sphere, but it does so in its own way, at a level of transcendence and authority. But this does not exhaust the demand feelings lay on expression. The power of expression that the student needs to develop in the process of moral empowerment involves a complex interaction between the languages of philosophy, of science, of religion, and of one or more forms of the arts.

In what follows it is argued that, in order to address continuity of thought, language, and action, an educational process concerned with moral empowerment needs to resolve at least two sets of issues. The first has to do with the question of "heart and mind" and the second with the "individual and collective." The lack of resolution of these two sets of issues perpetuates an illusory tension regarding the role science and the arts play in education and contributes to the vision of a fragmented self in its various formations—an emotivist, a computer, a modern being motivated by self-interest, a calculating rationalist, or a smoothly functioning cog in the machinery created by the state or the market, among others—which we have already rejected as candidates for the "subject of understanding."

Oneness of Heart and Mind

Feelings and emotions, up to now, have not entered explicitly into the exploration of the concept of capability, although they are clearly present in considerations of spiritual qualities, attitudes, habits, and, somewhat differently, in understanding concepts. The decision not to treat emotions directly at the level of educational objectives, as is done for example in Bloom's taxonomy, but indirectly through attributes that define capabilities, has important philosophical underpinnings that need to be made explicit. What is being questioned is the division of the subject of understanding into the "emotional" and the "rational" attached to the heart and the mind respectively. To seek unity between the heart and mind, of course, is not to deny the value of virtues traditionally associated with the heart. What is needed is an approach that addresses the cultivation of desirable emotions without creating a false duality, thus safeguarding the integrity of the individual and resisting alienation from the world. The language in which moral capabilities are conceived and discussed needs to counteract the language of modern life in which strong undercurrents contribute to ever separating fragmented spheres of being. The desired language was described to some extent in chapter 4 in the discussion of spiritual qualities as a particular category of virtues constituting properties of the human soul. Fostering spiritual qualities would be a fundamental concern in the development of every capability, independent of its particular emphasis on the intellectual, the social, or the moral.

The division of virtues into the intellectual and the moral—the former identified with the rational and the latter with the nutritive and desiring parts of the soul—has made it difficult for education to see the many unifying threads that if strengthened would contribute to the student's wholeness of character and organic unity with the world. Some would attribute the origins of this separation to Aristotle's words: "philosophic wisdom and understanding and practical wisdom being intellectual, liberality and temperance moral,"[6] and his suggestion that the growth of the former requires teaching, while the latter "come about as a result of habit . . ."[7] Randall Curren reminds us that this widely accepted distinction emerges from a rather simplistic account of Aristotelian virtues, since Aristotle "also holds that no one is fully virtuous or has true moral virtue without having the intellectual virtue of practical wisdom, . . . and he holds that no one can become practically wise without first possessing natural or habitual moral virtue . . ."[8] Yet the crude interpretation persists in many a practice of education.[9]

According to Midgley, ". . . many things on the current intellectual scene tend to make us disconnect feeling from thought, by narrowing our notions of both, and so to make human life as a whole unintelligible."[10] She points to the tendency to use words such as "heart" and "feeling" to "describe just a few selected sentiments which are somewhat detached from the practical business of living—notably romantic, compassionate and tender sentiments—as if non-romantic actions did not involve any feeling." Mean and vindictive action, she reminds us, "flows from and implies mean and vindictive feeling, and does so just as much when it is considered as when it is impulsive."[11] She further argues that while there is the possibility of tension between thought and feeling, and between feeling and action, they are nevertheless interwoven: "We are in fact so constituted that we cannot act at all if feeling really fails. When it does fail, as in cases of extreme apathy and depression, people stop acting . . ." And, "feelings, to be effective, must take shape as thoughts, and thoughts, to be effective, must be powered by suitable feelings."[12]

The most obvious connection between feelings and action is motivation—the former motivate the latter. But this is only one aspect of the relationship between emotions and actions in which thought and language play essential roles. Some of the emotions that move us to act with fear or anger, for example, are temporary; learning to eliminate them when unwarranted and to manage them when justified, as would be anger toward injustice, can be an outcome expected from an educational process concerned with moral empowerment. Other feelings such as jealousy and greed can become permanent features of character and need to be taken into account accordingly. But all of these belong to the category of "self-referential" emotions. "Our interpretation of the world is inveterately self-referential," Peters has observed. "We find difficulty in peering out and seeing the world and others as they are, undistorted by our own fears, hopes and wishes."[13] Addressing feelings in the process of fostering spiritual qualities and cultivating understanding obliges an educational program to pay attention to the development of "self-transcending emotions," corresponding to "appraisals which lack this self-referential character, notably love, respect, the sense of justice and concern for truth." This, according to Peters, is "probably the most effective way of loosening the hold on us of the more primitive, self-referential ones."[14]

Focusing on "self-transcending emotions" requires the critical examination of a common assumption that everything which has anything to do with rational thought is abstract in its pure form and only later is it applied to concrete situations. Thus, in the realm of morality, principles are considered "products of reason," affectively neutral and inert. "Fairness" and "considering people's interest," for example, are assumed to be abstractions for which meaning has to be found in concrete traditions.[15] Conversely all emotions are situated in particular circumstances infused with subjective states. Nel Noddings goes so far as to state that "caring," which is essentially "nonrational" engrossment in those cared for, is in danger of being gradually or abruptly "transformed into abstract problem solving."[16] She advocates that "rational-objective thinking is to be put in the service of caring"; recommends that "we must at the right moments turn it away from the abstract toward which it tends and back to the concrete"; and argues that at times we must "suspend" it "in favor of subjective thinking and reflection, allowing time and space for *seeing* and *feeling*."[17]

This contrast between reason and emotion is misconceived. Peters' use of the word appraisal in relation to emotion is significant. He argues that in so far as emotions involve a certain type of cognition in the form of appraisals, they are, "basically forms of cognition."[18] Another way to see cognition at work in the expression of emotions is via the operation of virtues,[19] particularly the category referred to as spiritual qualities in this book and incorporated into the notion of capability. None can dispute that virtues of this category have emotional and attitudinal dimensions which, when distorted, will hinder their inherent powers from manifesting themselves. "Kindness" with an attitude of superiority becomes paternalism, and "generosity" with feelings of pity could be a vehicle for perpetuating dependence. Appropriate emotions are needed commensurate with the integrity of spiritual qualities, and these emotions are not blind. Moral acts of benevolence, courage, and fortitude, even when manifested habitually, are not bereft of thought. And the seeing that endows those acts with significance does not require the suspension of rational thinking as Noddings proposes.

A concept that is particularly helpful when we seek unity of mind and heart is that of "perception," which entered our discussion in chapter 7. While it is not possible to undertake here an adequate examination of the concept, a line of inquiry suggests itself. We have already argued against the duality of the "subjective" and the "objective" in chapter 5, and have tried to position the subject of understanding in an extended reality. Within this reality, there is a spiritual as well as an intellectual dimension to perception in which both reason and feeling take part. To become increasingly empowered, the student stands in need of ever expanding "spiritual perception" and a language in which it can be expressed. Spiritual perception in the sense being used here includes McDowell's "sensitivity" to a "certain sort of requirement which situations impose on behaviour," which he identifies as perceptual capacity. The example he offers to clarify his point is kindness. The "reliably kind behaviour" of a kind person "is not the outcome of a blind, non-rational habit or instinct." On being kind in each occasion, the kind individual has a reliable sensitivity to the requirement which the situation imposes on behavior. McDowell holds that "the deliverances of a reliable sensitivity are cases of knowledge" and "the sensitivity is, we might say, a sort of perceptual capacity."[20]

Enhancing this perceptual capacity in the subject of understanding is an essential task of an empowering educational process. But this is only one aspect of the development of spiritual perception. As discussed in previous chapters, an expanded rationality in which reason and faith are not held in opposition to each other has to be adopted. Openness to an extended reality that includes the spiritual dimension has to be fostered—an openness which in turn creates receptivity to the intimations of that reality and enlarges the range of perception beyond the empirical and the logical. The corresponding faculties of the human soul—the "spiritual eye" and the "spiritual ear"—have to be sharpened. And for a Bahá'í-inspired educational process, susceptibilities to the workings of an all-embracing divine purpose have to be cultivated and developed.

It should also be remembered that it is difficult to conceive of the kind of active morality a process of moral empowerment is to engender, without passion. We often hear that to think rationally one needs to examine issues and situations dispassionately. But is the expanded rationality to be developed in an educational process concerned with moral empowerment divested of passion? According to Peters, "there are attitudes and appraisals which are the passionate side of the life of reason."[21] Science and any other rational activity presuppose normative standards such as consistency, relevance, impartiality, truthfulness, accuracy, clarity, and respect for evidence and other people. These standards are "intimately connected with the passion for truth which gives point to rational activities."[22]

In Peters' view, distinct disciplines of knowledge are "more precise articulations of the more generalized passions which begin to exert an influence when reasoning of a less precise sort gets under weigh," when, for example, "primitive constructiveness passes into the love of order and system."[23] The same is true in the moral realm. In helping students to enhance their moral capabilities, the educational process needs to ensure that cultivating spiritual perception goes hand in hand with the transformation of passion from lower to higher forms. The two developments go forward when ample attention is given to both the nurturing of understanding and the fostering of spiritual qualities.

The Interplay Between the Individual and the Collective

Those capabilities that bring to the fore the moral dimension of *knowing*, *being*, and *doing* are to a great degree shaped by concepts and notions that define personhood within a complex web of communal and social relations. Capabilities refer to the attributes of individuals; in an educational program, it is the individual who progressively advances in a set of capabilities. But the discussion of the previous chapters should have made it clear that advancing along the path of moral empowerment is deemed possible only if the student is immersed in the life of society. It is worth mentioning here that Sen has been criticized for adopting "methodological individualism" in his capability approach to development. He has responded to his critics by saying that the approach's concern with "people's ability to live the kind of lives they have reason to value brings in social influences both in terms of what they value (for example, 'taking part in the life of the community') and what influences operate on their values (for example, the relevance of public reasoning in individual assessment)." Further, he has suggested that "perhaps the misconstruction in this critique arises from its unwillingness to distinguish adequately between the individual characteristics that are used in the capability approach and the social influences that operate on them."[24]

In an educational process focused on the development of capabilities, raising awareness of the influence social forces exert on one's thought, language, and action will obviously have to be addressed. So too will be the ability to analyze the operation of such forces and the way to deal with them. But somehow this treatment of social forces does not seem to go far enough toward the creation of the kind of relationship between the individual and society that is being suggested here. While the ability to articulate the effects of the negative forces operating in society—greed, prejudices of many kinds, unbridled individualism and oppression, to name a few—plays some role in the development of capabilities, when overemphasized, it leads to cynicism and alienation. What is needed is a strong sense of belonging to the whole, not the detachment of a critical outsider. In chapter 2 we argued that no tension should exist between the processes of personal and collective transformation and that, in fact, they should be considered two inseparable dimensions of one movement. But tension can only be avoided if the language that is used to express thought and spur action describes a self that has incorporated into its very conception strong connections with other individuals, with the community, and with the institutions of society. A Bahá'í-inspired program would naturally consider the bond that connects us with the Divine as well.

MacIntyre offers penetrating insights in this respect. He identifies a sharp split in the current social order between "the realm of the organisational" in which the ends are not to be questioned and "the realm of the personal" in which, by contrast, there is nothing but disputation about personal values. The two sides of the political debates that fan the supposed opposition between the individual and the collective are the "self-defined protagonist of planning and organization" and the "self-defined protagonist of individual liberty." The apparent opposition masks the deep agreement between the two parties. For both, there are only two possible modes of social life: "one in which the free and arbitrary choices of individuals are sovereign and one in which the bureaucracy is sovereign, precisely so that it may limit the free and arbitrary choices of individuals."[25] According to MacIntyre, these two apparently antagonistic ways of life are, in fact, partners in a common culture, and it is in this culture that the emotivist self finds an ideal home.

The capabilities that are to be developed by the student in the process of moral empowerment, must enable her to transcend manipulative and authoritarian relationships that exist between individuals and social organizations—the results of arbitrary freedom and control. Once again, language is a vital concern here. So much of the language of our age—whether the language of the emotivist in which it is hard to distinguish between sentences expressing preferences and evaluative statements, or the bureaucratic language of injunctions and rules—not only reflects the culture MacIntyre sharply criticizes but also plays a central role in shaping it. To achieve, even on a modest scale, the transformation of essential relationships—requiring as mentioned in chapter 2 an expanded notion of power as well as new explanations of individuality and collectivity—a different language has to be allowed to evolve, the language of harmonious and reciprocal relationships whereby institutions act as channels for the release of human potential and individuals aspire to contribute to the shaping of such institutions.

What are some of those characteristics of the language in which moral capabilities have to be expressed that directly bear on relationships between the individual and society? To begin, the way person-hood is discussed must necessarily avoid narrow and misconstrued notions of "self." At the individual level, the concept of self seems to have become barren and the modern age evokes the sense of a loss of identity, heightened in moments of sincere introspection. This is ironic when one witnesses how often the word "self" is associated in to-day's language of many a practice with those of "image," "confidence," "assertiveness," and "actualization." But do these associations give rise to anything more than empty notions of "grandeur" and "ego"? To say, for example, that an individual measures herself mainly by the degree of confidence she has acquired or by her self-image is to reduce personhood; the individual in this reduced form struggles to reconcile herself with the collective. Taylor points out that although "self-image" is often associated with appearing in a good light in the eyes of others and caring about how we match up to certain social standards, it is not essential to who we are:

> On the contrary, what is usually studied under this head is what we can identify, outside the sterilized, "value-free" language of social science, as the all-too-human weakness of "ego" and "im-age" in the everyday sense of these terms (themselves, of course, incorporated into the vernacular from social science). The ideally strong character would be maximally free of them, would not be deterred by the adverse opinions of others, and would be able to face unflinchingly the truth about himself or herself.[26]

As an alternative, Taylor suggests "orientation to the good" as a crucial feature of the desired individuality, one that cannot be depicted with-out reference to its surroundings:

> What I am as a self, my identity, is essentially defined by the way things have significance for me . . . and the issue of my identity

is worked out, only through a language of interpretation which I have come to accept as a valid articulation of these issues . . . we are only selves insofar as we move in a certain space of questions, as we seek and find an orientation to the good.[27]

To continue with Taylor's line of reasoning, our orientation to good—which is constitutive of who we are—involves articulation and continuing clarification of significant issues, which cannot be done by a lone self. A self exists only within "webs of interlocution": those "conversation partners" who in the early part of life were essential to our self-definition and with whom we first learn "our languages of moral and spiritual discernment," as well as others who are now crucial to our "continuing grasp of languages of self-understanding." An important attribute of this language is that it only exists and can only be "maintained within a language community."[28] Rootedness in a community, however, does not imply conformity:

A human being can always be original, can step beyond the limits of thought and vision of contemporaries, can even be quite misunderstood by them. But the drive to original vision will be hampered, will ultimately be lost in inner confusion, unless it can be placed in some way in relation to the language and vision of others.[29]

Taylor, in probing "the relations of identity and community," distinguishes "the possible place of we-identities as against merely convergent I-identities, and the consequent role of common as against convergent goods."[30] It is not that I-identity knows no familial or communal bonds; such bonds are necessarily formed as individuals pursue their own inclinations, goals, and life plans. In the corresponding worldview collective action also has a place, but its purpose is to obtain benefits which individuals on their own could not secure.

Taylor's views point to a dynamic relationship between the individual and the community, the individual being rooted in the community but not necessarily conforming to it. Rootedness, however, is significant to the identity of the protagonist of moral empowerment only if certain conditions are present. Just as the individual does not represent an absolute value independent of the spiritual qualities with which she is adorned, of the vision that inspires her thoughts, of the goals that spur her to action, and of the efforts she exerts to advance material and spiritual civilization, likewise, the community cannot represent an absolute value in and of itself. Its character matters. There is no shortage of communities today fighting each other over their vision of common good that elicit a strong sense of belonging from their members. The ideal of multicultural communities that simply tolerate one another is a poor alternative, and is proving, in the final analysis, to be empty. Moral empowerment as described here implies building communities that come to embrace the diversity of culture, language, and history, yet are bound by their consciousness of the oneness of humanity. One can imagine how such communities can be environments in which individual and collective creative powers are consistently nurtured and directed toward the betterment of society. And it is in the context of the processes of life in such ideal communities that insights into the future relationship between the individual and the community can be gained.

To explore the nature of this relationship in more depth, however, some kind of theoretical framework on language and thought seems to be needed. Vygotsky's work offers valuable insight in this respect. According to Ellen Watson, Vygotsky avoids the problems associated with approaches—originated from the classical empiricist tradition— that consider thought primary and language its expression, in which the mind is the passive recipient and organizer of images produced by external objects. His work, however, does not embrace the radical social constructivism of approaches on the opposite camp, which consider language primary and responsible for shaping thought, and as a result, face the problem of communication across communities with varied languages. His theory lies somewhere between the two approaches.[31]

Vygotsky's work suggests that, in order to understand the uniqueness of human behavior, we need to consider both the historical character and the social nature of human experience. With regard to the former, Vygotsky writes: "Man makes use not just of physically inherited experience: throughout his life, his work and his behaviour draw broadly on the experience of the former generations, which is not transmitted at birth from father to son. We may call this historical experience."[32] As to the social character of human experience, it relies on interpersonal communication allowing a person to draw "on the almost infinite pool of experiences of others." Individual experience itself "becomes just one element in the field of experiences" available to each person.[33] On the old psychological question of knowing another person's mind, Vygotsky wrote that "We are aware of ourselves, for we are aware of others, and in the same way as we know others; and this is as it is because we in relation to ourselves are in the same [position] as others are to us."[34] He observed that children understand others first and themselves later:

> ... the child first learns to understand others and only afterwards, following the same model, learns to understand himself. It would be more exact to say that we know ourselves to the extent that we know others, or, even more exact, that we are conscious of ourselves only to the extent that we are another for ourselves, that is, a stranger.[35]

As René Van der Veer and Jaan Valsiner explain, Vygotsky reaches the conclusion that language, "the tool of social interaction, is at the same time the tool of intimate interaction with oneself."[36]

This brief reference to Vygotsky only hints at the kind of language in which the development of every set of capabilities has to be conceptualized, if the resulting individuality of the student is not to contradict the very aim of a program seeking moral empowerment. This is of particular importance because in an empowering process, the student has to be fully aware of the objectives of every activity and be able to reflect on how advancing in a given capability is helping to fulfill his or her twofold moral purpose. There is a rise in consciousness as the student advances in a capability, but this consciousness is not the property of the individual alone. The student has to be aware, and work within a rising collective consciousness that, as Evald Ilyenkov puts it, "is not simply the individual consciousness repeated many times" but rather "a historically formed and historically developing system of 'objective representations,' forms and patterns of the 'objective spirit' of humanity's 'collective reason.'"[37] A premise of this book has been that the rising "consciousness of the oneness of humankind" is the most fundamental manifestation of the spirit of humanity today and should permeate every aspect of education seeking moral empowerment. Further, according to Vygotsky, "The social dimension of consciousness is primary in time and in fact. The individual dimension of consciousness is derivative and secondary."[38] In his interpretation of Vygotsky's thought, Alex Kozulin underscores the "implicit conclusion" that if consciousness is to become a subject of psychological study, some other layer of reality should be referred to in the course of the explanation, and he goes on to suggest that "socially meaningful activity" may serve as such a layer.[39] Accordingly, in the process of moral empowerment, the student should be able to assess his or her own growing consciousness with the aid of socially meaningful activity. This brings added meaning to our arguments in previous chapters that moral empowerment needs to be associated with progressively more effective and complex acts of service to the community—and by extension to the whole of humanity. When this is achieved, the consciousness of the oneness of humankind, always in danger of being a mere abstraction, is given concrete shape through the notion of service. The motivation to act on society is generated within the individual who, while not driven by selfish interest, is, nevertheless, seeking intellectual and moral growth. The way is open to a fundamental orientation to personhood that is not sabotaged by notions of individualism. The so-called enlightened self-interest foresees the possibility of converging goods, but the urge to commit oneself to the common good defines a different identity. There is an even more complete sense of identity that the consciousness of the oneness of humankind nurtures.

Service, described in general terms in chapter 4 and through examples in chapter 8, embraces a category of actions that impels individuals to come face to face with the collective side of their identity, to recognize in practice not only the common good but also the interconnectedness of all things. Walking the path of service in the company of others—developing capabilities related to the moral dimension of the path, capabilities that have a direct bearing on the acts of service, and capabilities associated with the intellectual heritage of humankind—helps to shape the student's identity; service "unites the fulfilment of individual potential with the advancement of society."[40]

CONCLUDING REMARKS

The aim of this inquiry has been to explore the nature of an evolving conceptual framework that could guide programs concerned with moral empowerment in the context of a Bahá'í-inspired discourse on education. The approach has been to identify concepts which could be considered vital elements of such a framework—largely gleaned from the work of one of the participants in the discourse that has made noteworthy and distinct contributions to it—and to analyze these concepts in light of relevant philosophical literature. The inquiry has been carried out on the basis of two premises: that we live in an age of transition from humanity's childhood to its maturity, and that a fundamental characteristic of this age is the growing consciousness of the oneness of humankind. These two interrelated convictions are in themselves elements of the evolving framework under consideration, setting direction for the development of Bahá'í-inspired discourse on education commensurate with the progressive realization of human potential, both at the individual and the collective levels.

The purpose of the inquiry, and the methodology adopted, required specific insights to be gained from the writings of a number of authors in ethics and philosophy of mind—insights that would make it possible to express each selected concept in a reflective language and to expand its meaning and application in relation to the other elements of the framework being considered. Since a sufficient number of ideas had to be introduced in order to give some shape to the framework, significant concepts, each of which could have been the topic of an entire book, had to be dealt with inadequately, and weighty themes

319

did not receive the attention they deserve. Further, given the nature of the inquiry, little attempt was made to go beyond the discussion of relevant insights and undertake a systematic critique of the work of each author.

If we look at the totality of the argument presented, it is clear that it did not advance an equal distance in the exploration of each concept. In relation to the question of power, for example, only a few tentative steps were taken. The need to go beyond the political conception of power was argued, but little was said about representations of power found in religious and philosophical literature that could enter the proper conception of moral empowerment. A more comprehensive investigation of these dimensions of power and how they may modify the way power is understood in the political realm is required, and relationships between power, justice, and freedom are among the significant topics that must be studied in great depth if a clear conception of moral empowerment is to emerge.

Issues related to understanding, a central element of the framework in question, were scrutinized in more detail. Understanding was examined as both a process and an attribute of the human soul and it was stated that the "subject," the "object," and the "process of understanding" have to be treated together in the discourse on education, this in anticipation of the role capabilities would play in the formulation of curricular objectives and the analysis of content. In an educational process seeking moral empowerment, it was argued, nurturing understanding and fostering spiritual qualities must go hand in hand. Yet, it is clear that the treatment in this book of "spiritual qualities" as a distinct category of virtues is only an initial step in a much needed systematic research—not bound to narrow studies in cognitive psychology—to clarify how these attributes of the human soul contribute to the development of capabilities.

In the search for the "subject of understanding," certain candidates, suggested by various theoretical approaches to education, were found to be inadequate, both because of their own shortcomings and on account of the relationship they establish with objects of understanding and of the manner in which they engage in the process of understanding. Yet, the examination of each candidate did offer insights into the desired characteristics of a potential protagonist of moral empowerment and opened the way for the discussion of the relationship between the subject and the object of understanding. In positioning the subject of understanding in the larger context of physical, social, and spiritual reality, the ontological elements of the conceptual framework being sought were briefly considered, and the relations that physicalism and naturalism in its various forms propose between the subject and object of understanding were deemed restrictive. The notion of an extended reality as well as Nagel's conception of objectivity made it possible to grant the subject of understanding with the boundlessness she needs in order to advance significantly in understanding, and to explore the methods by which she can reach certain milestones along the way.

Reflections on the nature of "objects of understanding" in an extended reality—the complexity of which demands not a single language, but multiple ones—led to the notion of complementarity between the languages of science and religion. But to argue complementarity, it was necessary to first demonstrate the compatibility of science and religion by identifying the parallels that exist between them as two overlapping systems of knowledge and practice. On that foundation, the claim could be advanced that in enhancing the understanding of the student—a process inseparable from fostering spiritual qualities—and in strengthening a desired set of convictions in action, an educational process seeking moral empowerment would need to draw on both science and religion as complementary sources of knowledge and use the languages of both properly. Although examples from FUNDAEC's experience illustrated how the two languages could be employed without losing the rigor of the former and the penetrating power of the latter, much more has to be said on the way educational materials and methods can express the true nature of scientific inquiry freed from the limitations of positivism and the profound insights of religion freed from dogma and rigid notions of truth—this in order to help students develop patterns of thought and action that reflect the coherence between the material and the spiritual.

Criteria for the selection and organization of objects of under-standing into a structured whole was another aspect of the conceptual framework examined in some detail. This was done under the title of integration; first the question of integration of knowledge itself was analyzed, and then, several values of knowledge were discussed, values that would govern the organization of the teaching-learning experi-ence. This led to an initial consideration of the intimacy of thought and action, a theme that was developed further in the context of the continuity of thought, language, and action. Congruent with Hirst's criticism of the kind of thinking that has given rise to hasty attempts at integration, it was argued that one can respect forms of knowledge without having to accept the rigidity in the method of teaching and in the presentation of content often associated with subject-based curricula. Certain challenges were also identified in an alternative ap-proach where social practices become the sole organizing principle of curricular design.

The introduction of the notion of capability helped bring together the desired elements of the framework of the educational process with eyes set on moral empowerment—elements discussed in the examina-tion of issues related to empowerment, understanding, complementar-ity, and integration. Once again, the treatment of the various features of capability as a way of thinking about the objectives, content, and methods of education has been uneven. Its comparison with the for-mulations set forth by Sen and Nussbaum is probably sufficient for our purposes. The role of knowledge in the development of capabili-ties—as far as the understanding of concepts and the assimilation of information is concerned—has been addressed to a reasonable extent.

But issues related to skills, attitudes, and habits have been left out almost entirely. And as mentioned above, the treatment of spiritual qualities has been only preliminary. Nevertheless, it is hoped that the discussion succeeded in demonstrating the value of capability as a central element associated with moral empowerment and in exposing some of the philosophical underpinnings of an educational process organized around the progressive development of capabilities.

It has been an intention of this inquiry to bring together a number of threads of educational thought, often kept separate, which would enable Bahá'í-inspired educational programs to weave the appropriate curricula. To the extent that such a purpose has been achieved, this book makes a modest contribution to the general discourse on education as well. That the experience repeatedly cited has not been concerned so much with schools per se but more with education in the context of the social and economic development of peoples has opened areas of inquiry which would have otherwise been neglected. These areas of inquiry are of vital importance and need to be explored further; for reflecting from time to time on the indispensable contributions it must make to the advancement of material and spiritual civilization helps education in general to resist the enticements of relativism prevalent in today's intellectual life and achieve higher and higher degrees of clarity about its aim and its mission.

NOTES

Chapter 1

1. Shoghi Effendi. (1947), Summary Statement -1947, Special UN Committee on Palestine.

2. Ibid.

3. Office of Social and Economic Development. (2008), *For the Betterment of the World: The Worldwide Bahá'í Community's Approach to Social and Economic Development.*

4. 'Abdu'l-Bahá, *Selections from the Writings of 'Abdu'l-Bahá,* no. 225.24.

5. Shoghi Effendi, *World Order of Bahá'u'lláh,* p. 43.

6. Bahá'í World Centre. (2001), *Century of Light,* no. 5.16.

7. 'Abdu'l-Bahá, *The Promulgation of Universal Peace: Talks Delivered by 'Abdu'lBahá during His Visit to the United States and Canada in 1912,* p. 618.

8. 'Abdu'l-Bahá, *Selections from the Writings of 'Abdu'l-Bahá,* no. 23.6

9. Bahá'u'lláh, *Gleanings from the Writings of Bahá'u'lláh,* no. 43.4.

10. FUNDAEC. (2006), *A Discourse on Social Action, Unit 1: Basic Concepts,* p 13.

11. Shoghi Effendi. (1990), *Compilation of Compilations Prepared by the Universal House of Justice, 1963–1990.* Maryborough, Victoria: Bahá'í Publications Australia, p. 84.

Chapter 2

1. Bahá'í International Community. (1995), *The Prosperity of Humankind,* ¶14.

2. The metaphor of the human body used here may bring to mind other attempts to describe society in organic terms. Émile Durkheim's model of organic solidarity is one example. Durkheim makes a distinction between mechanical and organic solidarity. Mechanical solidarity is a feature of less advanced, more homogenous and highly religious societies, whereas organic solidarity represents the higher evolutionary stage in social order marked by complexity, differentiation, and interdependence as seen in modern industrialized society. However, it is important to note that Bahá'ís are not necessarily promoting such an organic model of social organization whatever its merits may be. They employ the metaphor only as a means to gain insight into the nature of the relationships that would govern a society approaching its stage of maturity. The distinguishing feature of the vision of social organization that spurs their efforts is the "consciousness of the oneness of humankind."

3. Bahá'í International Community, *The Prosperity of Humankind,* ¶16.

4. The habit of assigning discrete meanings to concepts in the political realm without regard to their application in other domains of life is not confined to the examination of the notion of power. Mulhall and Swift point out, for example, that Rawls' concept of justice is to contribute to the shaping of a particular political framework, one that excludes structures that are not viewed, strictly speaking, as political: "Justice as fairness, Rawls . . . claims, is a purely political conception of justice. By this he means that its scope is restricted to the basic structure of constitutional democratic regimes (applying only to their most fundamental social, political and economic institutions, and not, for example, to churches, universities and hospitals); that it does not depend upon the truth of any particular comprehensive philosophical,

religious or moral doctrines about human well-being; and that it is formulated only in terms of certain fundamental ideas that are implicit in the public political culture of democratic societies." Mulhall, S. and Swift, A. (1995), "The Social Self in Political Theory: The Communitarian Critique of the Liberal Subject." In D. Bakhurst and C. Sypnowich (eds), *The Social Self.* Thousand Oaks, CA: Sage Publications, pp. 107–8

5. Russell, B. (2004), *Power: A New Social Analysis.* Routledge Classics, p. 23.

6. Weber, M. (1997), *The Theory of Social and Economic Organization.* New York: The Free Press, p. 152.

7. Lukes, S. (2005), *Power: A Radical View.* (2nd ed.). London: Palgrave: Macmillan.

8. Dahl, R. A. (1957), "The Concept of Power." *Behavioral Science,* 2, 201–15, pp. 202–3.

9. Dahl, R. A. (2005), *Who Governs?: Democracy and Power in an American City.* Yale University Press, p. 336.

10. See Bachrach, P. and Baratz, M. S. (1970), *Power and Poverty: Theory and Practice.* Oxford: Oxford University Press.

11. Ibid., p. 39.

12. Ibid., p. 44.

13. Ibid., p. 43.

14. Lukes, S. (2005), p. 26.

15. Hindess, B. (1996), *Discourses of Power: From Hobbes to Foucault.* Oxford: Blackwell Publishers Ltd, p. 73.

16. Lukes, S. (2005), pp. 12–3.

17. Buckley, J. and Erricker, J. (2004), "Citizenship Education in the Postmodern Moment." In H. Alexander (ed.), *Spirituality and Ethics in Education.* Brighton-Portland: Sussex Academic Press, p. 174.

18. Freire, P. (2000), *Education for Critical Consciousness.* New York: Continuum, p. 17.

19. Ibid., p. 18.

20. Ibid.

21. Freire, P. (1998), *Pedagogy of the Oppressed* (M. B. Ramos, Trans.). New York: Continuum, p. 56.

22. Ibid., p. 62.

23. Ibid., p. 66.

24. Lukes, S. (2005), p. 34.

25. Hobbes, T. (2011), *Leviathan.* Toronto: Broadview Press.

26. Ibid.

27. Foucault, M. (1976), *The History of Sexuality* (R. Hurley, Trans.). (Vol. 1: An Introduction). New York: Vintage Books, p. 92.

28. Foucault, M. (1972–1977), *Power/Knowledge: Selected Interviews and Other Writings.* New York: Pantheon Books, p. 102.

29. Foucault, M. (1976), p. 93.

30. Foucault, M. (1972–1977), p. 96.

31. Hindess, B. (1996), p. 1.

32. Arbab, F. (2000), "Promoting a Discourse on Science, Religion, and Development." In S. M. P. Harper (ed.), *The Lab the Temple and the Market: Reflections at the intersection of Science, Religion, and Development.* Ottawa, ON: International Development Research Centre, pp. 162–3.

33. Hobbes, T. (2011).

34. Bellous, J. and Pearson, A. (1995), "Empowerment and Teacher Education." *Studies in Philosophy and Education,* 14 (7), 49–62, p. 54.

35. Arendt, H. (1958), *The Human Condition.* (2nd ed.). Chicago: University of Chicago Press, p. 200.

36. Arendt, H. (1970), *On Violence.* New York: Harcourt Brace & Company, p. 54.

37. Arendt, H. (1958), p. 203.

38. Mill, J. S. (1987), *Utilitarianism.* Amherst, NY: Prometheus Books, p.16.

39. Bentham, J. (1907), *An Introduction to the Principles of Morals and Legislation.* Oxford: Clarendon Press, pp. 1–2.

40. Mill, J. S. (1987), p. 17.

41. Kant, I. (1998), *Groundwork of the Metaphysics of Morals, Cambridge Texts in the History of Philosophy.* (M. Gregor, Trans.). Cambridge University Press, p. 25.

42. Ibid., p. 14.

43. Ibid., p. 15.

44. Ibid., p. 31.

45. Taylor, C. (1982), "The Diversity of Goods." In A. Sen and B. Williams (eds), *Utilitarianism and Beyond.* Cambridge: Cambridge University Press, p. 129.

46. Ibid., p. 130.

47. Ibid.

48. Arbab, F. (2000), p. 186.

49. Young, M. F. D. (2008), "Curriculum studies and the problem of knowledge: Updating the Enlightenment?" In M. F. D. Young (ed.), *Bringing Knowledge Back In: From social constructivism to social realism in the sociology of education.* London: Routledge, p. 82.

50. FUNDAEC. (2008), *A Discourse on Social Action,* Unit 2: *Education,* p. 47.

Chapter 3

1. FUNDAEC. (2005), *Curriculum Development,* p. 28.

2. See, for instance, how teachers are advised to teach students concepts in general through an approach called "concept attainment" using the concept of fruit as an example, in Woolfolk, A. E. (2010), *Educational Psychology.* Upper Saddle River, NJ: Prentice Hall.

3. FUNDAEC. (2005), p. 11.

4. Peters, R. S. (1966), *Ethics and Education.* London: George Allen & Unwin Ltd, pp. 35–6.

5. Arendt, H. (2006), *Between Past and Future.* Penguin Books, pp. 177–80.

6. Ibid.

7. The antecedents of the ideas that shaped the behavioral-objective model of teaching according to Dunne "go back to the beginning of the century and to the attempts made then to forge a new science of education that would replace the mixture of rhetoric, traditional lore, and practical know-how that had constituted the old pedagogy." Dunne, J. (1992), *Back to the Rough Ground: 'Phronesis' and 'Techne' in Modern Philosophy and in Aristotle*. Notre Dame, IN: University of Notre Dame Press, p. 2.

8. Dunne, J. (1992), pp. 4–5.

9. Benjamin Bloom edited in 1956 the Taxonomy of Educational Objectives which is a classification of educational goals or learning objectives. The taxonomy has come to be associated with his name. Bloom draws a parallel with the work of biologists who "have found their taxonomy markedly helpful as a means of insuring accuracy of communication about their science." Bloom, B. S. (1956), *Taxonomy of Educational Objectives, Handbook 1: Cognitive Domain*. New York: Longman, p. 1.

10. Tyler, R. W. (1949), *Basic Principles of Curriculum and Instruction*. Chicago: University of Chicago Press, p. 30.

11. Anderson, W. A. and Krathwohl, D. R. (2000), *Taxonomy for Learning, Teaching, and Assessing: A Revision of Bloom's Taxonomy of Educational Objectives*. Pearson, pp. 4–5.

12. Ibid., pp. 13–4.

13. Dunne, J. (1988), "Teaching and the Limits of Technique: An Analysis of the Behavioural-Objectives Model." *The Irish Journal of Education*, 22 (2), 66–90, pp. 69–70.

14. Gagne, R. M. & Briggs, L. J. (1974), *Principles of instructional design* (2nd ed.). New York: Holt, Rinehart &Winston, p. 119.

15. Bloom, B. S., Hastings, T. & Madaus, G. F. (1971), *Handbook of summative and formative evaluation*. New York: McGraw Hill, p. 33.

16. Dunne, J. (1988), p. 70.

17. Ibid.

18. Ibid., p. 71.

19. Mager, R. F. (1997), *Preparing Instructional Objectives: A critical tool in the development of effective instruction*. (3rd ed.). Center for Effective Performance, p. 102.

20. Dunne, J. (1988), p. 85.

21. Ibid., p. 69.

22. Taylor, C. (1982), "The Diversity of Goods." In A. Sen and B. Williams (eds), *Utilitarianism and Beyond*. Cambridge: Cambridge University Press, p. 130.

23. The cognitive movement is intimately associated with the breakthrough that occurred in the so-called cognitive sciences in the mid-twentieth century, eliciting collaboration among a number of discrete disciplines: "Cognitive science is a child of the 1950s, the product of a time when psychology, anthropology and linguistics were redefining themselves and computer science and neuroscience as disciplines were coming into existence. Psychology could not participate in the cognitive revolution until it had freed itself from behaviorism, thus restoring cognition to scientific respectability. By then, it was becoming clear in several disciplines that the solution to some of their problems depended crucially on solving problems traditionally allocated to other disciplines." Miller, G. A. (2003), "The cognitive revolution: a historical perspective," *TRENDS in Cognitive Sciences*, 7 (3): 141–44.

24. Bruner, J. (1999), *The Culture of Education*. (5th ed.). Cambridge, MA: Harvard University Press, p. 1.

25. Ibid., pp. 1–3.

26. Pinker, S. (2003), *The Blank Slate: The Modern Denial of Human Nature*. Penguin Books, p. 32.

27. Bruner, J. (1999), pp. 8–11.

28. Ibid., p. 10.

29. Gardner, H. (1987), *The Mind's New Science: A History of the Cognitive Revolution*. Basic Books, p. 6.

30. Bruner, J. (1999), p. 5.

31. Ibid., p. 6.

32. Ibid.

33. Ibid., p. 8.

34. Ibid., pp. 2–3.

35. Ibid., p. 9.

36. These are the kinds of "rules" or operations that are possible in computation. They must, for example, be specifiable in advance, and free from ambiguity. They must, in their ensemble, be computationally consistent. Any alteration to operations necessary as a result of a prior feedback should adhere to a consistent, prearranged systematicity. They may be contingent, but they cannot encompass unforeseeable contingencies. Ibid., p. 6.

37. Bruner, J. (2006b), *In Search of Pedagogy: The selected works of Jerome S. Bruner.* (Vol. II). London: Routledge, p. 82.

38. Bruner, J. (1999), p. 3.

39. "Primary process" is part of a constellation of concepts used by Freud in psychoanalysis. His model of the mind consisted of three parts: ego, id, and super-ego. Id contains everything that is present at birth; above all it is the expression of physical instincts in forms unknown to us. It is "the dark, inaccessible part of our personality; what little we know of it we have learnt from our dream-work and of the construction of neurotic symptoms, and most of that is of a negative character . . . it has no organization, produces no collective will, but only a striving to bring about the satisfaction of instinctive needs subject to the observance of the pleasure principle." [Freud, S. (1991), *New Introductory Lectures on Psycho-analysis,* p. 85.] Freud made a distinction between two varieties of mental functioning: primary process and secondary process. The former employs various mechanisms such as symbolism and hallucinatory wish-fulfillment that operate in dreams as id is frustrated by lack of gratification in the real world. Secondary process is governed by reason and the reality principle. It is used by ego which is that part of the mind derived from id, representing conscious-

ness. Many psychoanalysts today consider Freud's concept of "primary process" as archaic, childish, and maladaptive.

40. Bruner, J. (2006b), pp. 82–3.

41. Bruner, J. (1999), p. 13.

42. Ibid., pp. 11–2.

43. Bakhurst, D. (2001), "Memory, Identity and the Future of Cultural Psychology." In D. Bakhurst and S. G. Shanker (eds), *Jerome Bruner: Language, Culture, Self.* Thousand Oaks, CA: Sage Publications, p. 195.

44. Glasersfeld, E. von. (1991), *Cognition, Construction of Knowledge and Teaching.* In Phillips, D.C. (1995), The Good, the Bad and the Ugly: The Many Faces of Constructivism. *Educational Researcher,* 24 (7): pp. 5–12.

45. Phillips, D. C. and Soltis, J. F. (2009), *Perspectives on Learning* (5th ed.). Columbia University: Teachers College Press.

46. Bakhurst would probably agree with Evald Ilyenkov's notion of the ideal for whom "real" does not simply refer to "everything man perceives as a thing outside his own consciousness" and "ideal" to "everything that is not conceived as such a thing." Ilyenkov points to a much more complex relationship between consciousness, will, and human activity. The man within which the ideal exists cannot be understood "as one individual with a brain, but as a real aggregate of real people collectively realizing their specifically human life activity." [Ilyenkov, E. (1977), "The Concept of the Ideal," *Philosophy in the USSR: Problems of Dialectical Materialism* (pp. 71–99). Moscow: Progress.] According to Bakhurst, "Ilyenkov developed a distinct solution to what he called 'the problem of the ideal'; that is, the problem of the place of the non-material in the natural world. The latter involves a resolute defence of the objectivity of ideal phenomena, which are said to exist as aspects of our spiritual culture, embodied in our environment. . . ." Bakhurst, D. (1997), "Meaning, Normativity and the Life of Mind." *Language and Communication,* 17(1): 33–51, p. 34.

47. Bakhurst, D. (2001), p. 188.

48. Ibid., p. 195.

49. Williams, B. (1993), *Morality: An Introduction to Ethics. (Canto ed.).* Cambridge: Cambridge University Press, p. 18.

50. MacIntyre, A. (1981), *After Virtue.* Notre Dame, IN: University of Notre Dame Press, p. 12.

51. Ibid., p. 8.

52. Ibid., pp. 10.

53. Gardiner, P. (1988), *Kierkegaard: A Very Short Introduction.* Oxford: Oxford University Press, pp. 44–5.

54. Ibid., pp. 49–50.

55. MacIntyre, A. (1981), pp. 39–40.

56. Ibid., p. 41.

57. Ibid., p. 24.

58. Ibid., p. 11.

59. Kymlicka, W. (2002), *Contemporary Political Philosophy: An Introduction.* (2nd ed.).

Oxford: Oxford University Press, pp. 220–8.

60. Sandel, M. J. (1998), *Liberalism and the Limits of Justice.* (2nd ed.). Cambridge: Cambridge University Press, p. 152.

61. Kymlicka, W. (2002), p. 225.

62. Ibid., p. 227.

63. Kierkegaard, S. (1983), *Fear and Trembling* and *Repetition.* (H. V. and E. H. Hong, Trans.). Princeton, NJ: Princeton University Press, p. 70.

64. Gardiner, P. (1988), p. 66.

65. Kierkegaard, S. (2009), *Concluding Unscientific Postscript.* Cambridge Texts in the History of Philosophy, (A. Hannay Trans.). Cambridge University Press, p. 203.

66. Ibid., p. 163.

67. Gardiner, P. (1988), p. 40.

68. Kierkegaard, S. (2010), *The Present Age: On the Death of Rebellion,* (A. Dru, Trans.). Harper Perennial Modern Thought, p. 52.

Chapter 4

1. Bakhurst, D. (1997), "Meaning, Normativity and the Life of Mind." *Language and Communication*, 17 (1), 33–51, p. 38.

2. 'Abdu'l-Bahá. *Tablet to August Forel*, p. 8.

3. 'Abdu'l-Bahá, *Some Answered Questions*, no. 61.2

4. Ibid., no. 55.6.

5. Ibid.

6. Ibid., no. 54.

7. Ibid., no. 66.3

8. MacIntyre, A. (1981), *After Virtue*. Notre Dame, IN: University of Notre Dame Press, p. 175.

9. Ibid., p. 177.

10. Ibid., pp. 175–6.

11. Ibid., pp. 176–7.

12. Ibid., p. 178.

13. Higgins, C. (2003), "MacIntyre's Moral Theory and the Possibility of an Aretaic Ethics of Teaching." *Journal of Philosophy of Education*, 37 (2), p. 281.

14. MacIntyre, A. (1981), p. 169.

15. Higgins, C. (2003), pp. 281–2.

16. Ibid., pp. 282–3.

17. MacIntyre, A. (1981), p. 178.

18. Anscombe, G. E. M. (1981), "Modern Moral Philosophy," *Ethics, Religion and Politics: Collected Philosophical Papers* (Vol. III). Minneapolis, MN: University of Minnesota Press, p. 38.

19. MacIntyre, A. (1994), "A Partial Response to my Critics." In J. Horton and S. Mendus (eds), *Critical Perspectives on the Work of Alasdair MacIntyre* (pp. 283–304). Oxford: Cambridge, Polity Press in association with Blackwell Publishers Ltd, p. 288.

20. MacIntyre, A. (1981), p. 28.

21. Ibid., p. 82.

22. Ibid., p. 83.

23. May, T. (2001), *Our Practices Our Selves, Or, What It Means To Be Human*. Philadelphia: Pennsylvania State University Press, p. 31.

24. Carr, D. (2003), "Character and Moral Choice in the Cultivation of Virtue." *Philosophy*, 78, p. 231.

25. Nussbaum, M. (1993), "Non-Relative Virtues: An Aristotelian Approach." In M. Nussbaum and A. Sen (eds), *The Quality of Life* (pp. 242–69). Oxford: Oxford University Press, p. 250.

26. Williams, B. (1985), *Ethics and the Limits of Philosophy*. Cambridge, MA: Harvard University Press, pp. 160–1.

27. Williams, B. (2008), "Human Rights and Relativism." In G. Hawthorn (ed.), *In the Beginning Was the Deed: Realism and Moralism in Political Argument*. Princeton, NJ: Princeton University Press, p. 68.

28. Ibid., pp. 68–9.

29. Murdoch, I. (1997), "The Sovereignty of Good Over Other Concepts." In R. Crisp and M. Slote (eds) (pp. 99–118). Oxford: Oxford University Press, pp. 104–5.

30. FUNDAEC. (2006), *A Discourse on Social Action*, Unit 1: Basic Concepts, p. 23.

31. Bahá'u'lláh, The Hidden Words, Persian, no. 1.

32. FUNDAEC. (2006), p. 31.

33. Bahá'u'lláh, *Gleanings from the Writings of Bahá'u'lláh*, no. 125.6.

34. FUNDAEC. (2004), Primary Elements of Descriptions, Unit 1: Properties, p. 51.

35. Ibid., p. 59.

36. Ibid., p. 63.

37. Maleuvre, D. (2011), *The Horizon: A History of Our Infinite Longing*. University of California Press, pp. 3–4.

38. Taylor, C. (1982), "The Diversity of Goods." In A. Sen and B. Williams (eds), *Utilitarianism and Beyond*. Cambridge: Cambridge University Press, p. 132.

39. Ibid., p. 136.

40. Ibid., p. 141.

41. Ibid.

42. 'Abdu'l-Bahá, *Selections from the Writings of 'Abdu'l-Bahá*, no. 12.1.

43. Johnston, D. (2011), *A Brief History of Justice*. Wiley-Blackwell, p. 2.

44. Ibid., p. 126.

45. Hume, D. (1998), *An Enquiry Concerning the Principles of Morals*. Oxford University Press, p. 15.

46. Smith, A. (2008), *The Wealth of Nations*. Oxford Paperbacks, p. 21.

47. Kant, I. (1991), *Kant Political Writing, Cambridge Texts in the History of Political Thought*. H. Reiss, (ed.). Cambridge University Press, p. 74.

48. Johnston, D. (2011), p. 164.

49. Kant, I. (1996), *The Metaphysics of Morals, Cambridge Texts in the History of Philosophy*. (M. Gregor, Trans.). Cambridge University Press, pp. 105–6

50. Johnston, D. (2011), p. 174.

51. Sidgwick, H. (1907), *The Methods of Ethics*. Macmillan and Company, p. 274.

52. Johnston, D. (2011), p. 176.

53. Ibid., p. 177.

54. Ibid., p. 181.

55. Ibid., p. 182.

56. Ibid., p. 197.

57. Rawls, J. (1999), *A Theory of Justice*. Belknap Press, p. 3.

58. Ibid.

59. Johnston, D. (2011), p. 202.

60. Ibid., pp. 211–2.

61. Rawls, J. (2001), *Justice as Fairness: A Restatement*. Belknap Press, pp. 42–3.

62. Ibid., p. 44.

63. Johnston, D. (2011), p. 214.

64. Ibid., pp. 218–22.

65. Bahá'u'lláh, The Hidden Words, Arabic, no. 2.

66. Bahá'u'lláh, *Gleanings from the Writings of Bahá'u'lláh*, no. 164.2.

67. Johnston, D. (2011), p. 190.

68. Bahá'u'lláh, *Tablets of Bahá'u'lláh*, p. 138.

69. Ibid., p. 67.

70. Johnston, D. (2011), p. 226.

71. Ibid., p. 227.

72. Shoghi Effendi. (1953), *Guidance for Today and Tomorrow: A Selection from the Writings of Shoghi Effendi*. London: Bahá'í Publishing Trust, p. 110.

73. See, for example, Putman, D. (1990), "The Compatibility of Justice and Kindness," *Philosophy* 65 (254).

74. Bahá'u'lláh, *Tablets of Bahá'u'lláh*, p. 167.

Chapter 5

1. Searle, J. R. (1995), *The Construction of Social Reality*. New York: The Free Press, p. 9.

2. Ibid., p. 15.

3. Ibid., p. 20.

4. Ibid., p. 25.

5. Searle, in response to his critics, states that he needs "an account of collective intentionality which is consistent with methodological individualism." [Searle, J. R. (1997), "Responses to Critics of the Construction of Social Reality." *Philosophy and Phenomenological Research*, 57 (2), 449–458.] His ontology is that of "individual human organisms and their mental states," and not of "a primitive ontology of actual human collectives"(p. 449). According to him, the "collective's existence consists entirely in the fact that there is a number of individual agents who think of themselves as part of the collective"(p. 450). By implication, "We-intentionality can *give rise* to mutual belief, but does not *reduce* to I-intentionality plus mutual belief"(p. 453).

6. Searle, J. R. (1995), pp. 38–9.

7. Ibid., p. 27.

8. Ibid., p. 41.

9. Ibid.

10. Ibid., p. 38.

11. Ibid., p. 35.

12. Ibid., p. 9.

13. See Glasersfeld, E. von. (1996), *Radical Constructivism: A Way of Knowing and Learning*. London: Routledge.

14. Nagel, T. (1986), *The View From Nowhere*. Oxford: Oxford University Press, p. 14.

15. Ibid.

16. Ibid., p. 15.

17. Ibid.

18. Ibid., p. 16.

19. Ibid., p. 4.

20. Williams, B. (1985), *Ethics and the Limits of Philosophy*. Cambridge, MA: Harvard University Press, p. 132.

21. Ibid., p. 136.

22. Ibid.

23. Ibid., pp. 1389.

24. Ibid., p. 139.

25. Nagel, T. (1986), p. 18.

26. Ibid., p. 17

27. Ibid., p. 18.

28. Ibid., p. 5.

29. Ibid., p. 26.

30. Ibid.

31. Ibid., p. 91.

32. Bohm, D. (2002), *Wholeness and the Implicate Order*. (2nd ed.). London: Routledge, p. 2.

33. Ibid., p. 9.

34. Ibid., p. 3.

35. Ibid., p. 4.

36. Ibid.

37. Ibid., p. 5.

38. Ibid., pp. 5–6.

39. Ibid., p. 6.

40. There are, of course, many subtleties to the way observation and theory interact. But the fact itself that observation statements are made in the context of a-priori knowledge is indisputable. A. F. Chalmers, for example, in his introductory book *What is this thing called Science* mentions three "components of the stand on the facts assumed to be the basis of science": a) "facts are directly given to careful, unprejudiced observers via the senses"; b) "facts are prior to and independent of theory"; and c) "facts constitute a firm and reliable foundation for scientific knowledge." He presents clear arguments showing that "each of these claims is faced with difficulties and, at best, can only be accepted in a highly qualified form." Chalmers, A. F. (1978), *What is this thing called Science?* (3rd ed.). Buckingham: Open University Press, pp. 3–4.

41. Bohm, D. (2002), p. 62.

42. FUNDAEC. (1999), *Constructing a Conceptual Framework for Social Action*, p. 113.

43. McGinn, M. (2009), "McDowell." In C. Belshaw and G. Kemp (eds), *12 Modern Philosophers*. Willey-Blackwell, pp. 216–7.

44. Ibid., p. 218.

45. Ibid.

46. McDowell, J. (1994), *Mind and World*. Cambridge, MA: Harvard University Press, p. xv.

47. McGinn, M. (2009), pp. 218–9.

48. Spontaneity is a term used by Kant in the *Critique of Pure Reason*. He tries to reconcile "the apparently incompatible dimensions of observed empirical data and a priori knowledge." In philosophy before Kant's time "the realm of a priori knowledge, the realm of 'pure reason,' had been the location of debates about the nature of God and

being, which did not rely on empirical evidence. The title *Critique of Pure Reason* indicates Kant's desire to question the basis of such debates. The vital element in the first Critique is the establishment of a series of necessary—a priori—rules of thought for the classification of phenomena, together with the idea that these rules are based on the 'spontaneous' nature of the mind. For Kant something is spontaneous when it takes place 'of its own accord,' rather than being caused by something else. It might seem odd that in cognition *spontaneity* functions in terms of necessary rules, but this is the crux of what Kant proposes. The idea is that the knowledge of natural necessity is only possible on the basis of something which is itself not necessitated. The borderline between deterministic nature, and human spontaneity, is the location of the most fundamental disputes in modernity about how human beings are to describe themselves." Bowie, A. (2003), *Introduction to German Philosophy From Kant to Habermas.* Cambridge: Polity Press, pp. 17–8.

49. Wright, C. (2002), "Human Nature?" In N. H. Smith (ed.), *Reading McDowell on Mind and World.* London: Routledge, p. 140.

50. Ibid., p. 141.

51. Ibid., p. 140.

52. Sellars, W. (1956), "Empiricism and the Philosophy of Mind." In H. Feigl and M. Scriven (eds), *Minnesota Studies in the Philosophy of Science* (Vol. 1). Minneapolis, MN: University of Minnesota Press, pp. 298–9.

53. McDowell, J. (1994), p. xiv.

54. Ibid., p. xv.

55. Ibid.

56. Wright, C. (2002), p. 144.

57. McDowell, J. (1994), p. xxiii.

58. Ibid., p. xix.

59. Ibid., p. 26.

60. Wright, C. (2002), p. 147.

61. McDowell, J. (1994), p. 32.

62. Nagel, T. (1986), p. 84.

63. McDowell, J. (1994), p. xx.

64. Ibid., p. 115.

65. Gadamer, H.-G. (2004a), *Truth and Method.* (J.Weinsheimer and D. G. Marshall, revised Trans.). (2nd Revised Ed.). London: Continuum (first published in 1975), p. 441.

66. McDowell, J. (1994), pp. 84–5.

67. Bahá'u'lláh, *Tablets of Bahá'u'lláh*, p. 142.

68. Bahá'u'lláh, *Gleanings from the Writings of Bahá'u'lláh*, no. 90.1.

69. Bahá'u'lláh, The Hidden Words, Persian, no. 29.

70. McDowell, J. (1994), p. 72.

71. Ibid.

72. 'Abdu'l-Bahá, *Some Answered Questions*, no. 16.4.

73. McDowell, J. (1994), p. 72.

Chapter 6

1. Hirst, P. H. (1974b), "Liberal Education and the Nature of Knowledge." In R. S. Peters (ed.), *Knowledge and the Curriculum: A collection of philosophical papers* (pp. 30–53). London and New York: Routledge & Kegan Paul.

2. Hirst, P. H. (1974c), "Morals, Religion and the Maintained School." In R. S. Peters (ed.), *Knowledge and the Curriculum: A collection of philosophical papers* (pp. 173–89). London and New York: Routledge & Kegan Paul, p. 184.

3. Ibid., p. 187.

4. Cowen, M. P. and Shenton, R. W. (1996), *Doctrines of Development.* London: Routledge, pp. 116–17.

5. Haq, M. U. (1976), *The Poverty Curtain: Choices for the Third World.* New York: Columbia University Press, p. 12.

6. Ibid., p. 3.

7. Laudan, L. (1982), "Commentary: Science at the Bar—Causes for Concern." *Science, Technology, and Human Values,* 7 (41), 16–19, p. 17.

8. FUNDAEC. (2000), *Science, Religion and Development,* p. 26.

9. Harman, W. (1994), "A Re-examination of the Metaphysical Foundations of Modern Science: Why is it Necessary?" In W. Harman and J. Clark (eds), *New Metaphysical Foundations of Modern Science.* Sausalito, CA: Institute of Noetic Sciences, p. 8.

10. Nelson, L. (1994), "On What We Say There Is and Why It Matters: A Feminist Perspective on Metaphysics and Science." In W. Harman and J. Clark (eds), *New Metaphysical Foundations of Modern Science.* Sausalito, CA: Institute of Noetic Sciences, p. 17.17ces, p. 17 A Feminist Perspective on Metaphysics and Scienceh ve on Metaphysics and Science't here:

11. Ibid., p. 35.

12. Ibid., p. 37.

13. Ibid., p. 35.

14. Ibid., p. 36.

15. Ibid., p. 30.

16. Blackburn, S. (2005), *Truth: A Guide.* Oxford: Oxford University Press.

17. Simon Blackburn in his book refers to William K. Clifford's classic essay, "The Ethics of Belief," and William James's reply to it.

18. Clifford, W. K. (1999), "The Ethics of Belief." In T. J. Madigan (ed.), *The Ethics of Belief and Other Essays.* Amherst, NY: Prometheus Books (originally published in Contemporary Review, 1877), p. 91.

19. James, W. (2005), "The Will to Believe." In J. Capps and D. Capps (eds), *James and Dewey on Belief and Experience.* Champaign, IL: University of Illinois Press (originally published in 1895), pp. 107–8.

20. Blackburn, S. (2005), p. 11.

21. Ibid., p. 13.

22. Blackburn sometimes uses the terms "belief" and "faith" interchangeably. He mentions that for an individual there are times when

it is expedient to believe in something untrue as well as occasions when it is uncomfortable and threatening to believe in something true. "Truth," however, "has rights and privileges of its own, and they are not the same as those of utility" (Blackburn, 2005, p. 9).

23. John Henry Newman was an innovative thinker in the field of theological epistemology and contributed to a number of significant intellectual developments throughout the nineteenth century.

24. Dunne, J. (1992), *Back to the Rough Ground: 'Phronesis' and 'Techne' in Modern Philosophy and in Aristotle.* Notre Dame, IN: University of Notre Dame Press, p. 32.

25. Newman, J. H. (1903), *An Essay in Aid of A Grammar of Assent.* London: Longmans, Green, and Co., p. 303.

26. Cited in Norris, T. (2009), "Faith." In I. Ker and T. Merrigan (eds), *The Cambridge Companion to John Newman Henry.* Cambridge University Press, p. 85.

27. Newman, J. H. (1903), p. 211

28. Dunne, J. (1992), pp. 36–7.

29. Newman, J. H. (1903), p. 311.

30. Dunne, J. (1992), p. 37.

31. 'Abdu'l-Bahá, *Selections from the Writings of 'Abdu'l-Bahá,* no. 129.2.

32. Peters, R. S. (1972), *Reason and Compassion.* London: Routledge & Kegan Paul, p. 111.

33. See Kuhn, T. S. (1996), *The Structure of Scientific Revolutions.* (Third ed.). Chicago: University of Chicago Press.

34. FUNDAEC. (2000), p. 27.

35. Arbab, F. (2000), "Promoting a Discourse on Science, Religion, and Development." In S. M. P. Harper (ed.), *The Lab the Temple and the Market: Reflections at the intersection of Science, Religion, and Development.* Ottawa, ON: International Development Research Centre, p. 184.

36. Taylor, C. (2007), *A Secular Age.* Cambridge, MA: The Belknap Press of Harvard University Press, pp. 90–2.

37. Fleck, L. (1979), *Genesis and Development of a Scientific Fact.* Chicago: University of Chicago Press, p. 42.

38. Ibid.

39. See Lakatos, I. (1978), *The Methodology of Scientific Research Programmes: Philosophical Papers, Volume 1.* Cambridge: Cambridge University Press.

40. Larvor, B. (1998), *Lakatos: An Introduction.* London: Routledge. p. 51.

41. Ibid., p. 52.

42. Ibid., p. 53.

43. Nagel, T. (1986), *The View From Nowhere.* Oxford: Oxford University Press, pp. 83–4.

44. Ibid., p. 84.

45. Ibid., pp. 84–5.

46. Ibid., p. 85.

47. Shoghi Effendi, *World Order of Bahá'u'lláh,* p. 112.

48. Bahá'u'lláh, The Kitáb-i-Íqán, ¶104.

49. Gadamer, H.-G. (2004a), *Truth and Method.* (J.Weinsheimer and D. G. Marshall, revised Trans.). (2nd Revised Ed.). London: Continuum (first published in 1975), p. 351.

50. FUNDAEC. (2000), p. 71.

51. Gardner, H. (1991), *The Unschooled Mind: How Children Think & How Schools Teach.* New York: Basic Books, p. 3.

52. Ibid.

53. Ibid., p. 5.

54. It is true that at a more advanced stage a student of physics recognizes the limitation of the theory, which after all is a model of reality. However, the conviction that matter is made of particles is fundamental to the overall thinking of a physicist. In his celebrated lectures on physics, for example, Richard Feynman states: "If, in some cataclysm, all of scientific knowledge were to be destroyed and only one sentence passed on to the next generation of creatures, what

statement would contain the most information in the fewest words? I believe it is the *atomic hypothesis* (or the atomic *fact*, or whatever you wish to call it) that *All things are made of atoms—little particles that move around in perpetual motion, attracting each other when they are a little distance apart, but repelling upon being squeezed into one another.*" Feynman, R. (1963), *Six Easy Pieces: Essentials of Physics Explained by Its Most Brilliant Teacher.* New York: Basic Books.

55. Okasha, S. (2002), *Philosophy of Science: A Very Short Introduction.* Oxford: Oxford University Press, p. 70.

56. FUNDAEC. (2009), *A Discourse on Social Action*, Unit 3: *Science*, p. 40.

57. See Williams' notion of convergence in chapter 4.

58. FUNDAEC. (2009), p. 62.

59. Flyvbjerg, B. (2001), *Making Social Science Matter: Why social inquiry fails and how it can succeed again* (S. Sampson, Trans.). Cambridge: Cambridge University Press, p. 18.

60. FUNDAEC. (2009), pp. 65–6.

61. Lawn, C. (2006), *Gadamer: A Guide for the Perplexed.* New York: Continuum, pp. 77–8.

62. Collingwood, R. G. (1938), *The Principles of Art.* Oxford: Clarendon Press, p. 111.

63. Dunne, J. (1992), p. 64, citations from [Collingwood, R.G. (1938), pp. 226–27.]

64. Ibid.

65. Iris Murdoch states that "the development of consciousness in human beings is inseparably connected with the use of metaphor." They are not "merely peripheral decorations or even useful models, they are fundamental forms of our awareness of our condition: metaphors of space, metaphors of movement, metaphors of vision." "Metaphors often carry a moral charge, which analysis in simpler and plainer terms is designed to remove." (Murdoch, 1997, p. 99). They can be "a mode of understanding, and so of acting upon, our condition." (pp. 110–11).

66. Haydon, G. (2006c), *Values in Education*. New York: Continuum. P. 126.

67. Ibid.

68. Gadamer, H.-G. (2004b), *Philosophical Hermeneutics*. (David, E. Linge, ed. and trans.). Berkeley: University of California Press, (first published in 1976), p. 75.

69. Gadamer, H.-G. (2004a), p. 454.

70. Ricoeur, P. (1986), *The Symbolism of Evil*. Beacon Press, p. 351.

71. Ibid., p. 349.

72. Stiver, D. (1996), *The Philosophy of Religious Language*. Blackwell Publishing, p. 92.

73. See Lawn, C. (2006), pp. 88-90.

74. Krell, D. F. (ed.). (1978), *Martin Heidegger: Basic Writings*. London: Routledge, p. 163.

75. Bahá'u'lláh, cited in Shoghi Effendi, *The Advent of Divine Justice*, pp. 24–5.

76. Gadamer, H.-G. (2004a), p. 304

77. Stiver, D. (1996), p. 93.

78. Ibid., p. 97.

79. Ibid., pp. 94–5.

80. Gadamer, H.-G. (2004a), p. 371.

81. Ibid., pp. 271–72.

82. Ibid., p. 281.

83. Stiver, D. (1996), p. 98.

84. Williams, B. (2002), *Truth and Truthfulness*. Princeton, New Jersey: Princeton University Press, p. 8.

85. Stiver, D. (1996), pp. 98–9.

86. Bernstein, R. J. (1983), *Beyond Objectivism and Relativism*. Philadelphia: University of Pennsylvania Press, p. 168.

Chapter 7

1. Hirst, P. H. (1974a), "Curriculum Integration." In R. S. Peters (ed.), *Knowledge and the Curriculum: A collection of philosophical papers*

(pp. 132–51). London and New York: Routledge & Kegan Paul, p. 133.

2. Ibid., pp. 133–7.

3. Ibid., p. 138.

4. Ibid., pp. 137–8.

5. Ibid., p. 138.

6. Ibid., pp. 141–2.

7. Ibid., pp. 144–5.

8. Ibid., p. 145.

9. Ibid., p. 146.

10. Ibid., p. 143.

11. Hirst, P. H. (1974e), "The Nature and Structure of Curriculum Objectives." In R. S. Peters (ed.), *Knowledge and the Curriculum: A collection of philosophical papers* (pp. 16–29). London and New York: Routledge & Kegan Paul, p. 25.

12. Phillips, D. C. (1993), "Paul Hirst's Structure, or, the Uses and Abuses of an Overworked Concept." In R. Barrow and P. White (eds), *Beyond Liberal Education: Essays in Honour of Paul H. Hirst.* London: Routledge, p. 81.

13. Ibid., p. 83.

14. Ibid., p. 84.

15. Ibid., p. 85.

16. Ibid., pp. 85–6.

17. Ibid., p. 89.

18. Ibid., p. 92.

19. Pring, R. (1993), "Liberal Education and Vocational Preparation." In R. Barrow and P. White (eds), *Beyond Liberal Education: Essays in honour of Paul H. Hirst.* London: Routledge, p. 52.

20. Oakeshott, M. (1975), "A Place of Learning," in *The Colorado College Studies,* 12, and reproduced in Fuller, T. (ed.) (1990), *The Voice of Liberal Learning: Michael Oakeshott on Education.* Yale University Press.

21. Pring, R. (1993), p. 57.

22. Young, M. F. D. (2008b), "Rethinking the relationship between the sociology of education and educational policy." In M. F. D. Young (ed.), *Bringing Knowledge Back In: From social constructivism to social realism in the sociology of education.* London: Routledge, p. 110.

23. Hirst, P. H. (1974a), p. 150.

24. Hirst, P. H. (1993), "Education, Knowledge and Practices." In R. Barrow and P. White (eds), *Beyond Liberal Education: Essays in Honour of Paul H. Hirst.* London: Routledge, p. 185.

25. Ibid., pp. 186–7.

26. Ibid.

27. Ibid., p. 188.

28. Ibid., pp. 189–90.

29. Ibid., p. 191.

30. Belth, M. (1965), *Education as a Discipline: A Study of the Role of Models in Thinking.* Boston: Allyn & Bacon, pp. 61–2.

31. Hirst, P. H. (1983), "Educational Theory." In P. H. Hirst (ed.), *Educational Theory and Its Foundation Disciplines.* London and New York: Routledge & Kegan Paul, pp. 16–19.

32. Hirst, P. H. (1993), p. 194.

33. Ibid., p. 195.

34. Ibid., p. 196.

35. Ibid., p. 197.

36. Ibid., p. 198.

37. Walsh, P. (1993), *Education and Meaning: Philosophy in Practice.* London: Cassell. p. 132.

38. Bahá'u'lláh, *Gleanings from the Writings of Bahá'u'lláh*, no. 132.5.

39. See Engeström, Y. (2015), *Learning By Expanding: An Activity -Theoretical Approach to Developmental Research.* (2nd ed.). Cambridge University Press, pp. 190–4.

40. Pring, R. (1993), p. 71.

41. Ibid.

42. Ibid., pp. 71–2.

43. Ibid., p. 72.

44. Cooper, D. E. (1993), "Truth and Liberal Education." In R. Barrow and P. White (eds), *Beyond Liberal Education: Essays in Honour of Paul H. Hirst.* London: Routledge, p. 37.

45. Degenhardt, M. A. B. (1982), *Education and the Value of Knowledge.* London: George Allen & Unwin, p. 81.

46. Walsh, P. (1993), p. 113.

47. Ibid., p. 105.

48. Ibid.

49. Ibid., p. 106.

50. Ibid., p. 109.

51. Ibid., p. 110.

52. Ibid., p. 111.

53. Ibid., p. 113.

54. Ibid., p. 115.

55. Bahá'u'lláh, *Tablets of Bahá'u'lláh,* p. 35.

56. Hamlyn, D. W. (1970), *The Theory of Knowledge.* London: The Macmillan Press Ltd, p. 248.

57. Dreyfus, H. L. (1980), *Mind Over Machine: The Power of Human Intuition and Expertise in the Era of the Computer.* Glencoe, IL: The Free Press, p. 19.

58. Ibid., p. 21.

59. Ibid., p. 22.

60. Ibid., p. 23.

61. Ibid., p. 24.

62. Ibid.

63. Ibid., p. 26.

64. Ibid., p. 27.

65. Ibid., p. 28.

66. Ibid., pp. 28–9.

67. Ibid., pp. 29–30.

68. Ibid., p. 30.

69. Ibid., p. 34.

70. Dreyfus, H. L. (2007), "The Return of the Myth of the Mental." *Inquiry,* 50 (4), 352–65, p. 364.

71. Dreyfus, H. L. (2005), "Overcoming the Myth of the Mental: How Philosophers Can Profit from the Phenomenology of Everyday Expertise" (APA Pacific Division Presidential Address 2005), *Proceedings and Addresses of the American Philosophical Association* 79:2 (November 2005), 47.

72. Dreyfus, H. L. (2007), p. 355.

73. Ibid., p. 354.

74. Ibid., p. 356.

75. Ibid., pp. 356–7.

76. McDowell, J. (2007a), "What Myth?" *Inquiry,* 50 (4), 338–51. p. 349.

77. Ibid., p. 340.

78. McDowell, J. (2007b), "Response to Dreyfus." *Inquiry,* 50 (4), 3367–0, p. 369

79. McDowell, J. (2007a), p. 344.

80. Dreyfus, H. L. (2007), p. 352.

81. Taylor, C. (2002), "Foundationalism and the inner-outer distinction." In N. H. Smith (ed.), *Reading McDowell on Mind and World.* London: Routledge, p. 113.

82. Arbab, F. (1994), *Lectures on Bahá'í-Inspired Curricula.* Riviera, Florida: Palabra Publications, pp. 12–14.

83. Ibid., p. 69.

84. Ibid., pp. 69–70.

85. Ibid., pp. 70–1.

Chapter 8

1. Esteva, G. (1993), "Development." In W. Sachs (ed.), *The Development Dictionary: A Guide to Knowledge As Power.* Johannesburg: Witwatersand University Press, p. 7.

2. Sen, A. (1999), *Development As Freedom.* New York: Anchor Books, p. 3.

3. Aristotle, E. N., Book I.

4. Sen, A. (1999), p. 18.

5. See chapters 1–4.

6. Nussbaum, M. (2003), "Capabilities as Fundamental Entitlements: Sen and Social Justice." *Feminist Economics,* 9 (2), 33–59. p. 44.

7. Gasper and Staveren. (2003), "Development As Freedom—And As What Else?" *Feminist Economics,* 9 (2), 137–61, p. 146.

8. Goulet, D. (1980), "Development Experts: the one eyed giants." *World Development,* 8 (7/8), 481–89, p. 484.

9. Ravetz, J. R. (1971), *Scientific Knowledge and its Social Problem:* Oxford University Press, p. 9.

10. Williams, B. (2001), "From Freedom to Liberty: The Construction of a Political Value." *Philosophy and Public Affairs,* 30 (1), 3–36, p. 4.

11. Nagel, T. (1986), *The View From Nowhere.* Oxford: Oxford University Press, p. 127.

12. Bahá'u'lláh, The Hidden Words, Persian, no. 42.

13. Ibid., no. 38.

14. Ibid., no. 47.

15. Bahá'u'lláh,, *The Tabernacle of Unity,* no. 1.11.

16. Bahá'u'lláh, The Hidden Words, Persian, no. 72.

17. Sen, A. (1999), pp. 18–9.

18. Ibid., p. 19.

19. Ibid., p. 11.

20. Ibid., p. xii.

21. Ibid., p. 189.

22. Sen, A. (1993), "Capability and Well-Being." In M. Nussbaum and A. Sen (eds), *The Quality of Life: A study prepared for Development Economics Research (WIDER) of the United Nations University.* Oxford: Oxford University Press, p. 30.

23. Ibid., p. 31.

24. Ibid., pp. 36–7.

25. Ibid., p. 38.

26. Ibid., p. 33.

27. Sen, A. (1999), p. 88.

28. Ibid., p. 89.

29. Ibid.

30. Ibid., p. 90.

31. A primary concern of the "capability approach" is the "identification of value-objects." The selection of objects of value is an evaluative exercise and the relative value of objects is determined through further evaluative procedures. The evaluative space in this approach is seen in terms of "functionings and capabilities to function." It includes "a variety of human acts and states as important in themselves," which are not evaluated merely on the basis of their ability to produce utility or the degree to which they yield such utility. Neither primary goods nor utility provide sufficient informational base for evaluation. Even when the list of goods includes such items as rights, opportunities, income, or wealth, "it still is concerned with good things rather than with what these good things *do* to human beings." And utility— whether seen as happiness and pleasure in the full utilitarian tradition, as desire fulfilment in its more modern formulations, or simply defined as some numerical representation of a person's observable choices— while concerned with "what these things do to human beings," uses "a metric that focusses not on the person's capabilities but on his mental reaction." Sen, A. (1979), Equality of What? *The Tanner Lecture on Human Values* (pp. 196–220). Delivered at Stanford University, p. 218.

32. Sen, A. (1993), p. 35.

33. Ibid.

34. Ibid., p. 36.

35. Ibid., p. 37.

36. Ibid., p. 39.

37. Sen, A. (1985), Well-Being, Agency and Freedom: The Dewey Lectures 1984, *Journal of philosophy*, Vol. 82, No. 4, pp. 196–221, p. 202.

38. Ibid.

39. Ibid., pp. 34–5.

40. Nussbaum, M. (2000), *Women and Human Development: The Capabilities Approach.* Cambridge: Cambridge University Press. pp. 70–1.

41. See John Rawls' discussion of "reflective equilibrium" in *A Theory of Justice.*

42. Nussbaum, M. (2000), p. 77.

43. Ibid., p. 81.

44. Ibid., p. 82.

45. Nussbaum, M. (1987), "Nature, Function and Capability: Aristotle on Political Distribution." [Online]. *WIDER Working Papers*, 31, last accessed June 2011, p. 44.

46. Nussbaum, M. (2009), "Education for Profit, Education for Freedom." *Liberal Education*, 95 (3), 6–13, p. 8.

47. Ibid., pp. 11–3.

48. Units are used here generically to refer to a combination of materials to be studied and discussed by a group with the aid of a tutor, as well as the corresponding "guided action research in the community," analysis of results and reflection on the nature of activity being undertaken.

Chapter 9

1. The concept of pedagogy is used here in the broad sense of the term, as everything that addresses the teaching-learning experience, rather than simply the act of teaching a student. The term covers several interrelated sets of issues: One set has to do with the work of the teacher, her knowledge of content and of approaches to teaching, communication with students and the manner of assistance provided

to them, integration of instruction in one subject area with others, and reflection upon and revision of personal practice. Another set of issues concerns the development of educational materials in order to structure learning. Yet another set of issues is focused on the student and the kind of environment that enhances his or her learning. Participation in learning, however, extends beyond the classroom; students are members of society and interact with its other members, its institutions, and the many forces operating within it.

2. Dewey, J. (1938), *Experience and Education*. New York: Collier Books, p. 17.

3. Freire, P. (1998), *Pedagogy of the Oppressed* (M. B. Ramos, Trans.). New York: Continuum, pp. 52–3.

4. Ibid., pp. 53–4.

5. Ibid., p. 61.

6. Ibid., pp. 60–1.

7. Ibid., pp. 61–2.

8. See chapter 2.

9. Freire, P. (2000), *Education for Critical Consciousness*. New York: Continuum, p. 57.

10. Freire, P. (1995), *Pedagogy of Hope: Reliving Pedagogy of the Oppressed*. New York: Continuum, pp. 133–4.

11. Shor, I. (1992), *Empowering Education: Critical Teaching for Social Change*. Chicago: University of Chicago Press, p. 35.

12. Freire, P. (2000), p. 18.

13. See Adler, M. J. (1990), *Reforming Education: The Opening of the American Mind*. New York: Collier Books.

14. Dunne, J. (1992), *Back to the Rough Ground: 'Phronesis' and 'Techne' in Modern Philosophy and in Aristotle*. Notre Dame, IN: University of Notre Dame Press, p. 62.

15. Bruner, J. (2006a), *In Search of Pedagogy: The selected works of Jerome S. Bruner*. (Vol. I). London: Routledge, p. 67.

16. Ibid., p. 68.

17. Ibid., p. 87.

18. See Bruner, J. (1999), *The Culture of Education.* (5th ed.). Cambridge, MA: Harvard University Press.

19. Bruner, J. (2006a), p. 24.

20. Dewey, J. (1991), *How We Think.* Amherst, NY: Prometheus Books (originally published in 1910), pp. 57–8.

21. Ibid., p. 58.

22. Ibid., pp. 58–9.

23. Ibid., p. 62.

24. Dewey, J. (2007), *Democracy and Education.* Teddington, Middlesex: The Echo Library (originally published in 1916), p. 162.

25. Dewey, J. (1991), p. 62.

26. Hirst, P. H. (1974d), "The Logical and Psychological Aspects of Teaching a Subject." In R. S. Peters (ed.), *Knowledge and the Curriculum: A Collection of Philosophical Papers,* (pp. 116–31). London and New York: Routledge & Kegan Paul, p. 130.

27. Pring, R. (1993), "Liberal Education and Vocational Preparation." In R. Barrow and P. White (eds), *Beyond Liberal Education: Essays in honour of Paul H. Hirst.* London: Routledge, p. 72.

28. FUNDAEC. (2007), *Matter, Unit 1: The Heating and Cooling of Matter.*

29. Reiss, M. J. (2001), Representing Science, *An Inaugural Professorial Lecture.* Institute of Education, University of London: Institute of Education Press, p. 6.

30. Ibid., pp. 6–7.

31. Ibid., p. 7.

32. See Bruner, J. (1961), "The Act of Discovery." *Harvard Educational Review,* 31, 21–32.

33. Bruner, J. (2006a), p. 60.

34. Bruner, J. (1973), *The Relevance of Education.* New York: W. W. Norton & Company, Inc., p. 68.

35. Ibid., p. xv.

36. Vygotsky, L. (1986), *Thought and Language.* Cambridge, MA: The M.I.T. Press, p. 194.

37. See FUNDAEC. (2007).

Chapter 10

1. In the case of the "Promoter of Community Well-Being" program, discussed in previous chapters, the immediate environments in question are those segments of the community with which the student interacts. These exist in a larger world of ideas that form the ethical environment. The concept of ethical environment has been examined in its complexity by Haydon who has also explored the way values education has to take account of it. [Haydon, G. (2006a), *Education, Philosophy and the Ethical Environment.* London: Routledge.] The development of the kind of capabilities suggested here presents one approach by the aid of which education can intervene in the ethical environment.

2. Dunne, J. (1992), *Back to the Rough Ground: 'Phronesis' and 'Techne' in Modern Philosophy and in Aristotle.* Notre Dame, IN: University of Notre Dame Press, p. 143.

3. Gadamer, H.-G. (2004a), *Truth and Method.* (J. Weinsheimer and D. G. Marshall, revised Trans.). (2nd Revised Ed.). London: Continuum (first published in 1975), p. 417.

4. Dunne, J. (1992), pp. 143–4.

5. The main characteristic of modern life according to Charles Taylor is the failure to find a believable framework which brings with it a quest for meaning intimately connected with language: ". . . the invocation of meaning . . . comes from our awareness of how much the search involves articulation. We find the sense of life through articulating it." Taylor, C. (1990), *Sources of Self: The Making of Modern Identity.* Cambridge, MA: Harvard University Press, p. 18.

6. Aristotle, E. N., Book I.

7. Ibid., Book II.

8. Curren, R. (1999), "Cultivating the Intellectual and Moral Virtues." In D. Carr and J. Steutel (eds), *Virtue Ethics and Moral Education*. London: Routledge, p. 68.

9. There are, of course, more nuanced definitions of virtues available. Haydon, for example, refers to them in these terms: "Virtues, whatever else may distinguish them, are complex dispositions of human beings which involve feeling and motivation as well as perception and reason." Haydon, G. (2006b), "Moral Education." In R. Curren (ed.), *A Companion to the Philosophy of Education* (Vol. 2, pp. 325–6). Oxford: Blackwell Publishing.

10. Midgley, M. (2003), *Heart and Mind: The varieties of moral experience*. London: Routledge Classics, p. 4.

11. Ibid.

12. Ibid.

13. Peters, R. S. (1975a), The Education of Emotions. In R. F. Dearden, P. H. Hirst and R. S. Peters (eds), *Education and Reason: Part 3 of Education and the Development of Reason*. London and New York: Routledge & Kegan Paul, p. 90.

14. Ibid.

15. Peters, R. S. (1981), *Moral Development and Moral Education*. New York: Harper Collins, pp. 63–7.

16. Noddings, N. (2003), *Caring: A Feminine Approach to Ethics and Moral Education*. Berkeley: University of California Press, p. 25.

17. Ibid., p. 26.

18. Peters, R. S. (1975a), p. 77.

19. MacIntyre explains, for example, that the process of transition from infantile intelligence to independent practical reasoning is one in which the impulse to satisfy purely personal desires gives way to an informed desire to pursue good. The "qualities that a child must develop, first to redirect and transform her or his desires, and subsequently to direct them consistently towards the goods of the different stages of her or his life" are "the intellectual and moral virtues." MacIntyre,

A. (1999), *Dependent Rational Animals: Why Human Beings Need the Virtues*. London: Duckworth Publishers, p. 87.

20. McDowell, J. (1979), "Virtue and Reason." In R. Crisp and M. Slote (eds), *Virtue Ethics*. Oxford: Oxford University Press, p. 142.

21. Peters, R. S. (1981), p. 68.

22. Ibid., p. 67.

23. Peters, R. S. (1975b), "Reason and Passion." In R. F. Dearden, P. H. Hirst and R. S. Peters (eds), *Reason: Part 2 of Education and the development of reason*. London and New York: Routledge & Kegan Paul, pp. 76–7.

24. Sen, A. (2009), *The Idea of Justice*. Cambridge, MA: Harvard University Press, pp. 244–5.

25. MacIntyre, A. (1981), *After Virtue*. Notre Dame, IN: University of Notre Dame Press, p. 33.

26. Taylor, C. (1990), p. 33.

27. Ibid., p. 34.

28. Ibid., pp. 35–6.

29. Ibid., p. 37.

30. Taylor, C. (2003), "Cross-purposes: The Liberal-Communitarian Debate." In D. Matravers and J. Pike (eds), *Debates in Contemporary Philosophy*. London: Routledge in association with Open University, p. 201.

31. See Watson, E. (1995), "What a Vygotskian Perspective Can Contribute to Contemporary Philosophy." In D. Bakhurst and C. Sypnowich (eds), *The Social Self*. Thousand Oaks, CA: Sage Publications, pp. 47–66.

32. Vygotsky, L. (1979), "Consciousness as a problem of the psychology of behaviour." In *Soviet Psychology*, 17, pp. 5–35, 13.

33. Kozulin, A. (1990), *Vygotsky's Psychology: A Biography of Ideas*. Cambridge, MA: Harvard University Press, p. 81.

34. Vygotsky, L. (1979), pp. 29–30.

35. Vygotsky, L. (1926), "Pedagogical Psychology." Moscow: Rabot-

nik Prosveshchenija, p. 179. In R. Van der Veer and J. Valsiner, (1991), *Understanding Vygotsky: A Quest for Synthesis.* Blackwell Publishers Ltd, pp. 57–8.

36. Van der Veer, R. and Valsiner, J. (1991), *Understanding Vygotsky: A Quest for Synthesis.* Blackwell Publishers Ltd, pp. 57–8.

37. Ilyenkov, E. (2014), "Dialectics of the Ideal: Evald Ilyenkov and Creative Soviet Marxism." Leiden: Brill, p. 47.

38. Vygotsky, L. (1979), p. 30.

39. Kozulin, A. (1990), pp. 83–4.

40. FUNDAEC. (2006), *A Discourse on Social Action,* Unit 1: *Basic Concepts,* p. 41.

BIBLIOGRAPHY

Works of Bahá'u'lláh

Gleanings from the Writings of Bahá'u'lláh. Translated by Shoghi Effendi. Wilmette, IL: Bahá'í Publishing, 2005.

The Hidden Words. Translated by Shoghi Effendi. Wilmette, IL: Bahá'í Publishing, 2002.

The Kitáb-i-Íqán: The Book of Certitude. Translated by Shoghi Effendi. Wilmette, IL: Bahá'í Publishing, 2003.

The Tabernacle of Unity: Bahá'u'lláh's Responses to Mánikchí Ṣáḥib and other Writings. Haifa, Israel: Bahá'í World Center, 2006.

Tablets of Bahá'u'lláh revealed after the Kitáb-i-Aqdas. Compiled by the Research Department of the Universal House of Justice. Translated by Habib Taherzadeh et al. Wilmette, IL: Bahá'í Publishing Trust, 1988.

Works of 'Abdu'l-Bahá

Promulgation of Universal Peace: Talks Delivered by 'Abdu'l-Bahá during His Visit to the United States and Canada in 1912. Compiled by Howard MacNutt. Wilmette, IL: Bahá'í Publishing, 2012.

Selections from the Writings of 'Abdu'l-Bahá. Compiled by the Research Department of the Universal House of Justice. Translated by a Committee at the Bahá'í World Center and Marzieh Gail. Wilmette, IL: Bahá'í Publishing, 2010.

Some Answered Questions. Collected and translated from the Persian by Laura Clifford Barney. Newly Revised by a Committee at the Bahá'í World Center. Wilmette, IL: Bahá'í Publishing, 2016.

"Tablet to Dr. Forel," *August Forel and the Bahá'í Faith.* Oxford: George Ronald, 1978.

Works of Shoghi Effendi

Advent of Divine Justice. 1st pocket-size ed. Wilmette, IL: Bahá'í Publishing Trust, 1990.

Guidance for Today and Tomorrow: A Selection from the Writings of Shoghi Effendi. London: Bahá'í Publishing Trust, 1953.

Summary Statement –1947, Special UN Committee on Palestine, 1947.

The World Order of Bahá'u'lláh: Selected Letters. 1st pocket-size ed. Wilmette, IL: Bahá'í Publishing Trust, 1991.

Compilations of Bahá'í Writings

Bahá'u'lláh, 'Abdu'l-Bahá, Shoghi Effendi and Universal House of Justice. *The Compilation of Compilations: Prepared by the Universal House of Justice, 1963–1990.* 2 vols. Australia: Bahá'í Publications Australia, 1991.

Other Works

Adler, M. J. (1990), *Reforming Education: The Opening of the American Mind.* New York: Collier Books.

Anderson, W. A. and Krathwohl, D. R. (2000), *Taxonomy for Learning, Teaching, and Assessing: A Revision of Bloom's Taxonomy of Educational Objectives.* Pearson.

Anscombe, G. E. M. (1981), "Modern Moral Philosophy," *Ethics, Religion and Politics: Collected Philosophical Papers* (Vol. III). Minneapolis, MN: University of Minnesota Press.

Arbab, F. (1994), *Lectures on Bahá'í-Inspired Curricula.* Riviera, Florida: Palabra Publications.

———. (2000), "Promoting a Discourse on Science, Religion, and Development." In S. M. P. Harper (ed.), *The Lab the Temple and the Market: Reflections at the intersection of Science, Religion, and Development.* Ottawa, ON: International Development Research Centre.

Arendt, H. (1958), *The Human Condition.* (2nd ed.). Chicago: University of Chicago Press.

———. (1970), *On Violence*. New York: Harcourt Brace & Company.

———. (2006), *Between Past and Future*. Penguin Books.

Aristotle. Nicomachean Ethics, Book I. [Online]. Available at: http://classics.mit.edu/Aristotle/nicomachaen.1.i.html. Last accessed 25 October 2015.

———. Nicomachean Ethics, Book II. [Online]. Available at: http://classics.mit.edu/Aristotle/nicomachaen.2.ii.html. Last accessed 25 October 2015.

Bachrach, P. and Baratz, M. S. (1970), *Power and Poverty: Theory and Practice*. Oxford: Oxford University Press.

Bahá'í International Community. (1995), *The Prosperity of Hunmankind*. Haifa, Israel: Bahá'í World Center.

Bahá'í World Center. (2001), *Century of Light*. Haifa, Israel: Bahá'í World Center.

Bakhurst, D. (1997), "Meaning, Normativity and the Life of Mind," *Language and Communication*, 17 (1), 33–51.

———. (2001), 'Memory, Identity and the Future of Cultural Psychology'. In D. Bakhurst and S. G. Shanker (eds), *Jerome Bruner: Language, Culture, Self*. Thousand Oaks, CA: Sage Publications.

Bellous, J. and Pearson, A. (1995), "Empowerment and Teacher Education," *Studies in Philosophy and Education*, 14 (7), 49–62.

Belth, M. (1965), *Education as a Discipline: A Study of the Role of Models in Thinking*. Boston: Allyn & Bacon.

Bentham, J. (1907), *An Introduction to the Principles of Morals and Legislation*. Oxford: Clarendon Press.

Bernstein, R. J. (1983), *Beyond Objectivism and Relativism*. Philadelphia: University of Pennsylvania Press.

Blackburn, S. (2005), *Truth: A Guide*. Oxford: Oxford University Press.

Bloom, B. S. (1956), *Taxonomy of Educational Objectives, Handbook 1: Cognitive Domain*. New York: Longman.

Bloom, B. S., Hastings, T. & Madaus, G. F. (1971), *Handbook of summative and formative evaluation*. New York: McGraw Hill.

Bohm, D. (2002), *Wholeness and the Implicate Order*. (2nd ed.). London: Routledge.

Bowie, A. (2003), *Introduction to German Philosophy From Kant to Habermas*. Cambridge: Polity Press.

Bruner, J. (1961), "The Act of Discovery," *Harvard Educational Review*, 31, 21–32.

———. (1973), *The Relevance of Education*. New York: W. W. Norton & Company, Inc.

———. (1999), *The Culture of Education*. (5th ed.). Cambridge, MA: Harvard University Press.

———. (2006a), *In Search of Pedagogy: The selected works of Jerome S. Bruner*. (Vol. I). London: Routledge.

———. (2006b), *In Search of Pedagogy: The selected works of Jerome S. Bruner*. (Vol. II). London: Routledge.

Buckley, J. and Erricker, J. (2004), "Citizenship Education in the Postmodern Moment." In H. Alexander (ed.), *Spirituality and Ethics in Education*. Brighton-Portland: Sussex Academic Press.

Carr, D. (2003), "Character and Moral Choice in the Cultivation of Virtue," *Philosophy*, 78.

Chalmers, A. F. (1978), *What is this thing called Science?* (3rd ed.). Buckingham: Open University Press.

Clifford, W. K. (1999), "The Ethics of Belief." In T. J. Madigan (ed.), *The Ethics of Belief and Other Essays*. Amherst, NY: Prometheus Books (originally published in Contemporary Review, 1877).

Collingwood, R. G. (1938), *The Principles of Art*. Oxford: Clarendon Press.

Cooper, D. E. (1993), "Truth and Liberal Education." In R. Barrow and P. White (eds), *Beyond Liberal Education: Essays in Honour of Paul H. Hirst*. Routledge.

Cowen, M. P. and Shenton, R. W. (1996), *Doctrines of Development*. London: Routledge.

Curren, R. (1999), "Cultivating the Intellectual and Moral Virtues." In D. Carr and J. Steutel (eds), *Virtue Ethics and Moral Education*. London: Routledge.

Dahl, R. A. (1957), "The Concept of Power," *Behavioral Science*, 2, 201–215.

———. (2005), *Who Governs?: Democracy and Power in an American City*. Yale University Press.

Degenhardt, M. A. B. (1982), *Education and the Value of Knowledge*. London: George Allen & Unwin.

Dewey, J. (1938), *Experience and Education*. New York: Collier Books.

———. (1991), *How We Think*. Amherst, NY: Prometheus Books (originally published in 1910).

———. (2007), *Democracy and Education*. Teddington, Middlesex: The Echo Library (originally published in 1916).

Dreyfus, H. L. (1980), *Mind Over Machine: The Power of Human Intuition and Expertise in the Era of the Computer*. Glencoe, IL: The Free Press.

———. (2005), "Overcoming the Myth of the Mental: How Philosophers Can Profit from the Phenomenology of Everyday Expertise" (APA Pacific Division Presidential Address 2005), *Proceedings and Addresses of the American Philosophical Association*, 79:2 (November 2005), 47.

———. (2007), "The Return of the Myth of the Mental," *Inquiry*, 50 (4), 352–65.

Dunne, J. (1988), "Teaching and the Limits of Technique: An Analysis of the Behavioural-Objectives Model," *The Irish Journal of Education*, 22 (2), 66–90.

———. (1992), *Back to the Rough Ground: 'Phronesis' and 'Techne' in Modern Philosophy and in Aristotle*. Notre Dame, IN: University of Notre Dame Press.

Engeström, Y. (2015), *Learning By Expanding: An Activity-Theoretical Approach to Developmental Research*. (2nd ed.). Cambridge University Press.

Esteva, G. (1993), "Development." In W. Sachs (ed.), *The Development Dictionary: A Guide to Knowledge As Power.* Johannesburg: Witwatersand University Press.

Feynman, R. (1963), *Six Easy Pieces: Essentials of Physics Explained by Its Most Brilliant Teacher.* New York: Basic Books.

Fleck, L. (1979), *Genesis and Development of a Scientific Fact.* Chicago: University of Chicago Press.

Flyvbjerg, B. (2001), *Making Social Science Matter: Why social inquiry fails and how it can succeed again* (S. Sampson, Trans.). Cambridge: Cambridge University Press.

Foucault, M. (1972–1977), *Power/Knowledge: Selected Interviews and Other Writings.* New York: Pantheon Books.

———. (1976), *The History of Sexuality* (R. Hurley, Trans.). (Vol. 1: An Introduction). New York: Vintage Books.

Freire, P. (1995), *Pedagogy of Hope: Reliving Pedagogy of the Oppressed.* New York: Continuum.

———. (1998), *Pedagogy of the Oppressed* (M. B. Ramos, Trans.). New York: Continuum.

———. (2000), *Education for Critical Consciousness.* New York: Continuum.

Freud, S. (1991), *New Introductory Lectures on Psycho-analysis.* Penguin Books.

FUNDAEC. (1999), *Constructing a Conceptual Framework for Social Action.* Cali, Colombia: Fundacion para la Aplicacion y Ensenanza de las Ciencias (FUNDAEC).

———. (2000), *Science, Religion and Development.* Cali, Colombia: Fundacion para la Aplicacion y Ensenanza de las Ciencias (FUNDAEC).

———. (2004), *Primary Elements of Descriptions, Unit 1: Properties.* Cali, Colombia: Fundacion para la Aplicacion y Ensenanza de las Ciencias (FUNDAEC).

———. (2005), *Curriculum Development.* Cali, Colombia: Fundacion para la Aplicacion y Ensenanza de las Ciencias (FUNDAEC).

———. (2006), *A Discourse on Social Action,* Unit 1*: Basic Concepts.* Cali, Colombia: Fundacion para la Aplicacion y Ensenanza de las Ciencias (FUNDAEC).

———. (2007), *Matter. Unit 1: The Heating and Cooling of Matter.* Cali, Colombia: Fundacion para la Aplicacion y Ensenanza de las Ciencias (FUNDAEC).

———. (2008), *A Discourse on Social Action,* Unit 2: *Education.* Cali, Colombia: Fundacion para la Aplicacion y Ensenanza de las Ciencias (FUNDAEC).

———. (2009), *A Discourse on Social Action,* Unit 3*: Science.* Cali, Colombia: Fundacion para la Aplicacion y Ensenanza de las Ciencias (FUNDAEC).

Gadamer, H.-G. (2004a), *Truth and Method.* (J. Weinsheimer and D. G. Marshall, revised Trans.). (2nd Revised Ed.). London: Continuum (first published in 1975).

———. (2004b), *Philosophical Hermeneutics.* (David, E. Linge, ed. and trans.). Berkeley: University of California Press, (first published in 1976).

Gagne, R. M. & Briggs, L. J. (1974), *Principles of instructional design* (2nd ed.). New York: Holt, Rinehart &Winston.

Gardiner, P. (1988), *Kierkegaard: A Very Short Introduction* Oxford: Oxford University Press.

Gardner, H. (1987), *The Mind's New Science: A History of the Cognitive Revolution.* Basic Books.

———. (1991), *The Unschooled Mind: How Children Think & How Schools Teach.* New York: Basic Books.

Gasper and Staveren. (2003), "Development As Freedom—And As What Else?" *Feminist Economics,* 9 (2), 137–61.

Glasersfeld, E. von. (1996), *Radical Constructivism: A Way of Knowing and Learning.* London: Routledge.

———. (1991), *Cognition, Construction of Knowledge and Teaching.* In Phillips, D. C. (1995), The Good, the Bad and the Ugly: The

Many Faces of Constructivism. *Educational Researcher,* 24 (7): pp. 5–12.

Goulet, D. (1980), "Development Experts: the one eyed giants," *World Development,* 8 (7/8), 481–89.

Hamlyn, D. W. (1970), *The Theory of Knowledge.* London: The Macmillan Press Ltd.

Haq, M. u. (1976), *The Poverty Curtain: Choices for the Third World.* New York: Columbia University Press.

Harman, W. (1994), "A Re-examination of the Metaphysical Foundations of Modern Science: Why is it necessary?" In W. Harman and J. Clark (eds), *New Metaphysical Foundations of Modern Science.* Sausalito, CA: Institute of Noetic Sciences.

Haydon, G. (2006a), *Education, Philosophy and the Ethical Environment.* London: Routledge.

———. (2006b), "Moral Education." In R. Curren (ed.), *A Companion to the Philosophy of Education* (Vol. 2, pp. 325–6). Oxford: Blackwell Publishing.

———. (2006c), *Values in Education.* New York: Continuum.

Higgins, C. (2003), "MacIntyre's Moral Theory and the Possibility of an Aretaic Ethics of Teaching," *Journal of Philosophy of Education,* 37 (2).

Hindess, B. (1996), *Discourses of Power: From Hobbes to Foucault.* Oxford: Blackwell Publishers Ltd.

Hirst, P. H. (1974a), "Curriculum Integration," In R. S. Peters (ed.), *Knowledge and the Curriculum: A collection of philosophical papers* (pp. 132–51). London and New York: Routledge & Kegan Paul.

———. (1974b), "Liberal Education and the Nature of Knowledge." In R. S. Peters (ed.), *Knowledge and the Curriculum: A collection of philosophical papers* (pp. 30–53). London and New York: Routledge & Kegan Paul.

———. (1974c), "Morals, Religion and the Maintained School." In R. S. Peters (ed.), *Knowledge and the Curriculum: A collection of philosophical papers* (pp. 173–89). London and New York: Routledge & Kegan Paul.

———. (1974d), "The Logical and Psychological Aspects of Teaching a Subject." In R. S. Peters (ed.), *Knowledge and the Curriculum: A Collection of Philosophical Papers* (pp. 116–31). London and New York: Routledge & Kegan Paul.

———. (1974e), "The Nature and Structure of Curriculum Objectives." In R. S. Peters (ed.), *Knowledge and the Curriculum: A collection of philosophical papers* (pp. 16–29). London and New York: Routledge & Kegan Paul.

———. (1983), "Educational Theory." In P. H. Hirst (ed.), *Educational Theory and Its Foundation Disciplines*. London and New York: Routledge & Kegan Paul.

———. (1993), "Education, Knowledge and Practices." In R. Barrow and P. White (eds), *Beyond Liberal Education: Essays in Honour of Paul H. Hirst*. London: Routledge.

Hobbes, T. (2011), *Leviathan*. Toronto: Broadview Press.

Hume, D. (1998), *An Enquiry Concerning the Principles of Morals*. Oxford University Press.

Ilyenkov, E. (1977), "The Concept of the Ideal," *Philosophy in the USSR: Problems of Dialectical Materialism* (pp. 71–99). Moscow: Progress.

———. (2014), "Dialectics of the Ideal: Evald Ilyenkov and Creative Soviet Marxism." Leiden: Brill, p. 47.

James, W. (2005), "The Will to Believe." In J. Capps and D. Capps (eds), *James and Dewey on Belief and Experience*. Champaign, IL: University of Illinois Press (originally published in 1895).

Johnston, D. (2011), *A Brief History of Justice*. Wiley-Blackwell.

Kant, I. (1991), *Kant Political Writing, Cambridge Texts in the History of Political Thought*. H. Reiss, (ed.). Cambridge University Press.

———. (1998), *Groundwork of the Metaphysics of Morals, Cambridge Texts in the History of Philosophy*. (M. Gregor, Trans.). Cambridge University Press.

———. (1996), *The Metaphysics of Morals, Cambridge Texts in the History of Philosophy.* (M. Gregor, Trans.). Cambridge University Press.

Kierkegaard, S. (2009), *Concluding Unscientific Postscript.* Cambridge Texts in the History of Philosophy, (A. Hannay, Trans.). Cambridge University Press.

———. (2010), *The Present Age: On the Death of Rebellion.* (A. Dru, Trans.). Harper Perennial Modern Thought.

———. (1983), *Fear and Trembling* and *Repetition.* (H. V. and E. H. Hong, Trans.). Princeton, NJ: Princeton University Press.

Kozulin, A. (1990), *Vygotsky's Psychology: A Biography of Ideas.* Cambridge, MA: Harvard University Press.

Krell, D. F. (ed.). (1978), *Martin Heidegger: Basic Writings.* London: Routledge.

Kuhn, T. S. (1996), *The Structure of Scientific Revolutions.* (Third ed.). Chicago: University of Chicago Press.

Kymlicka, W. (2002), *Contemporary Political Philosophy: An Introduction.* (2nd ed.). Oxford: Oxford University Press.

Lakatos, I. (1978), *The Methodology of Scientific Research Programmes: Philosophical Papers, Volume 1.* Cambridge: Cambridge University Press.

Larvor, B. (1998), *Lakatos: An Introduction.* London: Routledge.

Laudan, L. (1982), "Commentary: Science at the Bar—Causes for Concern," *Science, Technology, and Human Values,* 7 (41), 16–19.

Lawn, C. (2006), *Gadamer: A Guide for the Perplexed.* New York: Continuum.

Lukes, S. (2005), *Power: A Radical View.* (2nd ed.). London: Palgrave: Macmillan.

MacIntyre, A. (1981), *After Virtue.* Notre Dame, IN: University of Notre Dame Press.

———. (1994), "A Partial Response to my Critics." In J. Horton and S. Mendus (eds), *Critical Perspectives on the Work of Alasdair Mac-*

Intyre (pp. 283–304). Oxford: Cambridge, Polity Press in association with Blackwell Publishers Ltd.

———. (1999), *Dependent Rational Animals: Why Human Beings Need the Virtues*. London: Duckworth Publishers.

Mager, R. F. (1997), *Preparing Instructional Objectives: A critical tool in the development of effective instruction*. (3rd ed.). Center for Effective Performance.

Maleuvre, D. (2011), *The Horizon: A History of Our Infinite Longing*. University of California Press.

May, T. (2001), *Our Practices Our Selves, Or, What It Means To Be Human*. Philadelphia: Pennsylvania State University Press.

McDowell, J. (1979), "Virtue and Reason." In R. Crisp and M. Slote (eds), *Virtue Ethics*. Oxford: Oxford University Press.

———. (1994), *Mind and World*. Cambridge, MA: Harvard University Press.

———. (2007a), "What Myth?" *Inquiry,* 50 (4), 338–51.

———. (2007b), "Response to Dreyfus," *Inquiry,* 50 (4), 336–70.

McGinn, M. (2009), "McDowell." In C. Belshaw and G. Kemp (eds), *12 Modern Philosophers*. Willey-Blackwell.

Midgley, M. (2003), *Heart and Mind: The varieties of moral experience*. London: Routledge Classics.

Mill, J. S. (1987), *Utilitarianism*. Amherst, NY: Prometheus Books.

Miller, G. A. (2003), "The cognitive revolution: a historical perspective," *TRENDS in Cognitive Sciences,* 7 (3): 141–44.

Mulhall, S. and Swift, A. (1995), "The Social Self in Political Theory: The Communitarian Critique of the Liberal Subject." In D. Bakhurst and C. Sypnowich (eds), *The Social Self.* Thousand Oaks, CA: Sage Publications.

Murdoch, I. (1997), "The Sovereignty of Good Over Other Concepts." In R. Crisp and M. Slote (eds) (pp. 99–118). Oxford: Oxford University Press.

Nagel, T. (1986), *The View From Nowhere*. Oxford: Oxford University Press.

Nelson, L. H. (1994), "On What We Say There Is and Why It Matters: A Feminist Perspective on Metaphysics and Science." In W. Harman and J. Clark (eds), *New Metaphysical Foundations of Modern Science*. Sausalito, CA: Institute of Noetic Sciences.

———. (1903), *An Essay in Aid of A Grammar of Assent*. London: Longmans, Green, and Co.

Noddings, N. (2003), *Caring: A Feminine Approach to Ethics and Moral Education*. Berkeley: University of California Press.

Norris, T. (2009), "Faith." In I. Ker and T. Merrigan (eds.), The Cambridge Companion to John Newman Henry. Cambridge University Press.

Nussbaum, M. (1987), "Nature, Function and Capability: Aristotle on Political Distribution," [Online]. *WIDER Working Papers*, 31, last accessed June 2011.

———. (1993), "Non-Relative Virtues: An Aristotelian Approach." In M. Nussbaum and A. Sen (eds), *The Quality of Life* (pp. 242–69). Oxford: Oxford University Press.

———. (2000), *Women and Human Development: The Capabilities Approach*. Cambridge: Cambridge University Press.

———. (2003), "Capabilities as Fundamental Entitlements: Sen and Social Justice," *Feminist Economics,* 9 (2), 33–59.

———. (2009), "Education for Profit, Education for Freedom," *Liberal Education,* 95 (3), 6–13.

Oakeshott, M. (1975), "A Place of Learning." In *The Colorado College Studies,* 12, and reproduced in Fuller, T. (ed.) (1990), *The Voice of Liberal Learning: Michael Oakeshott on Education*. Yale University Press.

Office of Social and Economic Development. (2008), *For the Betterment of the World: The Worldwide Bahá'í Community's Approach to Social and Economic Development.*

Okasha, S. (2002), *Philosophy of Science: A Very Short Introduction.* Oxford: Oxford University Press.

Peters, R. S. (1966), *Ethics and Education.* London: George Allen & Unwin Ltd.

———. (1972), *Reason and Compassion.* London: Routledge & Kegan Paul.

———. (1975a), "The Education of Emotions." In R. F. Dearden, P. H. Hirst and R. S. Peters (eds), *Education and Reason: Part 3 of Education and the development of reason.* London and New York: Routledge & Kegan Paul.

———. (1975b), "Reason and Passion." In R. F. Dearden, P. H. Hirst and R. S. Peters (eds), *Reason: Part 2 of Education and the development of reason.* London and New York: Routledge & Kegan Paul.

———. (1981), *Moral Development and Moral Education.* New York: Harper Collins.

Phillips, D. C. (1993), "Paul Hirst's Structure, or, the Uses and Abuses of an Overworked Concept." In R. Barrow and P. White (eds), *Beyond Liberal Education: Essays in Honour of Paul H. Hirst.* London: Routledge.

———. and Soltis, J. F. (2009), *Perspectives on Learning* (5th ed.). Columbia University: Teachers College Press.

Pinker, S. (2003), *The Blank Slate: The Modern Denial of Human Nature.* Penguin Books.

Pring, R. (1993), "Liberal Education and Vocational Preparation." In R. Barrow and P. White (eds), *Beyond Liberal Education: Essays in honour of Paul H. Hirst.* London: Routledge.

Putman, D. (1990), "The Compatibility of Justice and Kindness," *Philosophy* 65 (254).

Ravetz, J. R. (1971), *Scientific Knowledge and its Social Problem:* Oxford University Press.

Rawls, J. (1999), *A Theory of Justice.* Belknap Press.

———. (2001), *Justice as Fairness: A Restatement*. Belknap Press.

Reiss, M. J. (2001), Representing Science, *An Inaugural Professorial Lecture*. Institute of Education, University of London: Institute of Education Press.

Ricoeur, P. (1986), *The Symbolism of Evil*. Beacon Press.

Russell, B. (2004), *Power: A New Social Analysis*. Routledge Classics, p. 23.

Sandel, M. J. (1998), *Liberalism and the Limits of Justice*. (2nd ed.). Cambridge: Cambridge University Press.

Searle, J. R. (1995), *The Construction of Social Reality*. New York: The Free Press.

———. (1997), "Responses to Critics of the Construction of Social Reality," *Philosophy and Phenomenological Research*, 57 (2), 449–58.

Sellars, W. (1956), "Empiricism and the Philosophy of Mind." In H. Feigl and M. Scriven (eds), *Minnesota Studies in the Philosophy of Science* (Vol. 1). Minneapolis, MN: University of Minnesota Press.

Sen, A. (1979), "Equality of What?" *The Tanner Lecture on Human Values* (pp. 196–220). Delivered at Stanford University.

———. (1985), "Well-Being, Agency and Freedom: The Dewey Lectures, 1984," *Journal of philosophy*, Vol. 82, No. 4, pp. 196–221.

———. (1993), "Capability and Well-Being." In M. Nussbaum and A. Sen (eds), *The Quality of Life: A study prepared for Development Economics Research (WIDER) of the United Nations University*. Oxford: Oxford University Press.

———. (1999), *Development As Freedom*. New York: Anchor Books.

———. (2009), *The Idea of Justice*. Cambridge, MA: Harvard University Press.

Shor, I. (1992), *Empowering Education: Critical Teaching for Social Change*. Chicago: University of Chicago Press.

Sidgwick, H. (1907), *The Methods of Ethics.* Macmillan and Company.

Smith, A. (2008), *The Wealth of Nations.* Oxford Paperbacks.

Stiver, D. (1996), *The Philosophy of Religious Language.* Blackwell Publishing.

Taylor, C. (1982), "The Diversity of Goods." In A. Sen and B. Williams (eds), *Utilitarianism and Beyond.* Cambridge: Cambridge University Press.

———. (1990), *Sources of Self: The Making of Modern Identity.* Cambridge, MA: Harvard University Press.

———. (2002), "Foundationalism and the inner-outer distinction." In N. H. Smith (ed.), *Reading McDowell on Mind and World.* London: Routledge.

———. (2003), "Cross-purposes: The Liberal-Communitarian Debate." In D. Matravers and J. Pike (eds), *Debates in Contemporary Philosophy.* London: Routledge in association with Open University.

———. (2007), *A Secular Age.* Cambridge, MA: The Belknap Press of Harvard University Press.

Tyler, R.W. (1949), *Basic Principles of Curriculum and Instruction.* Chicago: University of Chicago Press.

Van der Veer, R. and Valsiner, J. (1991), *Understanding Vygotsky: A Quest for Synthesis.* Oxford: Blackwell Publishers Ltd.

Vygotsky, L. (1926), "Pedagogical Psychology." Moscow: Rabotnik Prosveshchenija, p. 179. In R. Van der Veer and J. Valsiner, (1991), *Understanding Vygotsky: A Quest for Synthesis.* Blackwell Publishers Ltd, pp. 57–8.

———. (1979), "Consciousness as problem of the psychology of behaviour," *Soviet Psychology,* 17, 5–35.

———. (1986), *Thought and Language.* Cambridge, MA: The M.I.T. Press.

Walsh, P. (1993), *Education and Meaning: Philosophy in Practice.* London: Cassell.

Watson, E. (1995), "What a Vygotskian Perspective Can Contribute to Contemporary Philosophy." In D. Bakhurst and C. Sypnowich (eds), *The Social Self.* Thousand Oaks, CA: Sage Publications.

Weber, M. (1997), *The Theory of Social and Economic Organization.* New York: The Free Press, p. 152.

Williams, B. (1985), *Ethics and the Limits of Philosophy.* Cambridge, MA: Harvard University Press.

———. (1993), *Morality: An Introduction to Ethics.* (Canto ed.). Cambridge: Cambridge University Press.

———. (2001), "From Freedom to Liberty: The Construction of a Political Value," *Philosophy and Public Affairs,* 30 (1), 3–36.

———. (2002), Truth and Truthfulness. Princeton, New Jersey: Princeton University Press.

———. (2008), "Human Rights and Relativism." In G. Hawthorn (ed.), *In the Beginning Was the Deed: Realism and Moralism in Political Argument.* Princeton, NJ: Princeton University Press.

Woolfolk, A. E. (2010), *Educational Psychology.* Upper Saddle River, NJ: Prentice Hall.

Wright, C. (2002), "Human Nature?" In N. H. Smith (ed.), *Reading McDowell on Mind and World.* London: Routledge.

Young, M. F. D. (2008a), "Curriculum studies and the problem of knowledge: Updating the Enlightenment?" In M. F. D. Young (ed.), *Bringing Knowledge Back In: From social constructivism to social realism in the sociology of education.* London: Routledge.

———. (2008b), "Rethinking the relationship between the sociology of education and educational policy." In M. F. D. Young (ed.), *Bringing Knowledge Back In: From social constructivism to social realism in the sociology of education.* London: Routledge.

INDEX

'Abdu'l-Bahá
    on human knowledge, 148–49
    on religion, 9
    on starting points of action,
        168–69
    see also Bahá'í Faith, teachings of
Abraham (Old Testament), 70–71
absolute conception of reality, no-
        tion of, 123, 129, 131, 150
action, reflection and
    in Bahá'í-inspired educational
        endeavors, 2, 5, 100, 122
    community programs of, 3,
        291–97, 354–48
    within evolving conceptual
        framework, 4, 14
    for teaching-learning experiences,
        266, 276
    unity of, 302–3
    see also reflection; thought,
        action and
actions, 25, 89, 124, 128, 193, 221
    convictions' complementarity
        with, 179–84, 197, 321–22
    feeling's tension with, 306–7
    human beings distinguished by,
        77, 85
    meaning in, 230, 245, 303
    power actualized in, 28, 199

rational, 166, 214
social, 10, 134–35, 158, 180–
    83, 187–88, 311, 355n1,
    357n1,
starting-points of, 168–69
see also agency/agents; doing;
    service, acts of; thought,
    action and
activity, human, 81, 193–95, 216,
    222, 258, 354n48
    see also human beings
Adler, M. J., 283
aestheticists/aesthetics, 64–66, 98,
    192–93
affordances, 236–38
agency/agents
    achievement of, 68, 260–61
    for capabilities development,
        257–58, 270
    functionings of, 25, 123–26
    individual, 338–39n5
    for moral empowerment, 199,
        258, 275
    perceptions by, 235, 239
    rational, 19, 35, 140, 143,
        237–38
    subjective, 70, 71
    trusteeship of, 154
    see also actions

377

BAHÁ'Í PUBLISHING

BAHÁ'Í PUBLISHING AND THE BAHÁ'Í FAITH

Bahá'í Publishing produces books based on the teachings of the Bahá'í Faith. Founded over 160 years ago, the Bahá'í Faith has spread to some 235 nations and territories and is now accepted by more than five million people. The word "Bahá'í" means "follower of Bahá'u'lláh." Bahá'u'lláh, the founder of the Bahá'í Faith, asserted that He is the Messenger of God for all of humanity in this day. The cornerstone of His teachings is the establishment of the spiritual unity of humankind, which will be achieved by personal transformation and the application of clearly identified spiritual principles. Bahá'ís also believe that there is but one religion and that all the Messengers of God—among them Abraham, Zoroaster, Moses, Krishna, Buddha, Jesus, and Muḥammad—have progressively revealed its nature. Together, the world's great religions are expressions of a single, unfolding divine plan. Human beings, not God's Messengers, are the source of religious divisions, prejudices, and hatreds.

The Bahá'í Faith is not a sect or denomination of another religion, nor is it a cult or a social movement. Rather, it is a globally recognized independent world religion founded on new books of scripture revealed by Bahá'u'lláh.

Bahá'í Publishing is an imprint of the National Spiritual Assembly of the Bahá'ís of the United States.

For more information about the Bahá'í Faith,
or to contact Bahá'ís near you,
visit http://www.bahai.us/
or call
1-800-22-UNITE